MW00423749

VULNERABLE MOMENTS

VULNERABLE MOMENTS

Deepening the Therapeutic Process

Martin S. Livingston, Ph.D.

JASON ARONSON INC.
Northvale, New Jersey
London

This book was set in 11 pt. New Baskerville by Pageworks of Old Saybrook and Lyme, CT, and printed and bound by Book-mart Press, Inc. of North Bergen, NJ.

10 9 8 7 6 5 4 3 2 1

Library of Congress Cataloging-in-Publication Data

Livingston, Martin S.
Vulnerable moments : deepening the therapeutic process / by Martin S. Livingston.
p. cm.
Includes index.
ISBN 0-7657-0310-6
1. Psychotherapist and patient. 2. Self-disclosure. 3. Self-containment (Personality trait) 4. Narcissistic injuries. I. Title.

RC480.8 .L584 2001
616.89'14—dc 21 00-052189

Printed in the United States of America on acid-free paper. For information and catalog write to Jason Aronson Inc., 230 Livingston Street, Northvale, NJ 07647-1726, or visit our website: www.aronson.com

Contents

Acknowledgments

Louisa R. Livingston, Ph.D., has been a tremendous help in the process of creating this book. Her loving support and encouragement have enriched my life and inspired the increase in my creativity and writing in recent years. She has also contributed a great deal to the book itself. Her editorial guidance through the early drafts and her help as a psychoanalyst in stimulating and discussing the ideas and case material as the book developed have been invaluable.

I would also like to thank the many patients who, in addition to stimulating my ideas and thoughts, also graciously, and of course anonymously, provided the substance of the book.

Finally, I want to express my appreciation to Eve Golden, M.D., whose amazing editorial skills allowed me to transform my material from a series of chapters into a book.

1

Identity, Vulnerability, and Change: An Introduction

> Narcissistic vulnerability is a ubiquitous burden of man, a part of the human condition from which no one is exempt.
>
> Heinz Kohut, 1977

In psychotherapy, as in life, there are times when people take the risk of experiencing and exposing aspects of themselves that they habitually hide from others, or even keep from their own awareness. This book is a study of vulnerability in the psychotherapeutic process: its nature, its importance, and the transforming experiences that I call "vulnerable moments."

The word *vulnerable* means "susceptible to being wounded," and people who relinquish their usual characterological defenses open themselves to wounds of many sorts, from peripheral encounters with shame and rejection to direct personal attacks and potentially devastating losses. Any of these can evoke memories of early traumas, and the fears of the dissolution of the existing sense of the self and its attachments that these recollections threaten. It is thus no wonder that protective shields become so deeply embedded in character. Still, at various times and for various reasons, they are lowered briefly, although seldom without an accompanying sense of confusion and, above all, danger. These occasions, when rigid barriers are softened and people open themselves to new experience, are the vulnerable moments that I explore in this book.

VULNERABILITY AND IDENTITY

The quest for identity is a lifelong process, since identity is not static, but is built and rebuilt over time. Old identities crumble, or at least fade into the background, to make way for new ones when our lives require them—when we re-form ourselves, as we periodically do, in response to changing circumstances and the passing of time. The process of rebuilding always involves periods of vulnerability, since a familiar personality protects us to some extent from the unknown, and to give it up is to give up that protection. But a sense of identity that remains unchanged for too long becomes brittle. If unchallenged, it may deteriorate into nothing but a protective shell, a pseudo-identity of established behaviors rather than the spontaneous manifestation of an individual's self. Rigid roles and codified patterns of relating are usually strategies for protecting a precarious sense of self, but like many protections they are also barriers; while they may in fact ward off feared experiences of depletion and fragmentation, they also block yearned-for experiences of freedom and intimacy. To the extent that rigid styles of relating hold at bay the anxiety, confusion, and sense of risk inherent in any growth process, including psychotherapy, they may be effective defenses against the experience of vulnerability; but at the same time they diminish the possibility of constructive change and the development of a flexible and meaningful sense of identity. The exploration and understanding of barriers to change and the underlying vulnerability that demands them is central to the therapeutic process. Without it, many patients never feel safe enough to open themselves to new possibilities.

The analytic process requires both the willingness to experience vulnerability and the capacity to tolerate it, despite the risks involved. It is precisely in moments of vulnerability that openness to new experience is possible. Vulnerability is both an inevitable concomitant of unfamiliar openness and a sign that something new is occurring, whether this be an experimental approach to previously foreclosed options, or a letting-go of rigid and limiting protective patterns. Although all of us, patients and therapists alike, find vulnerability uncomfortable and often seek to avoid it, nevertheless vulnerable moments are pivotal opportunities for change, and in treatment they should be welcomed as valuable, as well as fearsome, occurrences.

This point needs some emphasis, because therapists are no more immune than their patients to concerns about vulnerability. The analyst in the analytic situation is vulnerable himself; there is growing recognition that vulnerability in the analyst is not only a fact but also a requirement of analytic work. An analyst who is not emotionally available to his patients cannot establish the safety in which the tendrils of early developmental needs can begin to unfold. To be "emotionally available" (Orange 1995, p. 5), the analyst must be willing to risk being authentically touched by the patient's struggle, and by the feelings that the patient's struggle brings up in him. The belief that an analyst is impervious, or even a blank screen or rigidly "neutral," no longer holds the sway that it once did, and a lively dialogue, both in self psychology and in the psychoanalytic community as a whole, is now clarifying the nature of analysis as an emotional engagement between two highly involved and vulnerable people.

Therapists are particularly vulnerable in their sensitivity to criticism about their clinical behavior, and this may become an issue, especially at times when a patient's vulnerability is apparent. Vulnerability often arouses compassion in its observers, and analysts, like others, respond to vulnerable moments in their patients. However, interpretation in an atmosphere of abstinence is still considered by many to be central to analytic practice, and so an upsurge of responsive tenderness may bring discomfort along with it, because it does not appear to fit the classical theoretical model: "If I were a better analyst, or, if the patient were healthier, then I wouldn't be responding this way."

Early in my analytic training, I discussed in supervision a session with a very upset patient and the interpretive reflection that I had made as the session ended. My supervisor thought that it was right on target, and that I had handled the session well. But I felt uneasy, and not until we were walking to the door did I suddenly remember something I had not mentioned: that the patient had looked into my eyes as he was leaving and that I had reached out and squeezed his arm gently. I confessed this, and it took a long time for my supervisor to respond. Finally, he said, in what I'm sure he meant as a reassuring tone, "I guess it was all right, as long as you don't consider it as part of the analysis."

Times have changed, however. We can now acknowledge that patients' moments of vulnerability *do* evoke feelings in analysts—sometimes tenderness and compassion, sometimes even less comfortable feelings, but feelings nonetheless. Even now that interpretation in an atmosphere of abstinence is a less monolithic expectation than it used to be, analysts (and their teachers and supervisors) are not always comfortable with the ebb and flow of spontaneous feelings in the analytic situation—what to do with them, what use to make of them, and when it is and isn't okay to have them. The study of vulnerability as a desirable and useful aspect of the therapeutic process provides a new context for the consideration of such questions.

To succeed in therapy, patients must allow themselves to be vulnerable, and they need their therapist to respond to, and share in, that vulnerability. The cohesive identity that we all hope will provide stability and meaning in our lives can never simply be found. It must be created, and identity is created through repeated experiences of vulnerability that contain by their nature the very anxiety and confusion that we often would prefer to escape. Psychotherapy is an attempt to facilitate change, but in the psychoanalytic therapies the important changes are not the changing behaviors or vanishing symptoms that can be seen on the surface. The aim of analytic process is the accrual of structure within the self, and the development of a healthy sense of identity that allows for flexibility and openness. The capacity to tolerate the experience of vulnerability without resorting unduly to self-limiting protective barriers is an essential characteristic of a healthy self and identity. It also plays an important role in the *development* of such a self, and so in therapy it is important that this capacity be recognized, nurtured, and utilized by both participants.

To some analysts this stance will be familiar, but to others it is a startling bit of reframing. There are still times when patients' fear of vulnerability (or the behavioral reflections of it) is experienced, by analysts, as resistance. Patients' "refusal" to be vulnerable can sorely test analysts' capacity to contain their own feelings of inadequacy and frustration. When the efficacy needs of analysts are not met, they too are subject to the feelings of disruption and the overreactions that go with the experience of selfobject failure. I will discuss this important phenomenon in detail later, but will illustrate it rather simply here, with a vignette from my own analysis.

I was not an easy patient. I clung tightly to the illusion that I was in treatment because it was an important experience for an analyst. I had not accepted a man as a source of warmth and support since the death of my father when I was little, and I approached analytic exploration as a fascinating but abstract procedure, and my analyst as an idealized figure whose wisdom I could internalize from a safe distance. This stance frustrated and provoked my analyst, who was a classical Freudian, and who saw it (with some accuracy) as subtly contemptuous. It provoked me, in turn, that he interpreted any disagreement or dissatisfaction of mine as resistance. Although I couldn't have put it into words at the time, I experienced his attitude as experience-distant, and felt that he was always scrutinizing my remarks for pathology. I did not feel at all safe enough to drop the barriers that would allow the exposure of a more needy and vulnerable self.

Despite his intent to remain neutral, my analyst's annoyance began to make itself felt, and he told me one day that I was untreatable. That got my attention, all right, but I pursued the comment in my usual intellectualizing style until he finally bellowed angrily, "If I continue to feel the way I do, that will be the end of the treatment!"

I left without showing how rejected and unwanted I felt, but I feared that there was something dreadfully and irrevocably wrong with me. Eventually, however, my upset led me to what was at the time an astounding discovery: I felt devastated—a new experience for me in my "grown-up" life. And if I was so distraught at the thought of losing my analyst and the analysis, then I *was* treatable, and he was wrong.

The next day I excitedly shared this revelation. I was still scared that he would throw me out, but the vision of my

> reaction as understandable and human had bolstered me. And he himself seemed like a different person. He listened to what I said. He even commented that he might have a "countertransference," as he put it, and that he would need to reflect on it. Things were different from then on. In the moment of joint vulnerability the day before, both of us had dropped our customary identity patterns briefly. It was a pivotal point, and the real beginning of my analysis.

This example illustrates how rigid identities protect against the danger of retraumatization, but at the same time limit openness to change and intimacy. I know that the cracks in my armor of distance, and the experience of vulnerability, were frightening to me, and I am equally sure that the cracks in his armor of neutrality were frightening to him—that he saw both his anger and his subsequent kindness as missteps. I see them now as emotional availability, cracks in rigid identities that he and I unknowingly had to co-create before the treatment could get off the ground. This story illustrates too the importance of the therapist's ability to come back to an empathic, responsive stance when it has been temporarily lost, as it frequently is between vulnerable parties. I hate to think how this encounter might have turned out if he had not been able to right himself, and had met my vulnerability with further aggression or interpretation.

Experiences like this occur where fear and longing intersect—where defenses and desires engage each other—and that is why a clinical focus on narcissistic vulnerability is so helpful in the process of psychotherapy. An expanded awareness and appreciation of the vicissitudes of the state of the self that we call vulnerability can help the therapist facilitate and deepen vulnerable moments, and use them to the fullest in the quest for therapeutic change. But, as the example above shows, it is not only the patient who puts himself at risk. A real involvement between patient and analyst is central to the analytic process, and any real process between two people requires of both the openness and risk-taking that we experience as vulnerability. Throughout this book I use clinical examples to demonstrate how a more enlightened attention can be paid to the vicissitudes of this important aspect of the therapeutic process. Most of the examples are comprehensive process reports, rather than excerpted vignettes, because my aim is to illustrate the slow deepening of therapeutic process, as opposed to encapsulated moments of insight. Short vignettes cannot convey the sense of development over time that longer process samples can. Also, to retain in my descriptions as much similarity as I can to the therapeutic process as it happened in fact, I will pay close attention to certain aspects of my own subjective experiences. To share these ideas on vulnerability in the context in which they occurred is, in itself, a vulnerable act, and in this book as in therapy I hope that it will enrich the process of communication.

2

Tenderness, Vulnerability, and Selfobject Relationships

> Regardless of theory, the problem of treatment is to hook up with the patient's *trying*, and to make it profitable in one way or another. Laurels go to the man who gives us new ways to visualize what a patient is trying for. And that Kohut has surely done.
>
> Lawrence Friedman, 1986

My emphasis on vulnerability and its place in the psychotherapeutic process grew out of my theoretical commitment to self psychology and intersubjectivism, and my clinical experience as a therapist working not only with individuals but also with couples and groups. Self psychology dictates a clinical focus on affect and on the vicissitudes of narcissistic needs and injuries, while intersubjectivity emphasizes the interplay between the differing subjectivities of patient and therapist, stressing that what happens between them cannot be understood separately from the intersubjective context in which it occurs. This view enhances and extends the concept of empathic attunement by providing additional reasons for trying to see the world through the patient's eyes: the therapist's subjective reality has a validity, but it is not a privileged objective truth any more than the patient's is. Both people's subjectivity must be taken into account and respected.

Within this theoretical framework, years as a group and couple therapist have powerfully influenced my own individual approach to psychotherapy. Group and couple therapy demand attention to the relational aspects of analytic work. Seeing the powerful forces—sometimes nurturing and sometimes destructive—that develop among people who share and communicate intimately teaches one to take very seriously the mutual influences that exist within relationships. I have seen over and over how great change can become possible when people feel safe enough to come together and reveal to each other the vulnerabilities we all share. My convictions about the power of these vulnerable moments and the importance of fostering them have given direction to my therapeutic work. My intention in this book is to communicate these convictions and to support and illustrate them. To that end I briefly outline here the aspects of self psychology and intersubjective theory that underlie my clinical use of vulnerable moments, and throughout the book I demonstrate the practical intersection between the two in clinical examples of individual, couple, and group psychotherapies.

BASIC CONCEPTS: A SELF-PSYCHOLOGICAL VIEW

Kohut (1974) had a series of cases that his classical assumptions did not seem to fit. He finally concluded that his patients' complaints that he did not understand them were justified. He began to look skeptically at classical views of transference: "I began to entertain the thought that these people were not concerned with me as a separate person but that they needed me as a set of functions which they had not acquired in early life; that what appeared to be their love and hate was in reality their need that I fulfill certain psychological functions for them and anger at me when I did not do so" (p. 889). Kohut came to believe that these missing functions were developmental necessities for the formation of a healthy sense of self, and that his patients' demands for them were not simply a repetition of inappropriate wishes from the past that they refused to relinquish.

His experience with these people convinced him that there are developmental needs that persist until they are fulfilled, and that some of the demands that arise in analysis are phase-appropriate and legitimate reflections of these needs that, having been suppressed in their original form, surface in the transference. Moreover, these transferential demands are expressed in the analytic relationship *when* and *because* the analyst's understanding has created for the patient a safe-enough surround to resume them. This means, Kohut (1984) said, that the analyst must grasp

> the patient's perception of his psychic reality and [accept] it as valid. This is tantamount to saying that the self psychologist does not confront the patient with an "objective" reality that is supposedly more "real" than his inner reality, but rather confirms the validity and legitimacy of the patient's own perception of reality, however contrary it might be to the accepted view of reality held by most adults and by society at large. [p. 173]

That was how Kohut came to believe in the centrality of empathy, which he described as "vicarious introspection" (1959). He proposed that the only proper data for psychoanalysis is obtained through *empathic immersion* in the patient's subjective experience. Only by feeling himself inside the patient's world, and imagining the patient's experience within it, can an analyst gather the data he needs to understand what the patient feels. He must see the world through the patient's eyes, without imposing his own values or judgments. (Kohut's idea of empathy as a psychoanalytic tool is often misunderstood. Empathy, as Kohut described it, includes an acknowledgment of separateness. He did not imply merger, or an overidentification that blurs the boundaries between two separate selves, but rather an appreciation of the validity of the patient's subjective experience. The analyst decenters from his own subjectivity, in part by reflecting on it and distinguishing it from concrete reality. He does not relinquish his own perceptions and values, only the belief that they may be imposed on the patient as a superior reality.)

Selfobject Transferences

Kohut ultimately concluded that the style of attachment to him that his patients manifested was the expression of legitimate developmental needs for affirmation and for the presence of an idealized protective figure; that is, that it was a reflection of what he called *selfobject needs,* and he thought that it represented an effort to resume derailed development.

Selfobject needs are fulfilled when the adequate provision of a needed developmental function enhances the development, maintenance, or restoration of the self. Kohut called this provision a *selfobject experience,* and he came to believe that repeated selfobject experiences are the developmental background out of which individuals form a cohesive, vital, and continuous sense of self; part of "good-enough" responsiveness from caregivers is precisely the provision of selfobject functions. He found that patients who did not sufficiently receive such responses in childhood sought them from their analysts, and he called the manifestation of these strivings, and the patterns of attachment that went with them, *selfobject transferences.* He made clear as well that the need for selfobject experiences of one kind or another persists throughout life, and that the presence of selfobject needs and longings was not in itself a manifestation of psychopathology. "In the view of self psychology man lives in a matrix of selfobjects from birth to death. He needs selfobjects for his psychological survival, just as he needs oxygen in his environment throughout his life for physiological survival" (Kohut 1978, p. 306).

Selfobject Relationships, Safety, Empathy, and Tenderness

When functions such as mirroring, calming, and affect regulation are not adequately provided by the selfobject surround, the child does not develop these capacities sufficiently. Thus the individual does not possess reliable tools for the maintenance of a vital sense of self. In Kohut's view, therefore, the answer to the question posed in his last book, *How Does Analysis Cure?* (1984) was by accepting, legitimizing, and interpreting unfolding selfobject transferences. The analyst's empathic responsiveness allows the patient to feel safe enough to seek, though at first very tentatively, the selfobject experiences that he failed to find with early caregivers and that he needs in order to resume an arrested process of self development.

The selfobject longings of children, patients, and indeed all of us encounter a variety of responses over a lifetime. Some of these responses enhance the exposure and vitality of the self, some are actively destructive to it, and some simply fail to provide anything useful. The latter two outcomes tend to suppress one's willingness to experience and share selfobject longings in favor of more defended self-states. For this reason, the establishment of a sense of safety in the psychoanalytic situation is all-important in self-psychological work, and a more primary focus of the therapist than perhaps is called for when the theoretical emphasis is on insight rather than on eliciting selfobject needs. The analyst's empathic listening encourages the engagement and unfolding of selfobject transference and the tentative hope for selfobject experience. As the therapeutic process deepens, earlier and earlier forms of the selfobject transferences arise and become available for interpretation. That is, when the patient feels safe enough in the analytic situation to permit the experience of suppressed longings, or at least to explore the fears that have forced these longings into concealment, the underlying personal meanings and affects associated with the patterns of response seen in the transference can be ever more deeply explored.

People generally wish for their selfobject longings to be met with what I refer to as tenderness—a spontaneous appreciation of the vulnerability being offered and the desire to treat it kindly. To believe that one's analyst is capable of this kind of response is an important aspect of feeling safe enough to expose long-suppressed selfobject longings.

This idea, like a number of similar ones, is sometimes misunderstood by clinicians working outside of the self psychology context. Self psychology does not prescribe that analysts *must* feel tender toward their patients as some imagine that an idealized mother does toward her child. Tenderness on demand would be inauthentic and undesirable, even if it were possible, and tenderness, as we will see presently, is not a permanent or enduring state of mind, but a momentary and responsive one.

It is the vulnerable patient's *wish* for tenderness, not any particular obligatory response to it, that is relevant in this context. Simply, a patient who believes that his analyst (or other significant figure) is capable of, and open to, the kind of caring responsiveness that he longs for is more likely to allow himself to take the risk of exposing vulnerable selfobject longings than one who does not.

Yet when Warkentin and Leland (1966) edited an issue of *Voices* on tenderness, they could find no papers on the subject, and they concluded that the concept frightens many people. They also found it hard to get therapists to write about the subject. A number of authors said that it was more difficult for them to express tenderness in their work, or to say anything meaningful about it, than to be aggressive, efficient, or technical. In one of the papers in that issue, Bowers and colleagues (1966) attributed some of this reticence to the possibility that tenderness is an experience that "tends to merge two people" (p. 7); perhaps therapists are reluctant to write about experiences where they feel themselves approaching merger, or what Stern (1983) has called "state-sharing." It may be too that tenderness is sometimes confused with sexuality, leaving analysts uncomfortable about expressing it; I am thinking both of Freud's (1915) stress on the importance of frustrating transferential (incestuous) demands and of Ferenczi's (1933) view of the trauma inflicted upon children when adults fail to understand their need for tenderness, and mistake it for, and respond to it as, sexual interest. However, in the more than thirty years that have passed since that *Voices* appeared, the analytic climate has changed greatly. It is now possible to consider tenderness less fearfully and defensively, and to delineate its place in the empathic experience of both patient and analyst.

Tenderness, as I see it, is a response to the experience of

shared vulnerability. Lathrop (1966) described it as "a spontaneous feeling of compassion and love directed not necessarily toward one that you love all the time. It is a sudden insight into something inside the other person that makes you compassionate. It is not pity. The suddenness of it is one of its essential characteristics" (p. 116). This "sudden insight" is the result of a shift in the self-states of both the patient and the therapist, a co-created (Lachmann and Beebe [1993, p. 51] say "mutually organized") event that enhances the receptivity to emotional insight without which interpretations cannot be mutative.

This kind of connection can feel very intimate, at times to a disturbing degree. With it may come memories of embarrassing and painful moments of unwelcome exposure, as well as the comforting and validating kinds of sharing that we generally prefer to associate with intimacy. The temporary blurring of boundaries between analyst and patient can occasionally challenge the analyst's sense of separateness and neutrality, and it can also give rise to momentary but profound feelings of closeness.

In any case, vulnerability evokes feelings in other people; this is one reason that vulnerable moments, as I see them, are always shared experiences. It is in part because of the power of this universal experience that empathic immersion in another's subjective world so frequently gives rise to feelings of tenderness toward that person. To work as a self psychologist, which by definition means maintaining selfobject bonds with one's patients and repairing the ruptures in these bonds, requires that one open oneself to sudden and at times intense experiences of shared vulnerability, and the tenderness that is a not uncommon response to them. These reactions may happen frequently or seldom, but the patient's sense that they are possible—one aspect of Orange's (1995) "emotional availability" (p. 125)—is an important source of security to a patient who fears vulnerability as a forerunner of fragmentation. The analyst's *capacity for* tenderness is an important part of the creation of safety, not a liability that undermines his neutrality. Without it, a too-vulnerable person, rather than exposing and sharing his vulnerability, will resort to rigid protection or succumb to the wish to be left alone.

The potential in vulnerable moments for sharing comes from the universality of the experience of vulnerability. We can all identify with how it feels, and with the wish for a benign and caring response to it. (This universality accounts for the potency of the modalities of couple and group therapy. However, it also may lead to difficulties in reporting and exploring these moments, because of the complexities in the intersubjective context once additional subjectivities are added. Both the potency and the difficulties will be explored in coming chapters.) The therapist uses his store of experiences of this kind to attune himself to the patient, and the patient's experiences of selfobject failure and narcissistic injury resonate with the analyst's own experiences of these kinds, if he will let them, establishing the deep empathic resonance that is so important to the analytic healing process. Analysts tend to stress the value of interpretation, and Kohut himself struggled hard to maintain the scientific validity of empathy as a value-neutral tool for data gathering, but he also reluctantly acknowledged empathy as a healing force in itself. We do not always receive the tender empathic response to our pain and selfobject longings that we wish for, even as children, but we do wish for it, and when it occurs it is a powerfully liberating experience.

The "attuned responsiveness" that Stolorow (1993, p. 40) describes as necessary to the intersubjective view of therapeutic action, often includes a component of tenderness. But empathic responsiveness should not therefore be mistaken as an attempt to prevent or to soothe away pain. On the contrary, an empathetic responsiveness to emerging vulnerability invites a deeper exploration and processing of underlying painful affect. Furthermore, not every response of even the most skilled clinician is always empathic. Empathy is a tool to create the safety within which selfobject transferences of all kinds, and their underlying organizing principles, can emerge, and a thwarted developmental process be resumed. Even the most skilled clinician cannot expect his responses to be empathic every single time. The goal is that responses should be empathically informed. That is different from the expectation that they appear caring, nonconfronting, or empathic all the time. The analyst's responses can take many forms, but ideally they are based on an accurate empathic grasp of the patient's needs. Well-timed limit setting, for example, can be an empathic response, although perhaps not welcomed as such by the patient. Inappropriate sympathy or indulgence, by contrast, however urgently solicited, is not empathic at all. An essential aspect of the analyst's attitude of empathic inquiry and responsiveness must always be his or her "commitment continually to investigate the *meaning* of his affective responsiveness, or its absence, for the patient. . . . Whether or not the analyst's affective responsiveness will itself have a beneficial or therapeutic effect will depend on its meaning for the patient" (Stolorow 1993, pp. 32–33).

Selfobject Failure and Rupture and Repair Sequences

The working-through process in self psychology, therefore, requires the progressive exposure and elucidation of ever deeper selfobject longings, and so differs sharply from the corresponding process as envisioned in the classical model. The aim is not the uncovering of deeper and deeper derivatives of repressed sexual and aggressive drives to be mourned and relinquished, nor the correction of transferential distortions, but the resumption of an arrested developmental process and the strengthening of the self, based in part on the legitimitization of selfobject needs and yearnings.

Self psychologists understand the structure-building aspects of working through differently as well: The therapeutic process deepens, and structure develops around repeated sequences of nontraumatic rupture and repair of the empathic bond. The analyst, like the parents of early childhood, cannot always provide perfect empathic responsiveness. The patient experiences these inevitable lapses as what Kohut called selfobject failures: the empathic bond breaks, and needed selfobject support is suddenly missing. These experiences are inevitable, and are precipitated by the unavoidable "inaccuracies of the analyst's understanding or simply [by] the foreignness, the remaining otherness of the analyst" (Kohut 1984, p. 177).

Many people have childhoods in which these failures are frequent and severe, and the central affect states required for the development of self (what we have been calling selfobject needs) are not responded to or are actively rejected. Such individuals, like all of us, experience a strong wish to express their own affects, needs, and demands, but they feel an equally pressing need to conform to the emotional needs of necessary caregivers if they have learned that doing so is required to maintain vital attachments. In this situation a fundamental conflict is established between the need for self-delineation and the need to maintain selfobject ties. Once this fundamental conflict is established, it is likely to persist and endure (Stolorow et al. 1987), leaving some people historically and characterologically inclined to submerge their own affective strivings and individuality in the interest of maintaining indispensable ties.

Therefore, selfobject failures trigger strong and variable emotional reactions. When these can be seen from the patient's point of view, accepted, and, at the right time, interpreted as understandable reactions to a subjectively painful experience, they become a part of the working through of the selfobject transference. Kohut (1984) stated, "If—a crucial 'if' indeed!—the analyst retains his analytic stance and, open-mindedly and nondefensively, attempts to resonate empathically with what the patient is experiencing" (p. 182), he may be rewarded by seeing a very difficult situation and a very difficult patient transformed into a working patient and an analytic process. (As will be seen in some of my case material, this is sometimes much more easily said than done.)

Such occasional nontraumatic failures in the empathic attunement of basically good-enough caregivers allows for the growth of required developmental capacities and of a secure sense of self. When mirroring, idealizing, or twinship functions are sufficiently provided, then the inevitably imperfect empathic responses are a frustration, but a tolerable one. Kohut (1972) referred to this kind of selfobject failure as "optimal frustration, in that it provides the opportunity for the child or patient to take in a function that was being provided by a selfobject, and to make it a part of the self. A parent's attuned responsiveness to a child's panic, for example, provides a calming function and helps the child avoid being overwhelmed and disorganized. Eventually, a tolerable delay in providing this soothing function serves as an opportunity for the child, in small increments, to develop the capacity to calm himself.

This self-soothing capacity is internalized and becomes part of the child's self organization. At first, the internalization includes a representation of the providing caregiver. As the process becomes more complete, the qualities and representation of the provider are no longer a part of the experience. The child neither mimics nor internalizes the personality characteristics of the provider. In contrast to a process of identification where these characteristics are taken in, it is only the *function* of self-soothing that becomes part of the self. Kohut (1977) referred to this process of building new psychological structure as "transmuting internalization" (p. 32). The term *transmuting* refers to the mutative change that makes the function a part of the self.

Furthermore, when frustration is followed by an empathic understanding of its subjective meaning, the sequence of rupture and repair is transformed from a failure into a selfobject experience, and eventually leads to a *strengthening* of the empathic bond. Also, the demonstration of the child's effect on the caregiver creates a self-strengthening experience of efficacy. In treatment, nontraumatic failures occur and are repaired through the analyst's empathic understanding of what the experience meant to the patient. One effect of this is that the patient begins to experience the bond with the analyst as an empathic connection, but no longer as a perfect empathic *merger*. Through repeated instances, the archaic demand for absolute attunement is gradually transformed into a reliance on a more mature form of empathic resonance. The demand for total empathic immersion, which implies no awareness of separation and therefore no need to make needs overtly known, gives way to the expectation that the analyst will repeatedly struggle to emotionally understand the patient's inner life. In effect this is a developmental path from archaic demands to a more mature use of available empathic responsiveness. Thus failures contribute to the developmental process.

When the analyst repeatedly succeeds in repairing breaks

in empathy and returning to an empathic stance, the patient has the experience of being deeply understood, or at least attentively responded to; that is, he feels that his selfobject needs are being met. A patient who comes to expect that these needs will be met is experiencing what Bacal (1995) called a selfobject relationship—"an intrapsychic experience of a link with a significant other who can be counted on to provide essential self-sustaining psychological functions" (p. 360). A selfobject *relationship,* in other words, refers to the expectation of the availability of selfobject *functions,* which include empathic responsiveness and the tenderness that is a part of it.

Optimal Responsiveness, Optimal Restraint

More recent writers, though strongly influenced by Kohut, have questioned his belief that optimal frustrations allow the child (or patient) to "take in" the selfobject function that was being provided by the good-enough other, and make it a part of the self. They suggest that it is not frustration itself that is curative in analysis, but rather that it is the analyst's understanding of the rupture that provides the essential healing experience. Stolorow and Atwood (1992), for example, think that the principal source of therapeutic action in the analytic process is the *transference meaning* of the investigation and interpretation of these ruptures and repairs. "It establishes the analyst in the transference as the secondarily longed-for, receptive, understanding parent who, through his attuned responsiveness, will 'hold' (Winnicott 1954) and thereby eventually alleviate the patient's painful emotional reaction to an experience of repetition of early developmental failure" (pp. 257–258).

When a parent fails to respond adequately to a child's need for selfobject experience, the child is overwhelmed; children cannot, on their own, always regulate and organize intense affective responses without having to resort to self-limiting or developmentally impairing protective measures. This is the original failure. Unfortunately, the same misattuned parent who was unresponsive to the original hurt is also unlikely to respond empathically to the child's protest or expression of anger or pain.

Therefore, a secondary failure usually accrues also, and it is in response to this that the analyst is able to provide a new experience. When the repair of empathic failures does occur, in analysis if not in childhood, there is a resumption of the patient's experience of the availability of a selfobject—a function that understands and organizes the affective disruption of current as well as past experiences of selfobject failure. This allows the resumption of the growth processes arrested by the selfobject failure, and the patient experiences as well his own efficacy in eliciting a selfobject experience in a new relationship.

Bacal (1985) thought that Kohut's (1971) concept of optimal frustration placed too much emphasis upon deprivation and frustration as key elements in the therapeutic process, and believed that the discussion of frustration versus gratification "becomes inevitably entangled in theoretical difficulties and endless debate" (p. 202). He proposed the concept of optimal responsiveness as a more meaningful view of what leads to growth in analysis. He defined optimal responsiveness as

> the responsivity of the analyst that is therapeutically most relevant at any particular moment in the context of a particular patient and his illness. Empathy or vicarious introspection is the process by which the therapist comes

> to understand the patient by tuning in to his inner world. Optimal responsiveness, on the other hand, refers to the therapist's acts of communicating his understanding to his patient. [p. 202]

He and several others (Terman 1988 and Lindon 1994, for example) have maintained that the analyst's empathically attuned responsiveness cannot be neglected as a curative factor. When a patient reveals a dream, for example, he is sharing a relatively unprocessed, unguarded, and intimate part of himself. Often, the dream expresses either shame-related fragile aspects of the self or equally precarious newly forming self patterns. These are presented for acceptance, mirroring, or other tender needs. Some degree of involved empathic responsiveness is crucial to further exploration and to encourage the unfolding therapeutic process.

Fosshage (1983), on the other hand, makes the point that there are pitfalls as well in insisting on too much responsiveness from the analyst (in the sense of providing too much interpretive assistance). He felt, for example, that the patient's active participation should be encouraged in a process of elaborating, rather than translating, the dream imagery. It is this kind of encouragement (in this example of the dreamer's involvement), along with the stress on the patient's affective experience, that in my view is central to the furtherance of the therapeutic process. The dream is already, in itself, an important element of this process and thus simply requires amplification rather than translation. (This concept is discussed in much greater practical detail in the clinical material that follows. To my way of thinking it forms a model for the analytic response to all of a patient's subjective productions. It is particularly relevant to work with dreams and will be demonstrated in greatest detail in Chapter 8.)

What Shane and Shane (1994) refer to as "optimal restraint" is another counterbalance to Bacal's concept of optimal responsiveness. They point out that empathic attunement does not always lead to overt response or to providing. Silence, or the decision not to gratify a request, may be the optimal nurturing response. This is certainly true in working with dreams, for instance, where too frequent interpretative comments may discourage the dreamer's own initiative and creativity.

The balance between responsiveness and restraint has been integrated by Bacal (1995) in a more recent elaboration of his concept:

> Optimal responsiveness rests upon what might be called a theory of specificity, that the therapeutic process entails the operation of a complex, more or less unique, therapeutic system for each analyst–patient couple, in which the analyst's task is to discover and to provide what is therapeutic for that particular patient. . . . Optimal responsiveness comprises the therapist's acts of communicating to his patient in ways that that particular patient experiences as usable for the cohesion, strengthening and growth of his self. As an encompassing principle, it informs the therapist's work.

This means that there can be no one definitive approach to dreams any more than to treatment as a whole. Each therapist–patient couple must develop its own approach through a process of mutual regulation and cueing.

RELATIONSHIP IN THE ANALYTIC PROCESS

The increasing emphasis on responsiveness rather than frustration is a reflection of a growing appreciation of the centrality of relationship in the analytic process. Bacal points out that self psychology "is, in essence, a relational theory, which explicates the self's experience of a variety of responses in significant relationships with particular others" (1998a, p. xiii). "While 'officially' self psychologists address only self-experience, both their written and their verbal communications are replete with references about the importance to the analysand of the experience of his or her *connection* to the analyst as selfobject. In other words, the *selfobject relationship* is tacitly recognized by self psychologists as the major vehicle for the maintenance and development of the self" (1995, p. 360).

EMOTIONAL AVAILABILITY

This recognition of the role of the selfobject relationship means that the analyst has to be willing to engage in the relationship. Orange (1995) describes emotional availability in the analyst as a nonspecific readiness to respond that can take many forms, and she views it as "an underlying and often overlooked element in the success or failure of therapeutic relationships" (p. 125). Patients come to expect this emotional availability and to count on it. (They learn to expect and count on it not only from the therapist, but also, in couple and group treatment, from each other.)

Like all people, patients and analysts possess an underlying awareness of the possibility of narcissistic injury, and so both parties enter the analytic engagement with their own needs for self-sustaining responsiveness, and their fears of its failure. Yet to be emotionally available, an analyst must be willing to be deeply moved, and even disturbed, by the emotions and experiences of his own life that are evoked by the patient's struggle, or, as Ehrenberg (1996) describes it, to take off his "psychic rubber gloves." This willingness often leads therapists to "feel vulnerable, not only to the patient but also to our own inevitably unfinished business. . . . We revisit our own pain" (Orange 1995, p. 132). This is one reason that analysts, with the active cooperation of patients, often abort the development of vulnerable moments, and why being self-reflective and alert to this tendency is essential to analytic work. I concur with Orange in her belief that the analyst's emotional availability is a key factor in establishing the safety in which the tendrils of the patient's early developmental needs can begin to unfold. For many patients, the experience of the analyst's emotional availability and understanding is essential to mutative change. For insight and understanding to have a mutative impact, they must develop within a relationship.

That affective experience in the here and now is needed for understanding to lead to enduring structural change is not a recent idea. Orange (1995) and Bacal and Newman (1990) have provided extensive descriptions of the development of this view. My intent here is only to establish a historical context for my assertion that analysts must be affectively alive and involved in a relational process—that is, vulnerable. The question is no longer whether insight or affective experience is most essential. They are both acknowledged requirements of therapeutic process, and discussion can now address the narrower question of their relative emphasis at specific moments with specific patients: in other words, what in each instance is "optimally responsive" (Bacal 1985).

Psychoanalysis has long held that it cures by making the unconscious conscious, and notwithstanding his focus on empathy, Kohut wanted very much to retain the traditional stress on interpretation as central to the therapeutic process. Just before his death, he asserted that his most important point in the book that would be published posthumously as *How Does Analysis Cure?* (1984) was that "analysis cures by giving explanations—interventions on the level of interpretation; not by 'understanding,' not by repeating and confirming what the patient feels and says, that's only the first step: but then [the analyst has] to move on and give an interpretation" (Kohut 1981, p. 532). This sequence from understanding to explaining is illustrated at length in Chapter 8.

However, Orange (1995), who has made an excellent survey of the historical background of the question of how psychoanalysis heals, points out that Kohut also hinted that "something besides interpretation may be involved in psychoanalytic cure" (p. 169). In fact, Kohut (1984) mentions as well the importance of the development of an empathic bond and the establishment of a mature selfobject experience as essential components of psychoanalytic cure. In the final address (Kohut 1981) cited above, he reluctantly acknowledged that, as much as he wanted to regard empathy as simply an informer of action and a scientific tool for data gathering, he had to note that "empathy, per se, is a therapeutic action in the broadest sense, a beneficial action in the broadest sense of the word. That seems to contradict everything I have said so far, and I wish I could just simply bypass it. But, since it is true, and I know it is true, and I've evidence for its being true, I must mention it. Namely, that the presence of empathy in the surrounding milieu . . . is . . . something positive" (p. 530). Although he wanted very much to remain both scientific and loyal to the traditional analytic emphasis on interpretation, he felt he had to include the empathic bond between patient and analyst as an element in the therapeutic process.

Orange makes clear that the recognition that relationship as well as interpretation is crucial to psychoanalytic cure has very early roots, and that it did not originate with Kohut. She feels that the dissenting voices that stressed the emotional quality of the bond between analyst and patient began in the 1930s; Ferenczi (1931), whom Orange gives as an early example, wondered whether the relationship itself might not be the curative factor.

INSIDE A COFFIN: VULNERABILITY, RUPTURE, AND REPAIR

The following clinical example[1] illustrates in detail the rupture and repair sequence and its role in the working-through process, and it touches as well upon questions of optimal responsiveness, and the risks and rewards of emotional availability in the analyst.

Clinical Example

Lisa and I have been at a painful impasse for months. Very apprehensively, in her effort to convey her experience of utter

1. This case material first appeared in Livingston, M. (1997). Inside a coffin: a recurrent daydream. *Voices* 33(2): 26–34, and is reprinted here by permission of the American Academy of Psychotherapy.

despair, she reveals a recurrent daydream that she has never before shared with anyone. "When I was little, I used to have this dream while I was awake. I'm inside a coffin. I'm removed, but I can see and hear. People seem to care about me. They miss me, but I'm isolated. They can't see that I'm alive. I make no further effort."

I know that this is a very painful image to Lisa, who grew up in a family unresponsive to her inner feelings and dreams. Yet I also allow myself some hope that her trusting me with this secret is a break in the impasse: that she at last feels safe enough to venture out. Before I can put my appreciation of this tendril of hope into words, however, Lisa adds, "I feel exactly that way, right now, with you." The few perfunctory words I manage sound hollow, even to my own ears, and for me, the rest of the session passes in a disturbing blur.

At her next session, Lisa says that it was hard to come. She lies down reluctantly and stares silently at the ceiling. When I ask her what made it hard to be here, she says that she feels that something is always expected of her. "I'm never going to get what I need here. I'm never going to be whole."

It's hard for me not to reassure her that nothing is expected of her and that she can get some of what she needs from treatment. I make understanding noises and wait for her to continue. She says that she had a dream last night that she doesn't remember except that there were demons and a devil.

We talk about this, but I'm not sure if we're really working together. I sense that she's cooperating, rather than freely speaking her mind. The affect in the room seems flattened, and it seems to me that we're both nervous about whether I can hear what she needs to express.

After a long silence I say gently, "I am experiencing you as having something to talk about that's difficult to bring in to the session." She is visibly touched at my noticing and begins to speak with more affect. "I'm really hurt—in a lot of pain—and I don't know if I can turn to you. Even when you seem to understand, there's something that you want from me. I often feel a tension with you—a wanting to be mean to you—and at the same time, a not wanting to hurt you. I think my bewilderment is that I don't know what I want from you right now, if anything."

I have been shaken by the previous session, but have done some serious self-supervision since then and am not totally unprepared for a difficult encounter. I do want to understand better what is going on between us, and I am committed to learning about my contribution to it. I encourage her to continue; I want to legitimize her anger and invite a more open exploration of her experience of selfobject failure. I ask her to tell me more about her fantasy of being mean to me.

Lisa offers some fantasies of exposing me as the bad guy I really am, and not giving me a chance to redeem myself. Also, she says she is testing me: "If you can stand up to the blame and care about what I need at the same time—I need you to say 'I don't care if you are hurting me, I know what you need and I'm here for you.'"

She goes on to say that she feels that she has to "get past" this feeling. She isn't sure why she's so mad at me. "I think that I just wanted to feel better at this point in my life and I don't. I thought you were going to give that to me. . . . Are we walking mindlessly or does one of us know how to get there?"

I am uncomfortably questioning myself when she adds in a contemptuous tone, "Why would I be coming here if there wasn't something you could do?" I don't know what to say. My silences leave her feeling isolated and abandoned, but anything I say provokes an attack that only widens the gulf between us.

Lisa continues, "I'm telling you that I'm in a coffin and you aren't doing anything to open it. I want you to say, 'I know that you're in there. You don't have to be. Come on out.' Why doesn't anybody help me? I'm doing what I know how to do."

I'm doing what I know how to do also, I think to myself. I am struggling to contain my response to feeling attacked so as not to deny Lisa the experience of expressing her rage. At the same time I try not to say anything that will invalidate her subjectivity, and to self-right and return to an empathic stance from my own experience as the object of her rage. It's not enough.

Lisa continues, "Where are you? It's not easy for me to tell you all this. So, what do you do? I have the window open and you don't come in. That makes me close up." Now I *have* to say something, but even as the words come out of my mouth, I know they're defensive and invalidate her experience of abandonment: "So you're really feeling that you opened the window and I didn't come in?" I think to myself, I might just as well have said something like, "How could you imagine that I'm not with you? How can you see me in such a wrong way? I'm really here and a good guy." As I hear my defensiveness it becomes easier to spot how I'm contributing to her desperation, at least after the fact, but still, the clinical moment is excruciating. But Lisa continues to try to get through. Maybe she's picked up that I've realized something and am beginning to "get it." She says, "I don't feel you in the coffin with me at all!"

At this point I can't contain my own feelings any longer despite my intention to see the world through her eyes, and I react with some hurt in my voice: "I feel like I was in with you and you kicked me out." Now she is *really* enraged. "I don't want to have to be perfect. . . . Maybe you were with me for three or four sessions. I need more! This feels like I'm a kid and I have to give something up before I'm ready." Still a bit incredulous that she can be so unaware of how hard I'm struggling to be with her, but softening and really wanting to know, I ask, "What am I asking you to give up?" "I picture an infant struggling with her mother," she replies. "The baby really wants to be embraced but she's fighting. The mother wants it to be easier to be with her. I want to be miserable and have you be with me. Don't ask me what I need, just give me help!"

I'm trying to absorb and explore with her what she needs me to be. "It sounds like, in a way, I'm holding out because of the way you're being." "It's either that," she replies in tears, "either that, or you just can't love me." After that brief moment of vulnerability, Lisa goes back to her anger. "What am I doing here? What are you doing for me? That is a *real* question! What do you add to the equation?"

"It sounds like you want me to prove that I'm adding something—that I'm worth something." My response is still a distance from the mark, but my heart is really struggling to be with her. She corrects me once again, but this time without contempt. "It's not about you proving that you're worth something. That sounds like a pouting statement!"

I finally "get it." Right here and in the moment, I am repeating the very trauma that she has been trying to get me to understand. "I am pouting!" my inner voice shouts. I am thinking about how difficult it is for me to hear how inadequate she finds me. I am refusing to see how deeply hurt she is because her attacking manner has put me off. She's right!

As is so often the case in these difficult impasses, it is not anything specific that the therapist manages to say at the key point. Lisa senses a shift within me. At this point, I am receptive in a deep way, and she knows it even before I can find words to express what I now understand. I grunt and she seems to read into that more meaning than I had been able to convey in all my interpretations. She continues, "It's not that I want you to prove anything to me. It's more that I am feeling hopeless. Give me hope!" She breaks down momentarily and cries. My eyes are also full of tears.

My reply is not eloquent. Nevertheless, it is from the depths of my sense of the despair of her experience and from my own struggles with loneliness through the years. "We've been out of the coffin together before and I am sure we will get out of it again. I think that the struggle is to really know what's keeping you in the coffin. I've been able to reach you in there before and to find a way out together. We need to see what's keeping us where we are—like my pouting."

As she is leaving, Lisa asks, "Do you think that I'm unreasonable?" I'm caught a bit off guard and I ramble a bit, but I manage to be authentic. "I think that it's reasonable for you to want me to help you get out of the coffin. I certainly feel that it's reasonable for you to want me to find a way not to leave you so isolated." Then, with some anguish along with my newfound self-acceptance, I make what feels like an admission. "At some moments I just can't. If I listen and leave myself out of it, you feel isolated—I'm too far away. If I express my own feelings or thoughts, it seems at those times that I'm too near. It seems to make it worse. It's an intrusion. I'm an intrusion. No! The answer is definitely no. It is not unreasonable for you to want help. I have often been able to help. I want to. At some moments, though, I can't." Lisa is quiet and tearful as she leaves. I think maybe also a bit hopeful.

I approach the next session with renewed confidence. My self-supervisory process has enabled me to make an important shift to a more empathic and grounded stance. I experienced the last encounter as a major breakthrough, a repair of the empathic break, and I am looking forward to a more cooperative, less in-crisis patient. I should know better.

"I've been having more thoughts about taking a break from therapy," Lisa begins. "Arguing with you about what you aren't doing for me is a waste of effort. I'm coming here because I want you to be able to help me. I don't feel that yesterday helped me. All that happened is that I got locked into something with you. If I say anything about my feelings, you get hurt and withdrawn. You said something about my getting upset if you express your feelings. All I hear you saying is that you feel trapped too." After a long pause she adds, "I really need you to add something here!"

"Actually," I respond, "I've been thinking a lot about last session. I think you're trying to tell me about all the ways that I'm still defensive—like when I was pouting. I think we need to look at how I do that and how it gets in your way. How it hurts you." "I'm very sensitive to that," she replies. "You're like all of them. I try to tell you what I need and you go off onto how that hurts you. I'm trying to tell you how big my need is and you want me to see that you're giving me something. . . . Then I have to give up needing. Then I have to understand and be reasonable."

I am concerned about her desperation, and try to be with her in her pain. Lisa feels my nonverbal responsiveness and begins to slow. At the end of the session she tearfully says, "I know that I'm missing something. I know that I need to be here. I just don't trust that you will stay with me long enough. You seem to understand and you seem to care. It isn't sustained enough. It hurts when it isn't."

In the weeks to follow Lisa begins to open up the depths of her despair. She speaks often about how unbearably painful it is "to feel caring and to know it's not enough. It will never be enough." Whenever she begins to need someone, like her parents, they think that they've given her enough. Then they leave her, or expect her to understand their needs. There are days when killing herself seems like the only possible relief. There are also days when she feels "in better spirits." She has begun to feel that her worth is recognized at work and that a few friends have taken her pain seriously. She has also begun to explore what she describes as "a fiery rage inside—one that I was never allowed to say out loud. If I did, I would be thrown out. I can't justify the rage. No one would take it seriously. . . . I am starting to take myself seriously." Then she adds (in case I might think that it's enough), "I am still angry that you didn't care enough to see before. I'm angry that you want me to be better, that you want me to be okay."

The work continues. Lisa's experience of herself and of me alternates. She rocks back and forth between resentment and pleasure, between an inability to mourn and the seeds of a capacity to do so, between grandiosity and worthlessness, and most poignantly, between hope and despair. She alternates between closeness and distance. Such is the nature of working through. Her daydream and my reflective self-awareness continue to provide a crucial key. The impasse has been unlocked, and the therapeutic process has resumed its unfolding.

Discussion

The extent of Lisa's traumatic experiences (in childhood, as they were relived in the transference, and in several important relationships outside of treatment) had remained essentially unshared up to this point. The content had been explored extensively, but the all-important, emotion-laden subjective meaning had not ever been successfully conveyed to anyone. Her daydream about the coffin succeeded where words alone had not, and played a significant role in the working-through process that followed. This is a good example of how a self-psychological healing process proceeds, as the establishment of an empathic bond within a new relational experience allows patient and analyst to explore the here and now as well as the genetic roots of selfobject failures within the transference. This example also illustrates the role of the analyst's repeated self-reflection, affective involvement, and vulnerability, and a judicious use of an analyst's self-disclosure in the service of the patient's needs. My choice to share my awareness that I was pouting was a vulnerable risk, and it contributed to our breaking through the impasse.

Trying on the Attributes

My initial sense that Lisa's sharing of her secret daydream about being in a coffin was a budding tendril of trust was, after all, on target. She had begun to consider the possibility that I was sincerely interested in her inner self and was really trying to "get" the deep significance of her painful experiences. But the process was not as easy as I had hoped it would be, and I was horribly shocked by her comment, "I feel exactly that way, right now, with you."

Lichtenberg and colleagues (1992) call allowing the patient's subjective reality to stand without questioning or opposing it "trying on the attributes." The therapist must contain all of his own responses to being seen in a way that contradicts, and even at times attacks, his own view of himself. Trying on the attributes requires not only that he contain defensive responses, but that he try to explore the aspects of himself and his behavior that actually fit the patient's view. Often, if the analyst will allow himself a vulnerable moment, the reward is self-discovery of a disowned aspect of his own personality. The attributes are tried on like an overcoat and may be shed in time, and it can be quite a relief to regain a perspective that is not entirely the patient's! The concept is similar to that of a "trial identification," as opposed to a more basic or ongoing identification. However, the concept of wearing the attributes stresses an intentional acceptance of the patient's perception that tests the analyst's ability to decenter from his own perspective and see the world, including himself, through the patient's eyes.

It was only with great difficulty that I was able to try on the attributes of the person who was failing Lisa, and thus was responsible for so much of her current despair. Yet in my need to see myself as understanding, I was letting her down once more. Once I got over the shock, however, a shift began. Self-reflection helped me return to an empathic stance from which I could really "get" the import of what she had been trying to tell me, and eventually, once the message began to sink in, I was able to be spontaneously responsive in a heartfelt manner, and to see with regret that I had indeed been failing her. That emotional understanding was key to our resolution of the impasse and repair of the empathic rupture in such a way that Lisa's engagement in the analytic process deepened and her growth could proceed.

Self-psychological psychotherapy depends on the establishment of a sense of safety in the therapeutic situation. Without it, long-suppressed selfobject needs will not make themselves apparent or accessible to exploration, and the development that depends on their fulfillment will not be able to resume. It is important that the analyst be emotionally available and open to intense shared experience, because selfobject longings by their nature demand response; unless patients come to expect a different kind of response than they received from their parents, they will maintain their characterological defenses against vulnerability and their early unmet developmental needs. A clinical focus on the patient's subjective experience of vulnerability encourages this sense of safety, and reinforces it by enhancing the rupture and repair sequence that is necessary for psychological growth.

3

The Therapist's Attitudes and Interventions

> What Kohut did not explicitly include in his theory (although there is ample evidence throughout his writing to indicate that he understood otherwise) is that it is not only a psychology of the self, it is also quintessentially a psychology of human relatedness.
>
> Howard Bacal, 1995

Everyone, patient or therapist, has an underlying awareness of vulnerability, although habitual protective patterns often limit an individual's conscious experience or expression of these feelings. Kohut (1977), in fact, commented that "narcissistic vulnerability is a ubiquitous burden of man, a part of the human condition from which no one is exempt" (p. 292). A self-psychological approach to the therapeutic process thus requires a clear understanding of narcissistic vulnerability. My own clinical perspective is unusual in its emphasis on the *subjective* experience of vulnerability, the clinical use of the fleeting vulnerable moments in which it is transiently accessible, and the tendency of other people both to be drawn to and to avoid these moments. This concept is not theoretically revolutionary, as the last chapter has shown; it is central and common to intersubjectivity (Stolorow et al. 1987) and specificity theory (Bacal 1999), as well as to mainstream self psychology. However, it warrants greater clinical attention. Vulnerable moments possess such leverage, and are such powerful agents for structural change, that a clinical focus specifically on narcissistic vulnerability is very useful.

VULNERABILITY AND THE THERAPEUTIC PROCESS

The concept of vulnerability is not as simple as it seems. In common usage it connotes primarily a burden and a danger, but in the context of psychotherapy it is more akin to the Chinese concept of crisis, whose written representation consists of two characters meaning "danger" and "opportunity." Everyone has had experiences where being open meant being unprotected in an unsupportive and invalidating world, and for that reason patients approach treatment, as Anna Ornstein (1974) has said, with both hope and dread. To lower one's defenses—to allow oneself to be vulnerable—is to face the possibility that the interpersonal traumas and selfobject failures of childhood may be repeated; yet that risk may be acceptable when it coexists with the hope of a new experience of responsiveness and connection.

The experience of vulnerability therefore consists of two simultaneous aspects: the danger of shame or humiliation, or of fragmentation of the self, and the promise of the new experiences that greater openness allows. Longed-for and long-lacking selfobject experiences (of validation, affirmation, affect regulation, intimacy, and so on) once more become possibilities. Vulnerable moments are opportunities to seek, and perhaps receive, the empathic responsiveness that is still yearned for behind defensive barriers.

This is why vulnerable moments are potentially pivotal moments of change. They are the times when long-suppressed selfobject longings, and the sensitive feelings related to them, are finally, and anxiously, permitted expression. A vulnerable individual feels that a tender weakness is being exposed and fears the possibility of shame and rejection, even when the newly experienced parts of the self may also involve aggressive or assertive expressions such as anger or an increased wish for separateness. However, the experience of vulnerability and its great clinical potential lie not in any specific affect, but in the dropping of customary modes of self-protection, and the increased availability of the true, rather than false, self; they lie in the subjective experience of newness and risk, and in the sense of being "seen," with all that that entails of danger and of promise.

> My first awareness of the power in such moments occurred when I was a patient in a group myself. I struggled for years to express myself in it and to feel part of it. But I kept hitting what felt like a silent wall when I tried to share my feelings, and I would retreat again and again to the comfortable role of "understander" and empathic listener. Finally after another fruitless attempt to communicate, I exploded at the group's unresponsiveness.
>
> After this outburst another patient told me that although she really wanted to listen and to be with me, she found herself preoccupied, and kept daydreaming about her father's death. She felt that she was letting me down, since that wasn't what I had been talking about. "Don't you see?"

the group leader said. "Whatever the surface content is, Marty is always trying to deal with what he felt when his father died." "And no one ever was interested," I added. With those words, I was able to relive, and express for the first time, the agony of a 3-year-old whose mother and family ran from his grief, and the group was able to share this with me. While the group failed to pick up my struggle to mourn, I felt that something was wrong with me. The group's discomfort had felt like a repeat of my childhood experience, and my fears that people would withdraw from my painful feelings prevented me from exposing myself enough to allow anyone in. When I at last relinquished my "understanding" defensive stance, however, the vulnerability that burst out in my hurt and anger allowed the group and me to bridge the gap that had been separating us. The result was an opening up for many of the members of previously inaccessible experiences of grief and loss.

A moment like that is often so powerful as to seem almost magical, both to the person who experiences it and to any others with whom he is engaged at the time. The opportunity to be open in an accepting and empathic relationship is an opportunity for people to soften previously rigid beliefs about relationships and about themselves. This softening allows the integration of previously disowned elements of the self, and thus the resumption of developmental processes that were arrested when the disowning occurred.

We all know that this experience of safety in openness is not easily come by. To lower defensive barriers against others is risky in itself, opening one as it does to shame, rejection, and other blows to the self-esteem. To go a step further and relinquish the constraints that one routinely imposes on one's own behavior brings up accompanying fears that needed caregivers will not tolerate one's authentic self, and will sever necessary ties—what Stolorow and colleagues (1987) have called the "fundamental conflict." Some people identify so deeply with their charactero-logic defenses that they fear to relax them at all lest a vital existing identity dissolve. An empathic surround is necessary for the mere contemplation of such softening, but even with one, exposure always includes dimensions of risk as well as of opportunity. The balance manifests itself differently in different people and in different circumstances. Vulnerability is not a single definable phenomenon, but rather a dimension of self-experience. It ranges from an open and fluid state of the self on one end of the continuum to a set of crystallized and fixed protective structures on the other. Sometimes a person experiences the sense of vulnerability precisely and can express it clearly; at other times, though, the self feels in such jeopardy, and in such imminent danger of fragmentation, as to require rigid protective maneuvers that preclude reflection, exploration, or open communication.

Openly "vulnerable" behavior, however, is not a requirement for therapeutic progress. The vulnerability that underlies even formidable defensive barriers can be reached, and released to do its therapeutic work. When the analyst understands and communicates a patient's precarious self-experience and the anxiety that it engenders about greater openness, *that* experience of having one's self-protective maneuvers empathically exposed and understood is a vulnerable moment in the potentially curative sense that I am describing, and in its aftermath a new set of expectations begins to be established within the patient.

Similarly, clinical work with vulnerability can foster change even before a patient's capacity to reflect upon, and thereby develop insight about, his own vulnerability is well developed. Again the essential factor is the analyst's emotional involvement and understanding, and this includes an understanding, to whatever degree possible, of rigid and nonreflective self-protective maneuvers. Often a co-created sudden insight into the rigid defensiveness of another's world is what triggers the tender responsiveness that enables a vulnerable moment.

A well-timed interpretation produces a shift in the patient's experience of himself, facilitating a change from one self-state to another—from a sense of aloneness and fear, for example, to a more cohesive sense of safety or connection. The therapeutic action of interpretation occurs in this transformation of self-states, as the internalization of capacities to regulate and change self-states become reliable capacities for self-soothing, self-stabilizing, and affect regulation.

Vulnerable moments enhance the capacity to effect changes in self-states in similar ways. Lachmann and Beebe (1993) stated, "In adult treatment, interpretations transform self-states with respect to such dimensions as intactness-fragmentation, depletion-vitality, and freedom of the self-regulatory range" (p. 50). Vulnerability-protectedness may be seen as another such dimension. In fact, the development of the capacity to tolerate the experience of vulnerability, and to move flexibly and appropriately along this dimension of vulnerability-protectiveness, is an important aspect of structure building.

Openness to others (the extent to which an individual permits access to his subjective experience) differs from vulnerability proper, which is an inner experience. Both wax and wane depending on circumstances, but the transformation of vulnerability into openness requires the development of a relationship in which it is safe enough to risk the communication and sharing outwardly of the inner experience. The analyst therefore must understand and be able to grasp empathically both experiences of vulnerability, and the defenses and protections that are mounted against them.

For reasons such as this, I consider an analyst's attitudes more important than his technique or his specific interventions. I agree with Orange and colleagues (1997) that "technically oriented thinking blinds us to the particularity of our patients, of ourselves, and of each psychoanalytic process" (p. 25). Every analytic dyad or triad must create its own process, and change its own procedures, when necessary. It is the patient's experience of the analyst and the personal meaning that the analyst's responses hold *for that particular patient* that determine what is therapeutic. For this reason I concentrate throughout this book on attitudes and understandings that can serve as guides for the therapist's interventions, rather than on specific technical recommendations, and first among these attitudes is the awareness of just how important the subjective experience of vulnerability is, and the kinds of attention that allow the analyst access to it.

Attention to self-states is very helpful in this regard. Most significant communications in psychotherapy convey some message or other about the state of the self, and attention to vulnerability, and to vulnerable moments, requires careful monitoring of fluctuations and transformations of the self-state of the patient.

Lachmann and Beebe (1993) describe changes in self-state as "mutually organized events that transform and reorganize experience and promote self-regulation, vitality, and cohesion" (p. 51). Such changes show themselves subtly, through variations in the tone of voice, the quality of emotionality, and other nonverbal cues. Attunement to these cues makes possible exploration of the underlying state of the patient's self. It brings to light changes in cohesion and fragmentation proneness, vitalization and depletion, and other dimensions of self-experience. As I have pointed out, vulnerability and self-protectiveness constitute one of these dimensions and an important aspect of self-experience.

The fact of the therapist's empathic immersion in the patient's subjective life in itself creates an intensity and a support for these moments, and empathic inquiry into the underlying state of the self encourages a shift even further toward the vulnerable end of this dimension. Such inquiry into moment-to-moment fluctuations in self-experience can take the form of questions such as, "What is it like to be George right now?" and "What were you experiencing just then?" Looking for the trigger of affective fluctuations is also often helpful to many patients. Vulnerability can be further fostered, and vulnerable moments intensified, by slowing down the process and focusing on emerging material that is directly related to the patient's self-state. Encouraging patients to "experience what they experience" or to "stay with the feeling" (Levitsky and Perls 1970) can lead to surprising moments of openness.

What Lachmann and Beebe (1993) and Stern (1983) call "state sharing" is another way the analyst can recognize emerging vulnerable moments. State sharing is an aspect of empathy, and it refers to the way that empathically connected people feel within themselves aspects of the other person's experience. An analyst who is open to this experience—who is "emotionally available," to use Orange's (1995) term—may find in his own inner experience a clue to what is going on in the patient. Even when there are no overt manifestations of a change in the patient's self-state, a change in his own self-experience may alert the prepared analyst to the possibility that something important is happening in his patient. Inquiry at such points may bring out the patient's part of this shared vulnerability, deepening the process for both.

VULNERABILITY AS BURDEN AND POTENTIAL DANGER

One of the powerful fears that underlie people's reluctance to soften their boundaries and to allow another intimate contact is the terror of changes in core patterns of relating to and organizing the subjective world. Intersubjectivists Stolorow and colleagues (1987) think that every individual organizes and understands his perceptions of other people, as well as of the world, according to his own unique "organizing principles." These principles operate unconsciously (until elucidated in psychotherapy); challenges to them feel discomforting and risky, and they may be an important source of vulnerable feelings, as forthcoming clinical examples will show.

Furthermore, "tragic man," as Kohut (1977) conceived him, has a precarious sense of self, which is vulnerable to depletion and fragmentation when the necessary supports for developmentally vital experiences are not sufficiently available. When the self is so vulnerable, the burden of protecting it may lead to fixed defensive and relational patterns and therefore a brittle sense of identity—what Kohut called the limiting of the individual's "striving to express the basic pattern of his self" (1977, p. 133). In this context any move toward change is experienced at least in part as a threat to the rigidly established identity. Thus protective shields are tightly held.

Therefore, one fundamental danger of vulnerability is the perception of what Slavin and Kriegman (1998) have called the "psychic undertow." This is a conflict that operates whenever any two individuals attempt to interact in an intimate way, and it derives from the fact that two different people have diverging interests, values, and needs (even if they are patient and analyst). Each individual attempts "to use the other, to pull the other into his or her subjective world, and to resist the pull, the undertow, in the opposite direction" (p. 249). Each uses the other (as a selfobject) in the service of constructing and maintaining a sense of self-experience and of the relational world. Each inevitably tries to define the other in his or her own terms, and at the same time both to accept and resist being defined in the terms of the partner. The relational world always includes significantly competing interests. Self-protection may therefore be maintained even at the cost of yearned-for intimacy, both in analysis and in an individual's outside life.

Slavin and Kriegman see the process of arriving at a "relatively less deceptive and self-deceptive discourse about such conflicting interests [as] fundamental to the viability of the analytic relationship—central to therapeutic action" (p. 258). Clearly, patients and analysts will both have a reason to avoid vulnerability if this "undertow" within the intersubjective context of the relationship is not dealt with analytically. One especially difficult aspect of the analytic situation in this regard is its asymmetry. In most intimate relationships there is much more reciprocity of dependency and more overlapping of interests. Many patients experience the asymmetry of the analytic situation as dangerous.

Slavin and Kriegman point out that this inevitable conflict is *not* the result of the patient's pathology projected on a blank screen, nor is it the result of the therapist's countertransference to a projective identification. It is not even wholly the result of the therapist's inability to sustain adequate empathic attunement with the patient's subjective reality. Conflicts of interest of this kind are woven into even the most cooperative relationships, including the analytic and marital ones (which will be discussed further in the latter context in Chapter 6). To permit the kind of vulnerability necessary in psychotherapy, a patient must trust that the analyst, although never totally free from his own agendas and needs, has a "good-enough" alliance with the patient's interests. It is not a coincidence that this same trust is the precondition for the reappearance of long-suppressed selfobject wishes.

VULNERABILITY AND THE PSYCHIC UNDERTOW

The following clinical example illustrates the difficulties that arise around the patient's awareness of such potential conflicts of interest, and the need that the analyst be open to this awareness, too. It also highlights the legitimization and working through of these fears, and the subsequent unfolding of selfobject longings and the risk of further vulnerability.

> Audrey was feeling a great deal of conflict about resuming her analysis after a six-month hiatus following the birth of her second child. On her return she scheduled a group and an individual session on the same night of the week so as to minimize the time away from her children. She wanted analysis, but she was reluctant to make that a priority when the wish to be at home with her children was so strong. She was also aware that she had been experiencing deeper yearnings for closeness with a female supervisor than she had felt

thus far with me, and she was considering working with a woman analyst closer to her suburban home.

After a period of being "stuck," Audrey cautiously expressed the worry that my values and needs might lead me to recommend that she continue with me, sacrificing her other strong wishes and values. I had to "wear the attributes" assigned to me by her perceptions, and seriously consider that my wishes about her work might in fact be based on my own needs and values. Once I was able to do that, we both stopped obsessing about the decision. For Audrey, confronting me with her fears about my potentially intrusive values and interests was a significant risk, in the face of her fears that I would be hurt or angry and withdraw emotionally, reenacting painful childhood experiences. For my part, it was difficult to examine the ways that my own "selfish" needs threaten to get in the way of my therapeutic responsiveness.

We continued with one session a week for several months, while Audrey consulted several women therapists. During that period we explored together her fears that I would not be able to decenter sufficiently from my own needs, and also the validity of her perception that I was contributing to the conflict. We came to understand her wish to have both her closeness with me and the freedom to value other experiences even more. Gradually our discussion included Audrey's awareness that with her parents she had never felt certain that she could explore her own values and needs freely and still maintain an essential bond with them. She feared that they would feel rejected and pull away from her. The yearning for someone to maintain a deep connection with her while she questioned and moved back and forth began to surface. She eventually decided to risk that commitment with me.

Vulnerable moments cannot be avoided in the analytic process. They are uncomfortable, yet at the very point that the patient (often the analyst, too) experiences this sense of risk and grave danger, there is the greatest openness to new experience. Vulnerability is incurred, at least sometimes in psychotherapy, by the willingness to accept hitherto avoided risks. Moments of vulnerability inevitably accompany new openness, and they are a sign of its presence; they should be welcomed in treatment with a tender empathic responsiveness.

New relational experiences, and the vulnerability inherent in them, interact with insight to lead to change in three important ways. From the self-psychological vantage point, the most important of these is the unfolding and working through of selfobject transferences, whether they arise between patient and analyst, in a marriage, or among the members of a group. As Kohut (1981) expressed it, "Interpretations are not intellectual constructions. If they are, they won't work; [they might work] accidentally, but not in principle" (p. 532). A second mutative process is the exploration of old experiences and the softening of previously rigid intrapsychic organizing principles (Stolorow et al. 1987). Finally, in the experience of a safe-enough selfobject surround, the process of a more creative interpersonal negotiation of overlapping and conflicting interests is possible (Slavin and Kriegman 1998).

These are essential elements of the process of psychoanalytic psychotherapy, no matter who the patient or what the modality of treatment. The centrality of relational experience is most obvious in couple therapy, and an extended discussion of vulnerability in couple work follows in Chapter 6. But it applies equally to the analytic process in individual and group treatment. In addition to the development of reflective self-awareness, insight, and the illumination of old, formative, organizing principles, relational experiences are important elements in the analytic process. The following clinical example illustrates all of these elements and their intersection with the experience of vulnerability.

IN SEARCH OF SELF: THE STRUGGLE TO ALLOW VULNERABILITY

The session to be presented here is an example of both one patient's struggle to risk the vulnerability of greater self-experience, and the importance of the therapeutic relationship. Although the patient's relational experience is not the focus in this session, it is clearly operating in the background. Roz's sense of a warm supportive connection with her analyst provides a foundation for the analytic work she is doing both in her sessions and in between.

Roz is in both individual and group therapy with me. The frequency of individual sessions has varied over several years from a brief period when she came three times a week, to her current schedule of one session every other week. The frequency has been controlled by logistical factors of time and money. However, issues regarding trust and involvement play a role as well, although she is now an involved analytic psychotherapy patient. Roz often lies on the couch in her sessions, but she moves about actively, at times turning to face the analyst, sometimes sitting or even standing up to portray what she is saying in movement and posture. Her body language and gestures as well as changes in the tone of her voice are very expressive. Yet she still struggles to experience her feelings fully, and she often speaks from her intellectual and rational side. It is as if even her gestures and expressiveness are in the service of conveying her ideas and thoughts, and fail to express a deeper feeling experience.

She begins by reporting that there have been several instances during the past weeks in which she has been aware of feeling "self-defensive." With a degree of pride she adds that she has been able to get herself not to get "vicious" and protect herself that way. Her 12-year-old daughter had been attacking her. "After a long period of listening to her attack, I could feel myself shrinking. It feels as if I'm reducing myself down to a cellular place, where I can be one—one—one. Mark [her husband] tried to intervene. He didn't say anything bad. It's almost like I was making an announcement. 'I'm going under.'

"I said to him, 'I really recognize what I'm doing. I know it. I recognize it in the set of my jaw.' It's a face that my mother made my entire adolescence. Her face was set in an expression that basically said, 'I'm not going to respond to your vicious attacks on me,' meaning you girls. But I'm just at the end of my rope—but I'm not going to say anything. I'm not going to make it worse. It's a feeling in my jaw . . . a sort of . . . my face is sort of projecting as much as I can of disgust, but without being exquisitely provocative to Debbie. So we're locked in this place. So now I have this face that my mother had. I know exactly what she felt."

After listening intently with occasional "umm hmms" and encouragement to continue, I try here to move Roz more toward her inner experience if I can. "What do you feel when that's going on?" I ask.

"Attacked, wounded, but I'll be God-damned if I'm going to expose myself to her. Because she's so . . . angry . . . and the face . . . the feeling doesn't acknowledge that she's wounded, that she's a child. It doesn't compute that way, unless I step back a little bit. Mark wanted me to step back more. He said, 'That's interesting. How did you feel as a kid when your mother had that face?' He was trying to put me back into that feeling, to get me to see Debbie and not to identify with my mother. I couldn't take his help. Even though I didn't put out the signal of . . . I was on my way down . . . shrinking . . . self-protection . . . and I couldn't . . . I felt deeply threatened by exposing my vulnerability. I didn't trust him. I can't trust anyone when I'm in that place. I can't trust. He wasn't doing it outwardly, but I felt 'You're not being my friend. You're anxious about Debbie. You want to engage me in this conversation for Debbie, not for my sake. I can't. I'm boycotting this conversation even though, in a funny way, I agree with it.' I just sort of ignored it and he kept pushing . . . and it got us into a very bad situation. It all took until a few hours ago to repair, because I wanted to blame him, and there was blame here, for his anxiety led him to push for a conversation. He wasn't reading my signals of being so in danger." Roz is doubly frightened about being vulnerable here. First of all, she experiences Mark, like her parents, as not being sensitive enough to her sense of endangerment. In addition to this, she also senses, correctly, an inherent conflict of interest. Mark, in his identity as a protective father, sees the situation largely through Debbie's subjective experience and his own childhood experiences. He cannot, at least not as fully as Roz needs at the moment, see the interaction through his wife's eyes and have her interest totally at heart.

"He wasn't realizing how frightened you were," I clarify. "Right," she responds, "and yet he was saying that I don't give him any signals. He says that I don't reach out, and I'm saying that it's all I can do to not act out. I mean, all my energy is going into self-protection. The expectation that I'll reach out from that position and expose that I'm frightened . . . that's just not my reality."

Trying to move further into her inner experience and to focus on her sense of underlying danger and vulnerability, I say, "So, you're needing to protect yourself. What are you protecting yourself from?"

"I'm protecting the exposure that I'm feeling weak. I'm protecting anybody seeing my weakness, because I'm assuming that they'll take advantage of it . . . that they'll hurt me further. It's so . . . it's so about not trusting. There's no trust of anybody, nobody. It's not only that they can't help me. It's that they don't want . . . I get into a paranoid thing. Nobody wants to help me. Nobody is my friend. Everyone, if given an opportunity, will hurt me. They see me as mean and bad and they will hurt me further if I show my weakness. They will hurt me. They will take pleasure in my weakness . . . and everybody gets lumped into that, Marty. Even my 12-year-old daughter gets lumped into that. Everyone gets lumped into that. It doesn't matter who you are or how weak you are. It's such a nontrusting survival place. It's not that I'm not able . . . lately, one out of every three or four times I can reverse it, but the effort to do that is so indescribably difficult at that moment when every cell in my body is screaming, 'Batten down the hatches, close it all up, get in there, enemy attack! Enemy attack!' At that moment, to go like this [she gestures open arms] . . . it's *so* hard.

"What I need is more tests of my capacity to do that in a relatively safe place. I did it a week ago at dinner. It's a lingering feeling of tearing. It feels like tearing apart. It's *so* painful to do that. It's like tearing a tendon."

I know that the pain she is talking about has to do with going against old, deeply ingrained organizing principles and that she is struggling to take in new experiences and to build alternative organizing principles. It's like she is tearing apart a constraining but established identity to leave room for a new sense of self to develop. I try a bit awkwardly to draw her out further. "It's painful not to attack," I suggest tentatively.

I am a bit off target and, as I hoped, she helps fine-tune my understanding. "No, it's not that it's so painful for me not to attack, but for me to go from . . . to move from everything inside me saying that they're attacking . . . enemy attack! They are attacking me. To go from that to an open . . . to expose vulnerability, it's just indescribably hard. It's so hard and it remains so hard, and my memory of the last time that happened was . . . what I'm climbing over . . . the mountain that I'm climbing over in that protection, is a huge amount of anger that I have to say isn't real. I have to . . . you know what it's like? It's like passing through a room of virtual reality where I have to tell myself, 'This isn't real. This is a projection of my own making.' It's like the movie *The Matrix,* where the computers that control human beings generate our version, our view of reality. None of it is real. We are being controlled by computer generated . . . Actually, reality is a completely bombed out apocalyptic postcomputer . . . the computers have won in the battle between man and machine and in order to keep us subjugated, they've completely controlled our version of reality. That's what it's like. It's like moving through a place where all my messages are 'They are attacking you. Mark is trying to control you.' All those messages are coming in and I'm going '*Don't* listen to this. This isn't real. This is your shit.' Then the messages go, 'It feels real. What do you mean it isn't real?'

"So it takes an enormous will, just like in *The Matrix.* There are three or four humans that have woken up and gone through it. It's sheer force of will. 'I'm not believing this.' Then you break through to 'Oh, oh,' but it still feels as if you're passing . . . *and the bullet wounds are real.* It isn't suddenly, 'Oh great, fine.' My memory of that moment at the dinner table with Mark and

Debbie where I stopped and looked at what was going on was about a week ago. I'm the monitor of manners at the table, just like my father was the monitor of manners. Debbie was scooping something up on her plate onto her fork and I was horrified. I said in a disapproving tone, 'Debbie, use your fork!' Debbie reacted explosively and the explosion went back and forth. Then I turned to Mark and I said, 'Did I do something? What happened here?' That was the first step. I was actually turning to him—knowing, *knowing*—I wasn't stupid. I knew that I was part of this, so I was turning to him. Maybe part of me thought that he would simply come on my side and postpone until later . . . talking about my contribution to this, but I didn't really believe that.

"This is how it went down. Mark responded to my question in a calm, serious voice. 'It was your tone, Roz.' This was all in front of Debbie. 'It wasn't what you said,' he continued. 'It was your tone, the Henry tone [her father] . . . a disapproving, withering tone . . . a disapproving of who she is.' I was silent. This is all tearing me up inside . . . tearing . . . tearing . . . and then I turned to Debbie and said 'I'm sorry.' She was so surprised and that was that. That was a really successful moment."

"You were really able to take in the information," I reflected with a deep feeling of warmth and building excitement. "Yes!" she exclaimed and then poignantly added, "Yes, but it was so painful. It was so painful. It was like I'm screaming at myself. All the while, there's this other voice."

"What is the pain about?" I ask gently, once again focusing on the underlying vulnerability and danger. "What I hear is your realizing, 'Oh, I had a tone.' So, I wonder what it is that's so very painful."

"What was so painful was to deafen myself . . . to pay attention to the little voice of new reality, which is telling me the truth.

The truth that I know from here and that I know from watching people in group and from watching myself. But it's a little voice compared to the really loud voice that's trying to control my reality the old way. The old voices of 'Don't let them see your weakness, don't let them see your weakness!'" Then in a playful exaggeration of a sinister voice, "They are the enemy!" We both laugh and then, after a quiet thoughtful pause, Roz begins to cry. Through the tears she continues, "Debbie is only 12. It doesn't matter who it is. It's like a police system, a powerful police system that depletes me . . . wants to keep me isolated . . . alone and isolated."

I reflect, "So, it's very painful to question that police system." Then after a long sigh, Roz replies, "It's so painful. It's so counterintuitive. It's counterintuitive in the deepest sense. It's countercyclical behavior and the headwinds are so powerfully trying to protect me from something that's no longer an enemy, not really. But I'm so well trained to protect myself . . . and I'm giving myself these signals that are . . . that keep me isolated."

I continue simply to reflect her subjective experience. All the while, though, I am subtly pursuing an inquiry into the deeper aspects of the patterns and organizing principles that serve as barriers to vulnerability and intimacy. "So, the signals protect you in some way, and at the same time, they keep you isolated."

"They don't protect me. They did once. They don't protect me. They just keep me . . . they protect me in a very short-term survival strategy. They protect me from exposing my weakness, but it's as if, you know, I've grown up behind a great wall. I've grown as the 'last emperor' and now I'm in the free world and it no longer matters, but the construct is so powerfully there. It did matter once. I mean it must have. It did matter, but that was like 'pre-memory.' I can't even remember about what would have happened if I exposed my weakness in the old regime. I mean, I can imagine either teasing or not being seen . . . or just black. I just don't have any experience of it. But the real . . . the pain of doing it now is so bad. It's just so hard to do it in the moment without anger, without acting out."

Vulnerability and the barriers to it are tied to very early, prereflective organizing principles and rigid building blocks of identity. It's no wonder that these old principles are not easily replaced by the new experience in therapy. Working through toward softening and questioning these principles and exposing shame-laden parts of the self is often, as is clear with Roz, a painful process.

Roz continues, "The rational construct is a tool of protection. It's not the thing itself that I'm protecting. I'm protecting . . . uhh . . . vulnerability, weakness. I don't trust that if I expose myself as being vulnerable, that I won't be attacked for being irrational."

Roz's terror of underlying irrationality involves both the fear of its being treated as shameful and a deeper fear of fragmentation. The contemptuous tone she uses at times is one of several barriers erected out of this terror. I move to open this up for exploration. I reflect tentatively, "So, what I hear is that what you're really frightened about being exposed is that it's irrational."

Roz is quiet and thoughtful, but seems to be calmer in response to my reflection. "Yes, that's why I cling to the facts. So I can say, 'Look, she was really doing that.'" I try to move her a step further. "So, you cling to the facts." Roz is clearly with me, nodding an assent. I add, "You cling to the facts rather than to your own experience." I am feeling tender toward Roz's struggle, but I want to be firm about this. "It's very hard to trust and express your own experience without having to be rational and prove a point."

Roz is touched. "Right. It exposes a weakness that I'm convinced, here in my body, will lead to devastation . . . will lead to . . ." She trails off and there is a rather long silence. I am feeling very connected to Roz at this point. I have my own history of painful isolating defenses. I am enjoying working with her and experience a deep empathic sense of "withness." A strong empathic bond and a selfobject relationship are intensely operating in the background. It is at times like this that explanations (interventions on an interpretative level) are most potent in opening up and deepening therapeutic process. Then, if the interpretive work succeeds, what we see is a facilitation of both vulnerable moments and the exploration of inner, subjective experience.

I become a bit more active than I have been up to this point, although I continue to speak quietly. "That tone in your voice with Debbie was protecting yourself from your experience of a danger." Roz seems particularly receptive. After a brief pause I continue. "So, you have a tendency to fall into a trap of trying to come up with facts that will justify what you're experiencing. Right? Not to take a look and know more about your own experience."

Roz nods and, with a tone of sadness, agrees. "Right, because to do that moves me behind the rational curtain. Then there's nothing to hang onto . . . nothing that's outside myself. Then it's all inside myself." I underline, "It's all in you—in your response, in your experience." "Yes, and all my responsibility too," she continues. "If it's just me, just my reality . . . I don't have a lot of experience. I don't have enough experience taking that seriously. To go there without . . . without hanging on to a plumb line down to some outside objective outside thing. . . ." Once again, Roz trails off and lies quietly.

I encourage her to explore further, to stay with and deepen her feelings. "So, can we do that now? Can you take a look at that experience with me? When the tone changed, what was the danger you experienced? What happened before you used that tone?" Roz speaks openly with a good deal of affect and introspection. "It's a . . . repulsion. So, that means I'm protecting something. What am I saying? What is that? Why should I be repulsed by Debbie's fear? I'm afraid of her output . . . afraid of her . . ."

"What was going on just before?" I inquire, sensing the importance of that vulnerable moment (both at the dinner table with her family and also in the here and now with me). Roz begins to re-create the key moment. "She was eating. I don't feel that way with Ann [her younger daughter], only with Debbie. When Ann puts her foot up on the table or some really egregious breach, I jump in and get alarmed, but I'm aware that I don't have the same level of revulsion that I do with Debbie. I don't have it. I'm firm, but I don't have that tone. The tone comes from a fear about Debbie."

"What are you afraid of?" I ask, keeping the focus on her affect in that key moment. Roz answers, "Her appetite . . . her . . . it's connected to her weight and her . . ." Again Roz trails off and I bring her back to the exploration of her own experience. "Does it have to do with you?" "Yes, because I can't feed her enough. You see, manners are also a way of regulating intake, regulating the speed and style with which something is going into her, and I feel like it's the dam or the breakwater of her intake that I can't satisfy. That scares me . . . her appetite . . . it scares me. It must be that I don't have enough, that she wants more from me that I can't give. Her appetite, on some level, feels like an accusation . . . like a manifestation of my not-enoughness, my not being enough, my not giving her enough. It really frightens me."

"It frightens you that she may have a hunger and that you're not giving enough," I reflect, encouraging her to continue. Roz continues, "I know that her hunger comes originally from my not giving her enough. I know that. I've talked to her about it. I know when it started . . . when I got so involved with my career and traveled a lot. It's clear to both of us." At this point Roz sighs deeply. After a long silence, which I do not interrupt, she sighs again.

Her eyes are full of tears and the silence seems to last a long time. Then, painfully, and with much more confusion than is usual in her composed clarity of expression, she continues. "My insistence on manners for her is a way of externalizing the rules of her demands, externalizing my need for her to regulate her need . . . and I know that must be true for my father, too. I mean, look, that's what men are for. That's what the whole thing is about. With men you're face to face with appetite and your crude mammalian need for nourishment . . . and so the shame . . . it's all rules to cover up your shame about that act and about that raw crude need, and so there are all these rules to disguise that what's going on here is '*I want! Give me!*'"

That phrase is abundantly clear and touching. Without understanding all the levels and details of the words that led up to it, I simply express my empathic grasp of the moment. "So, you're frightened if your '*I want! Give me!*' isn't disguised. "Yes, that's right," she responds as the moment continues to intensify. "It frightens me deeply. It strips the skin off the whole thing which is she wants more than she needs . . . she wants more than I can give and I'm at fault. It's my fault. I created it."

MENTAL HEALTH RESOURCES
44 W BRIDGE ST
CATSKILL, NY 12414
518-943-3559

C O P Y
03/10/2005 10:26
Sale:

Transaction # 13
Card Type: VISA
Acc: ************4910
Entry: Swiped
Total: 34.54

Reference No.: 914500765
Auth Code: 032060
Response:APPROVAL 032060
Sequence Number: 0013

"Both that it's your creation and that you can't satisfy it," I reflect. Roz says, "Yes, and the only thing I can do now is insist on the disguise . . . and that must have been what my father was feeling with me." I grunt to let her know that I'm following and ask her to flesh that out. "Well," she responds, "he must have been so afraid of any display of appetite, food, sex, need. When my sister and I had passionate fights, he would say in the most withering tone, 'You sound like a bunch of fishwives,' relegating us, with a precise clarity, to some lower species. That was just totally humiliating.

"What is really amazing, Marty, though, is that we all played along with it. Kids will play along. If I had a husband who allowed that, who institutionalized it the way my mother did, Debbie would *never* be able to stand up to that. We never said, 'Ohh, no.' Never once did my mother question him. Never once did he turn it back on himself and say 'What's that about? Me maybe?' That's astounding! What would happen?"

I reflect her question back to her slightly differently. "What would happen if, as a kid, you could do what Debbie does? If you could question him." Roz says, "Yes, that's right, Debbie does. I'm more porous than Dad. Dad was impermeable. Debbie has someone else to go to, who isn't always going to point to me and say 'That's God, that's perfect.' So she gets a break. She's having my experience, but with valves."

"She can protest," I underscore. Roz responds, "Yeah, it would be better if she didn't have the whole experience though. She's going to have my issues. The difference is that she isn't going to be trapped without a way of protesting for eighteen or twenty years the way I did until I came here. So it is better, but it's the same experience with all kinds of levers and pulls and stuff. I'm at work trying to change it while it's still her current experience. I have another six or seven years.

"I know why my father didn't try to change things like that. You need someone with you, pushing you. Now I push myself. It's so hard and I don't have someone with me all the time going 'Yay, you're doing so well. You're working so well.' Mark will acknowledge it every once in a while, but mainly he's impatient for the remainder of the job. So I feel like women must feel who start out weighing 300 pounds and then, when they're down to 200, they're still fat. I want to say, 'But I've lost 100 pounds.'

"I run into myself all the time. I'm always running into my protective shit . . . my walls. I just feel like I need more opportunities, more safe opportunities, and Mark is pretty safe, as safe as I could get for someone who's involved. If I can do it eight or ten times in a row, then I can break into my new self. I'm like a crustacean . . . like the one in the dream I worked with in group last month [this dream is presented in Chapter 8]. I'm like a crustacean with a crust, a shell. If I can break the pattern, I could break out of my crust into a new self . . . skinless and raw though, like in the dream. I'd break free of my crust. It no longer fits me, Marty. It hampers me, but it really works to protect me. Mark has no idea that I'm vulnerable at that moment. It really hides it. He has to remember that we talked about it before."

Returning once again to the affect, I point out, "So, it's hard for him to see how scared you are." "Yeah," she responds. "That's the point. It's really a successful adaptation, and you can imagine how well it works with people who don't know me that well. It doesn't even enter their mind that I'm weak at that point."

"It doesn't enter their mind that there's a danger that that hunger will be unbridled," I add. "You mean that's why I'm doing it?" Roz asks. I respond, "I think that's the danger you experience. You know, when you say weakness, I think the fear is in the boundlessness." I'm trying to clarify, but feeling a bit off the mark, I add, "I guess there's more to it," looking for further clarification from her. She says, "It's the need that seems by definition unsatisfiable. It feels like there's a voice saying, 'No, no, no. None of you understands. Don't ask me to expose my needs. You don't know how big it is. Don't give me that shit. You can't help me. Don't ask me to come out. You can't help me. You're lying. You're lying by asking me to come out. Don't ask me to trust you, because if I come out . . . you can't help me!'"

"What will happen?" I ask, excited at how alive her feelings are in the room. I want to understand more of the repetitive transferential fears involved. I am also interested, despite some trepidation, to see my contribution to her experience. Roz says, "What will happen is that you'll see how big it is and you'll say, 'Oh.' You'll ask me to go back in. You'll turn away. You'll be disgusted. I don't believe you. You don't know what you're asking. You're too weak for my need. That's why I don't trust. Nobody is strong enough for my need!"

After a pause, she continues. "The good thing with Debbie is that a big part of her experience is that as bad as my withering look feels, as bad as it makes her feel, she never loses sight of the fact that it's my weakness, my lack of courage. So when I walk out of an interaction she'll say to me, 'There you go again, you're so uncourageous. You're so weak.' It wouldn't have occurred to me with my father. No, no, it's me. I'm disgusting."

Sensing a chance to get back to her need to protest and the pain of being unable to do so, I underline, "It wouldn't have occurred to you." Roz is responsive and takes it a bit further. "Not on any level. I know she takes in that she's disgusting too, but she's able to see that her mother is weak."

"I think that you took it in also, but you couldn't say it," I point out, trying again to focus on the experience of protest and the inability to protest. I sense that that is where the vulnerability and affect are most centered. “I don’t know,” she replies. “Why do you think I took it in?” “Because you always talk about protecting your father, about protecting his image,” I elaborate. “Right,” Roz agrees and I continue. “So, you had some sense that it was his weakness.” “Yes, that’s right. It had to remain a secret,” she says thoughtfully. Then, after a pause, I return to the interchange with her daughter, “So, when Debbie is saying, ‘This need is too much for you,’ she’s saying it’s your weakness.”

“Uh huh,” Roz reflects. “I always get there . . . let her know that it’s my weakness. She cries and says, ‘I know, Mommy,’ and hugs me. I’m always stunned by her forgiveness. I expect her to be repelled and say, ‘No, Mom, you’re supposed to be strong.’ I’m amazed that it feels good to her. I feel like I’m doing something wrong by exposing my weakness. Mark says it’s a good thing, but something in me is saying, ‘It’s wrong! This is wrong. She should continue to feel I’m strong.’ She’s flooded with relief, but it still feels wrong for a parent to expose weakness. It feels weird. I don’t know what I would have felt if Dad would have done that. I guess I would have felt like Debbie and been able to forgive myself, but at some point it’s too late. I don’t want him to . . . I don’t want to hear about his weakness. You get locked into the story and ‘Don’t fuck it up now!’ So as Dad gets older he’s starting to ask for advice . . . like about a car . . . and it’s deeply disorienting. The whole family knows that we don’t want that story to change now.”

“It’s disorienting once it’s been established,” I reflect. “Very disorienting. It’s too late now,” Roz responds. I add, “But even when you were a kid, to question it would have been very disorienting.” “Well, you have to have something. It has to be safe to do that, to say that out loud. There has to be some witness in the house going, ‘You’re right.’ I mean, Mark makes that possible for Debbie and my occasional switching helps, too. She hangs on to that. She says, 'I remember Mom said.' When I'm in my good mode I say, 'Debbie, please remember this.' There is another version in the house. When I was a kid there was no other version going on. I want to have that experience now."

"Of questioning that old version?" I underline tentatively. "Yes," she continues. "In the moment when the old version surfaces, it's like a little voice saying, 'No, keep going, keep going.' It feels like a weak insistent rebellion against a much more powerful . . . a much, much more powerful version of reality." Then in a very timid voice she illustrates, "It's going, 'excuse me.'" "Like a little *new* voice," I reflect.

"Yes," Roz replies less hesitantly. "It has to be made stronger. It does surface. It's not that I don't hear it. I just kept choosing not to obey it. Then, every time it fails, it makes me feel even worse, like I've let it down, let myself down." Roz notices, as she often does, that the time is up. She gets up and as we walk to the door she lets me know that she is having some scheduling difficulties with our next several appointments. I assure her that I will try to reschedule and I comment, "It's a real struggle to make room for the new experiences. So many things keep interfering."

CONCLUSION

The general focus in self psychology on empathic immersion and the creation of safety in the clinical environment is easily extended to include a focus on vulnerability and its value as a therapeutic tool. The safety created by the self psychologist's empathic immersion in the patient's subjective experience (along with his or her attention to breaks in this empathic bond) is central to the promotion of change, since it is the safety of the empathic bond that allows the unfolding and thus exploration of the patient's longings. These longings, and the perceived risks of pursuing them, give rise to the experience of vulnerability.

The analyst's recognition of, and attitude toward, vulnerable moments is therefore crucial to the analytic process. Yet the importance of these moments is often overlooked. Therapists sometimes fail to focus on them when they occur. They may be allowed to dissipate too quickly, with no measures taken to sustain or protect them. Perhaps the possibility of touching, or even exposing, the therapist's own emotional vulnerability sometimes leads to this neglect. I will discuss this possibility later on. But it may also simply be the lack of sufficient understanding and appreciation of the importance of these moments. In any case, when vulnerable moments are not protected, the potential to deepen a healing intensity and intimacy is lost.

4

The Therapist's Vulnerability

Before I built a wall I'd ask to know
What I was walling in or walling out.
Robert Frost, "Mending Wall"[1]

A therapist's capacity to facilitate and deepen the vulnerable moments that arise in his patients is closely related to his willingness to permit, tolerate, and make use of his own vulnerability. This willingness, moreover, as an aspect of the therapist's personality and subjectivity, is central in a more general way to the analytic process itself. The nature and extent of its centrality may not be fully clear, and the therapist's vulnerability is not usually discussed in precisely those terms, but it is clearly included in the ongoing dialogue in the psychoanalytic community about the extent to which treatment requires an emotional entanglement between two highly involved and vulnerable people.

---

1. From *The Poetry of Robert Frost* edited by Edward Connery Latham, © 1969 by Henry Holt & Co., LLC. Reprinted by permission of Henry Holt & Co., LLC.

The experience of vulnerability, in therapist as in patient, is internal, and often privately held. It may sometimes involve or provoke external behavior, such as an act of self-disclosure or even the taking of a dramatic risk. But vulnerability and self-disclosure are different, though related, issues, and by "the therapist's vulnerability" I mean the *experience* of vulnerability, not what is or is not overtly disclosed to the patient. The transcript of a session in which the therapist felt particularly vulnerable might not necessarily reveal anything unusual in his remarks or behavior, as I will demonstrate shortly. Even when the therapist does act openly in some way upon a vulnerable moment of his own, momentary overt responses such as those are not the essence of analytic vulnerability, which is rather a day-in, day-out attitude. A therapist trying to maintain the emotional availability and empathic stance that is central to self psychology must maintain an openness to his own inner experience.

The willingness to experience and reflect upon a wide range of affect and personal associations is a necessary aspect of what Kohut (1959) meant when he defined empathy as "vicarious introspection." Empathic immersion demands of its practitioners that they be aware of, able to reflect on, and able to separate, their own subjectivity and the patient's. A therapist who sustains a disciplined attention to this process will experience frequently the arousal of painful, problematic, and conflicting feelings, as the following clinical example illustrates.

EARLY MORNING REFLECTIONS: AN EXAMPLE OF THE THERAPIST'S VULNERABILITY

My meetings with this patient are both exciting and hard work. It has been that way as long as I've been seeing Nancy, and I always look forward to her sessions. In the few months that she's been in treatment with me I have been moved many times by what I experience as her underlying vulnerability. Although Nancy does not express it openly, I feel that there is a deep sense of deprivation, and a yearning for emotional responsiveness and comfort lying just beneath her surface.

Most of the time, though, my efforts to respond and to reflect an empathic grasp of her moment-to-moment experience are met with annoyance. Nancy often experiences my reflections as inexact. At other times she feels dissatisfied that I am simply saying back to her what she has already said. "My father could always repeat my exact words. Then he would be angry that I didn't feel understood. He just doesn't get it."

In spite of this, I feel that a relationship is steadily developing. She has told me that she has never expressed, or even felt, annoyance at anyone as quickly as she does with me. I am drawn to her. I think that she needs to experience my wish to connect with her in order to feel safe enough to expose and explore suppressed yearnings and to resume an arrested developmental process. At the same time, she is critical of my inexactness, and she seems to keep me at some distance. I think she experiences me as sincerely trying to understand her and wanting to find the right point of closeness or distance with her.

Nancy seems reluctant to experience her feelings, and awkward in expressing them. She desperately fears not making sense. She describes her father as caring and supportive, but unable to relate to her emotionality. Her experience is that when she fails to make sense he is disparaging and cold.

As the session begins, I feel intensely connected and caring. I am troubled by my inability to make rational sense of my experience and my expectation. I am aware of my wish to be closer and also of her need for me to be at just the right distance. I feel a sense of tension and excitement in sustaining my attentiveness and at the same time reflecting on my own subjectivity.

Nancy starts by observing that I seem tired. We talk a bit about her fear that if I'm tired I will not be eager or able to be "present." Then she shifts to an awareness that she was not eager to come to the session. She is concerned about something going on at work today and wants to hold herself together. "I need to be strong . . . to be able to function and to focus." She also comments that she's feeling flat. She talks of being concerned about making sense so that I will be able to hear her.

I find myself leaning forward in my chair, feeling intense and connection-seeking. I am aware of fantasies of holding her and comforting her. Nancy explores her fear of feeling too much and her need to be appropriate and to make sense. She talks about how easily she feels defensive, and with some emotion, she connects this to never expecting either her father or her mother to respond with any understanding or attention to her feelings. Her flatness clearly seems to me to be related to the suppression of the yearnings I'm picking up and containing.

I'm aware that I'm choosing to maintain my intense connection, although at times I'm afraid that it reflects my need more than hers, that colleagues would call it overinvolvement and worry about enactment, that my mother would think it selfish. Nancy continues to talk with increasing aliveness as I ponder some of my uneasiness and yet remain connection-seeking. She talks about her dad's putting her down—criticizing any expression of feeling that didn't make sense or seem "appropriate" to him. My associations run to my mother's need to have everything "make sense"—that is, to have me submit to her view of the world. I also remember her concern that something was wrong with me if I wanted too much, especially too much closeness or, at other moments, "too much" separate thoughts and feelings.

Nancy's yearnings and fears are very like my own. The struggle to contain her suppressed impulses and to maintain an optimal closeness and distance has echoes in my own history. On another level, as the reader may have surmised already, Nancy represents the longed-for "good mother" whom I will be able to satisfy and carry off into the sunset. As the session continues, Nancy remembers moments when she feels a passion (usually an idealistic passion about her work). The flatness she often feels makes her sad, and the sadness and a sense of vulnerability deepen toward the end of the session. She talks about being afraid to reveal some parts of herself and finally of her fear of being more intense.

I know that my own intensity, and my willingness to reflect on the entangled relationship developing between us, is facilitating the unfolding of Nancy's vulnerability and openness to new experience. At the same time, I am aware that there are pitfalls in either too much or too little involvement. How close can I fly to the sun? I believe my ability to experience and contain this array of feelings and to continue to return to a position of empathic inquiry into Nancy's subjectivity, is central to the therapeutic process. In moments

> like this, a nondefensive exploration of the patient's experience of the interaction between us is particularly essential.
>
> I begin to feel more comfortably committed and less vulnerable. But there is more than one way that the analyst is a vulnerable participant in the treatment process. As I become less concerned about outside judgments, I begin to reflect on pitfalls within the relationship itself. "What happens when the analyst, in allowing himself to be more vulnerable, is injured? What if I am so connection-seeking and Nancy becomes more disparaging or pulls away?" On some level the analyst must expect to go through a whole range of experiences with his patients. The more vulnerable he is the more difficult it is to contain these experiences—that is, to keep self-righting and returning to an empathic stance—without reacting in a hurt, punitive, or withdrawing manner. Each of us responds to narcissistic injury in his or her own way and no one is immune from this burden. In my work with Nancy, at least, my sense of vulnerability is clear and accessible to awareness.

To enter the tangled and unique relationship with each patient that is required to achieve what Bacal (1985) calls "optimal responsiveness" leaves one vulnerable, because vulnerability is an openness to new experiences, whatever they may bring, and however intense, painful, or shame-threatening they may be. The (theoretical) old-time classical analyst was protected from these experiences to some degree by the prescribed role of "blank screen" and interpreter of transference distortions. The relational self psychologist, however, and most current analytic practitioners, whatever their theoretical persuasion, must be emotionally present and involved without the comfort and protection of rigidly dictated roles and behavior. Increasingly the analytic world recognizes that the structure of treatment must respond to the needs of each unique patient–analyst dyad. Thus, without predefined, unchanging roles and techniques, the vulnerable analyst must repeatedly contain and reflect on not only the patient's anxieties and conflicts, but also his own. This requires consistent and concentrated self-discipline and the courage to sustain an openness to new experience and a reflective attitude, rather than the easier habits of avoiding proscribed behavior or adhering to rules of technique.

THE THERAPIST'S VULNERABILITY AND THE "NON-DIFFICULT PATIENT"[2]

It is generally recognized that the therapist's use of his own subjective experience of the patient and the analytic interaction must serve as "a central guide for inquiry and intervention" (Fosshage 1993). The therapist's use of his own subjectivity (his countertransferential responsiveness), and the extent to which it makes him vulnerable, is well known with regard to the group that has often been referred to as "difficult patients" (see, for example, Brandchaft and Stolorow 1988). These patients frequently elicit uncomfortable or conflict-laden responses in the therapist. Their subjective experience of the world, including and often especially their experience of the therapist, at times diverges significantly from the therapist's view of the world and

2. This material first appeared in Livingston, M. (1996). Countertransference and curative process with "non-difficult" patients. In *Progress in Self Psychology*, vol. 12, ed. A. Goldberg, pp. 123–140. Hillsdale, NJ: Analytic Press, and reprinted here by permission of The Analytic Press.

of himself. This intersubjective disjunction leads to stormy transference–countertransference impasses that challenge the therapist's capacity to be aware of, and use, his subjective reactions.

However, the awareness and use of countertransference are just as important in certain subtler analytic situations. They inform the therapeutic process in the treatment of a group of patients who do *not* provoke uncomfortable reactions in the therapist, and they also require that the therapist remain open and therefore vulnerable, although the risks of such openness may not be as immediately apparent.

I call this group of patients "non-difficult," to distinguish them from both the difficult patients described above and from the usual run of analytic patients with whom work is a lively and varied process. These patients are perhaps *too* easy. They pose no threat to the therapist's identity, organizing principles, or sanity. Work with them proceeds without stormy empathic ruptures or rage-filled demonstrations of the therapist's failures as a selfobject. In fact, the work is so even-tempered and uneventful that it lacks a sense of vitality, and it tends to be very slow. Hence, the term *non-difficult,* because clearly "easy" does not apply to therapies that produce minimal results with years of effort.

Since these patients do not display what are frequently referred to as negative transferential responses, and since neither therapist nor patient experiences either great discomfort or a sense of impasse, these cases tend not to be brought into supervision in a desperate call for help the way work with "difficult" patients often is. In fact, they are seldom mentioned in supervision or written about at all. Yet the lack of vitality in these sessions—their very "non-difficulty"—is a warning sign that calls for supervision, or at least a self-supervisory process to sharpen the therapist's self-awareness.

In a previous project (Livingston 1996), I presented an illustration of such a self-supervisory process, and its particular relevance with one of these "non-difficult" patients. I took detailed notes on a series of sessions, including my own subjective experiences. I was trying to deepen my understanding of what was taking place in what felt like a stuck treatment process, since I hoped both to sharpen my own self-awareness and to revitalize the work. I offer a new look at this effort now, because my inner experience in that process demonstrates the vulnerability that turned out to play a key role in the treatment process. On the surface, the patient did not elicit any difficult countertransferential response. Through a disciplined self-reflective process, however, both my own vulnerability and the importance of my exploration of it came to light.

CLINICAL EXAMPLE

Mrs. A. is the mother of three grown children who represent her most alive sense of self. The liveliness displayed in her children and in her discussion of them is controlled and diminished in the rest of her life, although her smile and an occasional glimmer of excitement in her eyes or in her voice suggest the seed of a lively self that is largely hidden from view. In the meantime, her overweight body has become a manifestation of her passivity.

Throughout the treatment a strong empathic bond had been sustained with very little sense of rupture and repair. It seemed important to me to allow a lengthy period of sustained empathic responsiveness, and to allow the patient to progress at her own pace. She seemed both appreciative and insistent on this, and she became very anxious when I made any attempts to explore her perceptions of me more deeply. In other words, a prolonged and uninterpreted idealizing transference was unfolding. This provided the patient with an essential nurturing experience, but at the same time it perhaps discouraged the necessary empathic inquiry into our relationship.

The atmosphere in the first session of this series is, as usual, friendly and warm, while lacking any sense of aliveness. My attention wanders while the patient talks at length about a situation at work, and then returns as she reports after a long silence, that she is "doing something to myself"—that is, numbing herself—so as not to feel anything or think anything. I (with my lapse of attention in mind) inquire if she has any awareness of what triggered her doing this to herself. She is visibly embarrassed and remains quiet.

My thoughts turn inward. I am aware that I am very comfortable with this patient. I feel no pressure to be anything more than a warm accepting listener or sometimes just a presence in the room as she sits in silence for varying amounts of time. I never feel impatient or frustrated with her, and in general do not feel any need to push her. I am comfortable with her slow, steady pace, and trust the gradual unfolding process. Yet I am aware that my attention varies greatly in intensity, and I find myself questioning this complacency. I decide to wonder aloud if her numbing herself might be related to some sense of fluctuation in my attentiveness to her, or in her own sense of connectedness.

As I embark on this self-supervision, I recognize that several years ago I had understood my own fluctuations of attention differently. I had seen them either as indications that I was picking up the patient's resistance, or as irrelevant mood changes in me. Now with self-psychological concepts to guide me, I am alert to the possibility that self-numbing might be a response to a perceived selfobject failure—my lapse of attention. I have a different understanding of resistance now, too, and am more inclined to think that her defensive numbing was a protection against the painful loss of my attunement, rather than that my lapse was simply a response to her numbness. In this moment I move closer to an empathic stance and also suggest a tentative "explanation" for her response. This seems to lead her into a more introspective and deeper therapeutic process.

She says that she has a sense of when she began to close off, but she hesitates to express it further except to reassure me briefly that it was a response to her own inner thoughts, and not to any action of mine. We both recognize that this is a clear pattern of hers—an invariant organizing principle. Blame is never attributed to me as a nurturant figure. On the contrary, she protects my possible vulnerability by placing the blame on herself. I offer a tentative interpretation, that a fear of losing her connection with me might make her reluctant to see my contribution to her distress.

Mrs. A. tells me that the trigger for her numbing herself was the awareness of a wish to be more connected. She is excited with this awareness, and says that both the numbing and the trigger were clearer this time than they have ever been before. Then she relates a fantasy that she often has in sessions: there are a thousand people staring in silence, waiting for her to say the right thing. She wants very much to satisfy them, but feels totally inadequate and has no idea what they want.

After the session, I wonder if my comfortable acceptance of her pace is a nurturing acceptance—the provision of a needed selfobject experience—or an interference with the necessary empathic inquiry into the interaction between us. And how does my belief in my undemandingness relate to the thousand people staring?

The patient before Mrs. A. the next day is distrustful and blaming. She tells me that I am a person who interferes with her process. I tentatively say that I've been feeling unable to say anything that will feel empathic to her. I am frustrated and uncomfortable, but as I say the words out loud, I feel peaceful. It becomes okay with me to have her see me as not good-enough.

Still, as Mrs. A.'s session begins, I breathe a sigh of relief. The atmosphere in the room is not charged. I find myself thinking about the contrast between my subjective state with her and my experience with the previous patient. As "difficult" patients do, Mrs. A.'s predecessor had confronted me with a role I didn't like—an intersubjective disjunction. But the very overtness of the disjunction had forced me to become self-reflective, which allowed me to return to a deeper grasp of the patient's experience and then to a more peaceful acceptance of the situation.

My thoughts return to the intersubjective context of the present moment. My attention is focused and my self-state is comfortable. My presence as a nurturing selfobject is accepted and appreciated. These contrasts make me wonder if some version of the difficult previous session lies beneath the surface of my relationship with Mrs. A. I am aware that I am far from eager for another such experience.

After a while, Mrs. A. relates that the long silence is her way of "getting a grip on myself." When she thinks about the last few sessions she feels as if she is "a pinball machine with a ball rolling around inside and hitting things—ringing buzzers and setting things off."

I begin to explore this rich imagery with her, but find my thoughts wandering. I also notice Mrs. A. has become silent again. I inquire as to what she is experiencing, thinking that my wandering has again triggered a feeling of abandonment and numbing. She flashes a lively smile and confirms this. She is aware of the trigger and is very reluctant to speak of it: "It is just totally against the rules."

But once expressed, the prohibition softens and she tells me about her experience of these moments, which is different from *my* expectation that she felt my inattention as abandonment or evidence of my lacks. On the contrary, *her* experience is that she felt momentarily scared and was afraid that if she explored, or even expressed, her fear, it might be met with disapproval or disdain. To prevent this, she numbed herself and also, as she experienced it, "made you disappear" by ignoring me.

She is afraid I will think her imagery is silly. I choose to disclose that I, too, experienced a "disappearing" at those moments. It feels risky to let her know that I was failing to sustain my end of our connection at that time. She might experience it as a selfobject failure and an abandonment—because after all, at some level, it is. But she seems enlivened by my disclosure. Apparently it validates her affective imagery. She becomes more open and tells me how afraid she is to expose these thoughts.

It appears to me that although she is afraid of, and attempting to limit, my disapproval at those moments, what her behavior actually limits is the exposure of her pain and fears to my responsiveness. I say this. She is quiet momentarily, digesting it. Then she reports a sense that her head is being "stuffed." Her association to this experience is that it is "like when you need to cry and you can't." This leads to the recounting of many childhood experiences with "croup" and "stuffed sinus problems."

As the session ends, I underline that what I heard as most

important was her taking of total responsibility for her parents' or my lapses, and that it was "against the rules" for her to see others as responsible. Mrs. A. leaves the session with some degree of excitement. "It was like a deal," she comments. I add as I say good-bye, "It doesn't sound like a good deal. Let's talk some more about it."

[The nature of the "non-difficult" impasse is coming into focus. Mrs. A.'s "deal" is an example of Brandchaft's (1994) "structures of pathological accommodation." She has developed a deeply learned pattern of accommodating to the needs of her selfobjects to maintain her connection to them and the borrowed cohesiveness it provides. She diminishes and controls all expression of her own wants and feelings because these would have made her parents uncomfortable. In other words, she sensed, early in her childhood, that her parents were very vulnerable to narcissistic injury. What was still not clear to me at this point was my contribution to this impasse.]

The following session begins with another long silence, during which I manage to sustain a good degree of quiet attentiveness. Mrs. A. smiles and describes her discomfort whenever she feels me paying attention to her. "It's as if I want it very much and at the same time I don't want it." Now she hears voices that she experiences as "not my own" and which she carefully distinguishes from a hallucination. "I hear a child's voice," she continues. "A child mimicking an adult. You know, like repeating a tone that she has heard an adult using. It says, "Leave me alone—stop pestering me.' Then it becomes a little girl's voice, clearly frightened and pleading to be left alone. Finally, it sounds like a warning." She looks up at me with a frightened expression on her face and explains, "This is a crazy place—a place I don't go." As the session ends she asks, "If I let the voices speak, will they ever go away?" I try to be reassuring through my manner and nonverbal encouragement. I restrict my verbal response to an empathic reflection. "I can see how scary it is to explore this place."

The next session begins with a sense of aliveness and immediacy. "I am nuts," she says. "Ready to explode. I think I've always had this fear. Now I'm so aware of it. I'm afraid I will fall apart and be all in pieces. I won't be able to put myself together and then you'll leave before I can. I'll be all alone and apart. It's much too scary when I'm alone. I have to get a grip on myself—to keep together."

For an instant, I am frightened by the poignancy of her expression. Her frequently hospitalized psychotic sister flashes into my mind. I want to call time-out for a diagnostic conference with myself. I have images of presenting this case after the patient falls apart and being asked how on earth I thought she was a candidate for four-times-a-week analytic treatment. (The vulnerability of the analyst is often related to fears of shame and judgments from colleagues or childhood authorities.)

I try to contain this process within myself without communicating any fear to her, and note that it is probably not unrelated to her fear of creating discomfort and rejection if she opens up. I reflect how painful and frightening being left at the end of a session (while in midprocess) can be. She relates a fantasy she's had of asking me to promise that I won't leave her while she's in pieces. She explains that when she's calm she knows that I wouldn't, but that when she's scared it's hard to hold onto that. Also, she adds, "Even though you have never rejected me all these years, I haven't shown you this crazy place yet—so it doesn't count."

The session continues to flow although the patient is still frightened. She describes how she sits poised to protect herself—to regain her grip at any moment. We explore some of the patterns of her life and she is impressed by how much she does to avoid these feelings. There is a great deal of sadness as she becomes aware of the cost of these protective devices in lost contact and intimacy.

The focus sharpens onto our relationship and her need to keep me at just the right distance—not too near, yet not too far away. "It's as if I look up every now and then to be sure I haven't pushed you to where you'll be unreachable. It's like I want to be sure you're on the shelf, but your attentiveness can't get too close because then I would feel all this crazy stuff coming out."

Mrs. A. begins the next session with a report that she had been thinking about the places where she is "not supposed to go." She now feels willing to go into them, but she explains, and I concur, that it was not possible just to decide to do it intentionally. What she feels she can do is that when it comes up she will be more on the side of going into the crazy feelings and sharing them with me than ever before.

She then relates some thoughts and associations to the "deal" not to bring up anything that might make me uncomfortable in return for being able to keep me at just the right distance. She begins to explore the genetic roots of the deal in a way that is clearer and emotionally more connected than ever before. She goes back and forth between observations of her experience with me and her role in not upsetting each family member from early childhood through recent years.

Later in the session, Mrs. A. recalls her mother's need for her to "fix things," and her own sense of having to draw a line in the sand "and not let anyone get too close." "If mother gets too close, she will suck something away from me and I won't have it anymore."

She reflects on how much of her life has followed from the view that it's not safe to let anyone too close. It's a principle that organizes her experience, yet she now realizes that it is, at least in part, erroneous. This is sad, but she notes that she had to draw that line or else she wouldn't have had any sense of herself. I reflect that it's understandable that she needed to hold to her way of viewing people in order to protect herself. I also reflect that it *is* sad that it blocked her from some of the closeness she so much wanted. As the session ends she exclaims painfully that until now she "couldn't even think about this organizing principle, it just operated."

In the next session Mrs. A. expresses the fear that I will become bored and give up on her. I ask if I'm behaving in a way that might trigger that fear. (I had been finishing my lunch as she came in, and I wonder aloud if that might have been a trigger.) She assures me that it was nothing I had done. She talks briefly about her sense that I had never given up on her, and how important that had been to her ability to keep coming even when she felt hopeless and discouraged.

I inquire, "If not me right now, whom did you experience as giving up on you?" She speaks with a lot of quiet emotion about her feelings around being an adopted child, or, as she has come to express it, a "given-away child." She thinks about her birth mother's having given her up, and her fear that it was because of something about her. "Even years later, she could have tried to find me. It's as if she's given up again."

She then talks about how important not giving up is to her. It forms a strong core of who she is. She talks about her sense that her father gave up on her. When he threatened to "send me back to the Indians," it seemed to her a result of her wanting so much. She relates, sadly, how she has erased so much of herself, hoping that he would approve of her. She was surprised that when he died, she felt a loss, even though she never felt he had given her very much.

Toward the end of this session, I offer my first interpretive comment in the past two sessions. Perhaps her sense of loss at her father's death was related to the finality. She had never given up her hope that if she "erased parts of myself" he would someday respond with the love and approval she yearned for. Now it was never to be. I affirm that her quality of never giving up was a strength that in many ways helped her survive and feel a sense of cohesion in herself. Then I add that perhaps it also kept her in a "bad deal"; she sacrificed parts of herself and experienced others as failing to keep their end of the bargain. I suggested that that must leave her yearning and unfulfilled.

She is obviously moved, and we sit quietly for a while. Then she says that she's begun to feel overwhelmed and is trying to understand it all. I say that sometimes it might be more important to just experience her feelings. I point out that there is no need to understand and keep it "under control" or even to put in words the sadness I could already see on her face. She cries quietly for a while and, as she leaves, rests her head on my shoulder in a very peaceful embrace.

Then in the next session, Mrs. A. tells me about a new awareness. The tension that begins shortly before every session has more content than she has been reporting. "I feel a pressure," she relates, "a questioning of what am I going to do with you. I think about ways to distract you or to occupy you. It's like I'm a lion tamer and you're the lion on a box. I have my whip and a chair and I have to watch you very carefully." She pauses briefly and I encourage her to go on. "I'm not allowed to say these things. If I do, or do anything at all to make you uncomfortable, then you will pounce. You will be on top of me—pinning me down and biting."

The rest of the session centers around how hard it is for her to see me this way. She knows that she trusts me more than she has ever trusted anyone, yet she also fears that I will pounce upon her if she breaks the deal and fails to keep me comfortable.

I tell her the story of a man who keeps snapping his fingers. When he's asked why he does this, he explains that it keeps the lions away. When his friend exclaims that there are no lions within thousands of miles his smug reply is, "See, it works!" We laugh together and talk briefly about how our "deal" is gradually and tentatively being challenged for the first time.

"A sated lion is no danger to anyone," Mrs. A. begins the following session, quoting something that she had read in a novel the night before. We both acknowledge the truth in this and leave its connection to the intersubjective context unverbalized for the moment.

"I feel a clear physical tension in my body," she reports. "I'm ready to fight you." She stops to let me know how confusing and crazy it feels to express these experiences. We talk briefly about her fear that I will feel blamed for her fears and about her difficulty in clarifying my contribution to the experience. I decide that more attempts to get her to talk about what I might be doing to trigger her fear would be counterproductive at that point.

My attempts at encouraging her to explore my role in perpetuating our "deal" seem unproductive as well. Asking her to express what is not in her awareness at the moment is itself an empathic break and seems to increase her sense of craziness. I acknowledge, in an attempt to repair the break, that my requests seem to make her more uncomfortable. She responds by again assuring me that the feelings are within her; at the same time she does seem relieved by my comment. She then speculates, "The lion could be in me too. I erase parts of me that could be dangerous. I keep a grip on things."

It occurs to me that there is a meaningful connection here. She is afraid of her own wanting and hunger as well as the other person's. There is probably little clarity of separate self and object in this experience. I choose my response here carefully, keeping in mind the sated lion with which she had begun the session. "What I hear you saying is that it's the hunger that feels dangerous." Her reply is spontaneous and includes a touch of play. "Sure, if I'm the meal." Then she quiets down and expresses an awareness that her response raised some fear right in this moment.

I sense that this moment presents an opportunity. I return to my temporarily suspended invitation that she include my presence and responses as contributing to what I now see clearly to have been an impasse. This has kept Mrs. A. from attributing any qualities to me that might create an intersubjective disjunction. She is not allowed to view me in any way that does not coincide with my view of myself. It is a soft and gentle impasse, the impasse of the "nondifficult patient," but it is, nevertheless, an impasse.

I sense that we have been working through this impasse over several sessions and feel a very quiet excitement. I inquire at this point if she "has ever seen me as hungry in some way." I sense that this material is within her awareness. There is a long pause during which I wait hopefully. My patience is rewarded as she very timidly, at first, explains: "It isn't really hungry—at least that's not the word. The word is different, but it has all the feelings we're talking about as hunger." Then with some growing sense of the validity of her experience, she says directly to me, "*Your interest scares me.* You look at me with intensity and interest. I want it and it's very scary."

I remain attentively silent as I realize that what I feel as one of my best qualities, my intense empathic listening stance, in some ways poses a danger to her emerging sense of self. This is a bittersweet and vulnerable moment for me. It's painful to hear that what I see as nurturing and wonderful can also be connected to something "bad." Memories flash through my mind like wildfire. I see myself as a little boy being interested in an aunt's beautiful inner thigh and feeling confused about what was all right. I remember people who have been uncomfortable with what they called my "overintensity." I somehow learned to channel that intense listening and wish for contact into my therapeutic stance, and I know that it's an important aspect of therapeutic process with many people. So in this moment, I feel excited at the effect of my willingness to sustain an attitude of empathic inquiry and to reflect on the organizing principles that have contributed to the slow, draining quality in the work with Mrs. A. I feel excited and optimistic that my self-supervision is freeing up the logjam and that there is room for increased spontaneity as well as some intersubjective disjunction. I also feel a bit confused and hurt.

I contain my own process pretty well and continue to listen attentively. This appears to be a good-enough response as it enables Mrs. A. to go on to explore her experience of my interest. She feels ashamed and confused. She is afraid that she is encouraging the interest—after all she does want it. She continues, "Maybe I'll encourage it and it will be a misinterpretation. Then I'll feel humiliated. I want it and I don't want it. I'm confused about whether it's wrong for me. Is it shameful? It isn't clear whether these feelings relate to something that happened. I know I was always uncomfortable with my parents' friends who really loved me. Their interest scared me. I didn't understand it. I told my mother I didn't want to go to visit them and she told me I was silly or that of course I wanted to see them. It colors my whole life. It certainly colors how I feel in therapy."

As she was leaving, she asked if tomorrow was my birthday as she thought. I acknowledged that it was, and she wished me a happy birthday. I said with a smile that it was nice that she remembered.

A half hour later she left a phone message on my machine. Tearfully, she said that she "realized that not all interest has to be bad." Then she cheered up and, as if it was an unimportant incident, said, "I'm really glad that you were pleased that I remembered your birthday."

I felt good in response to the message. I understood it on two levels. Having finally let me know that my interest scared her, she is beginning to feel nurtured by it. Also, on a second level, Mrs. A. experienced my pleasure at her remembering my birthday as an affirmation that her interest in me is not shameful or bad. On the contrary, it is received as pleasurable.

CONCLUSION

The impasse of the non-difficult patient often centers, as it did with Mrs. A., around a need to maintain the appearance of intersubjective conjunction. Patients like Mrs. A. are afraid to risk voicing a subjective impression that does not match the analyst's view of the world, and especially of himself. To understand more fully the patient's subjective experiences, the analyst must deepen his own reflective self-awareness and any contribution that he might be making to avoiding an awareness of disjunction. In the self-supervisory process presented I was clearly guided by several self-psychological and intersubjective concepts. These pointed up my discomfort in "wearing the attributes" that Mrs. A. needed to express. The concepts helped me to digest the validity of her perceptions of me and the subjective meanings my words and actions had for her. However, the key to really decentering and focusing on the patient's experience was a vulnerable willingness to go deeper into my own subjectivity and to see how it interfered with the process. The patient's analysis took off as the analyst's self-analysis and willingness to experience some vulnerable moments took off.

Trying to function simultaneously as a vulnerable human being and as an analyst, with an analyst's sense of responsibility and disciplined self-reflection, is not for the faint of heart. However, as Darlene Ehrenberg (1996) has pointed out, "The most subtle aspects of our own experience, however inappropriate or threatening they may seem at any given moment, can become our best guide to how to open the work and to how to make contact in a meaningful way. . . . Our very vulnerability often becomes our most sensitive instrument, and paradoxically thereby, a source of analytic power and strength" (p. 281).

5

Issues of Self-Disclosure

Extreme positions about how much the therapist can or should remain inexpressive and anonymous reflect two significant fears. On the one hand, psychotherapy is about understanding and helping the patient; careless self-disclosure risks flooding the session with the *therapist's* feelings, needs, and opinions, thus overwhelming or burdening the person he is there to help. Although we no longer believe in the possibility of a blank-screen analyst on whom the patient projects distortions from the past, we still have obligations to focus primarily on the patient's needs, and to establish conditions that will allow the transference to unfold. These obligations can be restated in current self-psychological terms, without the blank-screen metaphor: when the therapist's empathic understanding forms the background of the process, the patient, and particularly the patient's subjective experience, is clearly the focus of treatment. A safety is provided that enables the patient to begin to experience and express selfobject needs that have been suppressed since childhood. It is an opportunity to resume an arrested development. If the therapist's needs are randomly expressed or even acted out, the patient's selfobject transference may not unfold, and indeed the patient may accommodate to the therapist as he did in childhood to early caregivers. Vulnerability will remain hidden and treatment will be blocked.

On the other hand, too rigid a stance of nondisclosure may overly reserve and constrain the therapist. Kohut (1984) addressed this danger in a well-known comment:

> I believe that gifted analysts—whatever their consciously held and openly professed theoretical beliefs—have always, subtly or not so subtly, discarded their straitlaced reserve in responding to those patients who, during childhood, were deprived of the emotional palpability of the selfobject. And they have thus provided for these patients . . . that minimum of emotional responsiveness without which the analytic work could not proceed optimally—just as normal mothers some decades ago continued to provide a lively emotional presence for their babies despite their lip service to the Watsonian principles of a distant efficiency that had been impressed on them by their pediatricians. [pp. 170–171]

Even Otto Fenichel (1941), an outstanding representative of the classical tradition, pointed out the danger that a "fear of . . . countertransference may lead an analyst to the suppression of all human freedom in his own reactions to patients" (p. 74), and that "the patient should always be able to rely on the humanness of the analyst" (p. 74). *Any* approach to the analyst's subjectivity that aims to control or eliminate his personhood runs the risk of reducing emotional availability, responsiveness, and spontaneity. In considering what makes for "judicious" self-disclosure, it is as valid to reflect on the rationale for *not* expressing a feeling (or revealing personal content, or answering a patient's question) as it is to think about the reasons to do it. The meaningful questions are always, What would be optimally responsive within a specific analytic dyad at any given moment? and What will facilitate the toleration of vulnerability and the unfolding of the transference, and thus the deepening of the treatment process, within this particular relational, intersubjective, context?

The analytic use of self-disclosure is related to the uses of vulnerability that I have been discussing, but the two are not identical and their separateness can easily be illustrated. (My work with Mrs. A. illustrates some aspects of this difference. The vulnerability that I had to deal with in reestablishing a vital therapeutic process was an inner experience and never directly shared with the patient. In contrast, there was also the matter of my birthday. Mrs. A. knew when it was; this was an inadvertent disclosure and not a planned intervention, but it does illustrate a quality of our relationship and it clearly became a part of the treatment situation. My decision to express my pleasure at her remembering is an example of a deliberate disclosure.) A therapist may choose to minimize what he discloses out of theoretical conviction or out of a sense of personal privacy. This need not be a defensive choice, it may not impede the analyst's emotional availability, and it may be based on factors very different from issues of self-reflection, narcissism, and self-protection that I have outlined above.

By the same token, just as an analyst's experience of vulnerability can be an inner or private experience that he or she might choose not to disclose to the patient, so self-disclosure is not necessarily based upon true vulnerability. The sharing of any particular piece of information or feeling might be a risk for one analyst and risk-free for another. And for the same analyst, sharing certain content might make him feel vulnerable with one patient, while the same sharing with a different patient might not entail any sense of risk or vulnerability at all.

Furthermore, personal sharing can at times even serve as a protection *against* vulnerability. Rather than moving the analytic dialogue forward into unexplored terrain, it may defensively maintain a fixed role-relationship or reflect a therapist's need to assert his own subjectivity. Inexperienced therapists' experiments with self-disclosure are sometimes an expression of their own mirroring needs, rather than a response to the needs of the patient or the analytic process. One common example of this is a therapist's describing his own resolution of a conflict with which the patient is struggling. The intention is to model a successful resolution, but the patient may end up feeling inadequate in comparison to an unrealistic perception of a "fully analyzed" or perfect analyst. I think of this kind of sharing as "pseudo-vulnerable." Vulnerability and its clinical value lie not in any particular content, but rather in their proximity to processes of newness, risk, and exploration.

In fact, content may have no meaning at all in a self-disclosure; sometimes it is simply the nondefensive sharing of a self-reflection that is important, rather than any particulars of genetic or personal content. That is why the best use of judicious self-disclosure is often in the intersubjective, here-and-now interaction of the analytic session, where the analyst's authentic owning of his or her contribution to the process is often essential to moving it forward. The following clinical example from my work with Nancy, which took place about a month after the one presented in Chapter 3 and which continues her preoccupation with the distance between us, is a good example of the usefulness of this type of disclosure.

SELF-DISCLOSURE IN THE HERE AND NOW OF THE SESSION

Nancy sits facing me and asks me if I'm tired. "You look tired," she adds. I answer casually, "No, I don't feel tired." I am caught off guard, and fail to explore her underlying concern about my availability, but a few minutes later I get another opportunity. "Are you getting bored?" she asks. This time I ask her to tell me more about her experience of me. "I'm afraid that you aren't staying present . . . that you aren't staying here with me," she says with some annoyance. I begin to reflect (a bit defensively) "You seem to be picking up slight fluctuations," but before I can finish my thought, she interrupts. "Yes, I'm afraid that you're leaving. *Are you?*"

This is the choice point. Do I try to explore her feelings further without sharing mine? I feel quite vulnerable here. I'm wondering if I can keep from repeating her father's failures, or whether she will discard me as being "just like him." These feelings are complicated by the conflict about closeness with Nancy that I mentioned in my discussion of the earlier session. I am also aware that my defensiveness has contributed to escalating the problem. There is an urgency in Nancy's wanting to know, and I am very aware that her experience of her father is that he is often distant—"not present," to use her words. I also know that her fruitless efforts to get him to understand her need that he be more available have left her feeling frustrated and helpless. I decide to share my experience of the moment and risk her seeing me as "just like" her father. "I think that at the point that you felt a fluctuation I had an association to what you were saying and that took me away some."

Nancy had been talking about seeing old friends at a

wedding. She wondered if they would see any change in her. "People resist seeing any changes. They treat me as if I was the same old person . . . as if I was the same as I was in college. I've come a long way since then." At that point I had experienced myself as very closely attuned to her. Actually what had happened was that Nancy's thoughts had triggered a personal association in me. I would be seeing my brothers and sister next week after a year and a half of having no contact with them. I wondered about how they see me now, and if they still see me as the same selfish kid I was when we were growing up.

In this case, I did not share the content of my association, just the fact of it. I felt that to talk about myself would take away from the centrality of Nancy's experience. I went on: "I had an association to a similar experience. Sometimes that helps me to deepen my understanding of what you're telling me about. It helps me to know what it might be like, but I guess it also takes me into my own thought and away from you."

Nancy thinks about this. "So you were really away some. My father did that a lot but he would never admit to it." Then with some excitement she noted, "Hey, look at that. I did what you did. I had an association and wandered a bit to thinking about my father and the past. Then when I realized it, and I wanted to, I could come back. I don't think that anyone will come back to me though. I get impatient when you aren't really present. It comes from not trusting that anyone will stay. There won't be enough time." She goes on to talk about her hunger for a deeper connection.

Perhaps the session might have led to a deepening without the disclosure of my drifting. It might have been pos-

> sible to understand her experience without validating her perception. But I think that if I had not owned my contribution to the distance between us, I would have run the risk of making it *her* problem, and repeating the traumatic situation she experienced with her father. Nancy and I are cocreating a new relational experience that includes my emotional availability. This judicious self-disclosure contributed to that process.

Ultimately, the decision to disclose, or not to, must always be based upon reflection on what the transferential meaning is likely to be to that specific patient at that specific time, and what constitutes optimal responsiveness just then within that specific analytic dyad. Certainly the analyst must always consider the intersubjective meaning of the disclosure. However, he must equally question the effect and personal meaning to the patient of any nondisclosure. These decisions are often made spontaneously in the heat of an interaction, and it is often not possible to think them out ahead of time. But a spirit of reflection and exploration of these meanings is central to the analytic process, and can inform even such on-the-fly decisions. Optimal responsiveness is really evaluated retrospectively in an ongoing process. It is not a set of rules for a self-conscious, constrained, or intellectualized decision making.

In fact, most self-disclosure is not an active intervention at all; inadvertent self-disclosure occurs constantly. The analyst as blank screen is an impossibility. We constantly disclose ourselves in our dress, the furnishings of our offices, our greetings to patients, and countless other ways. Even the choice to remain private—not to disclose certain information, or not to express certain emotional reactions—is in itself a disclosure, and provides information about our choices. Self-disclosure can never be eliminated from the analytic relationship, so it is less important to argue for or against it than to explore what any interaction means within a particular analyst–patient relationship.

The exploration of the usefulness and risks of therapist self-disclosure is further complicated by the fact that the effect of the disclosure or nondisclosure in any particular session is less important than its effect on the analytic relationship. Some patients need the analyst to remain at a distance, not just at one particular moment, but as a basic stance; when parents have been overstimulating or intrusive, a patient may feel threatened and overwhelmed if boundaries are not clearly respected. Some patients grew up as parentified children, caring for their parent's needs at the expense of their own. For these individuals, the analyst's sharing of any vulnerable material may become a signal to reenact a childhood accommodation.

However, many patients need to co-create a relationship in which the analyst's humanness is clearly evident. They will allow the unfolding of their selfobject yearnings only in a relationship that they experience as not too unbalanced, perhaps because, as Eda Goldstein (1992) suggests, "Self-disclosure is helpful in helping patients to deal with feelings of humiliation, difference, aloneness . . . and to become more revealing themselves." The issue becomes not simply the effect of a specific disclosure in a particular session, but the general effect of freedom or restraint in the expression of the analyst's humanness and emotional availability on the analytic relationship. The relational context enhances or detracts from the mutative power of noninterpretive provisions as well as of interpretive interventions.

ON THE USE OF SELF-DISCLOSURE IN ENABLING A PATIENT TO BEGIN TO OPEN UP AN EXPLORATORY PROCESS

Richard is an intelligent young lawyer who entered treatment at his wife's urging. He is friendly and cooperative and he quickly formed an attachment to me. He seems to be an ideal candidate for analytic work. But there is a catch. He does not easily engage in an exploratory process. He is willing to answer any questions I ask, but he draws a blank when I ask about his inner experience, or suggest that he tell me more about something. My quiet listening quickly brings us to an uncomfortable dead end. Sessions often begin with comments like, "This was an easy week. I don't know what to talk about," or with a report of the day's events.

The session I want to describe marks the beginning of a change in our relationship. It shows how the use of the therapist's vulnerability in the decision to self-disclose was able to help the patient engage in a selfobject relationship, begin to feel comfortable in therapy, and become more revealing of himself.

The session begins typically as Richard reports the day's events. He made a wrong prediction to a client. There was no dire result, but he felt very bad about having made an error. After a brief description of the details of the data that went into his prediction, he stops. The silence is uncomfortable for both of us. This is unusual for me, but unlike the silences that feel like part of an unfolding process, this one seems to be setting off feelings of inadequacy and shame in Richard that he is unable to express verbally. I feel vulnerable because I know that remaining passive, or following my usual patterns, will not work. A riskier intervention is going to be called for, although at this point I don't yet know what form it will take.

"Look inside," I suggest. "It isn't the content that's important. It's your experience that I want to know more about." My awkward probe touches something. "Turbulence," he replies briefly. That is then followed by more silence and discomfort.

"You aren't used to looking inside, at your experience," I comment in an attempt to be empathic. Richard nods sadly. "Tell me more about the turbulence," I ask, this time feeling more connected to how difficult the exploration is for my patient. Richard responds to my change in tone and says, "It's about feeling wrong. I'm afraid that I'll lose credibility."

I encourage him to go further. "Tell me about what might happen, about what you would like to prevent." Richard tries to respond, but it's a bit like pulling teeth. I try to open up his experience further. "Can you say more about what it's like to be wrong? What was it like as a kid?"

"My mother used to criticize me a lot. 'Stand straight, Richard. Your nose is too long, Richard. You are too serious all the time.'" I try to move closer to his inner experience; I can feel his emotion, but it's still difficult for him to put it into words. "What was it like for little Richie?" I ask.

"I felt that she was disappointed in me . . . that she felt that I wasn't good enough," he responds. He is still focused on his mother's experience rather than his own. I try to draw him out a little further, although I am beginning to recognize the risk that he may experience me as disappointed or unsatisfied. It's a tough line to walk and I'm concerned that I might not be sufficiently empathic. However, I am feeling increasingly close to him in the struggle, so I feel trusting of my intuition and I proceed: "You're good at perceiving her responses and very concerned about them. I'd like to know more about what *you* feel. You're a little boy and your mommy is disappointed. Then she goes away. What does that feel like?"

"I feel a shrinking in my body. I couldn't stand tall. That's why she always told me to stand straight." I lean forward and encourage him to continue, hoping that we've found an inroad. "Good. Your body is a clue to your feeling. Tell me more." But his response is discouraging. "I don't know what to say . . . just insignificant."

I feel my discouragement building. I am beginning to grasp the feelings that Richard's struggle has triggered in me, and I feel vulnerable in my worry about what it will feel like if I continue to be open to them.

I feel my own body taking a posture similar to Richard's, and I'm touched by the poignancy in the single word *insignificant.* I decide to enter the exploration more fully and to share a painful association of my own to Richard's experience. I tell him that I'm thinking about a photograph that my stepfather had loved but that I had hated. "For him, it was a picture of his happy family. My brother is so expansive . . . smiling . . . They're all smiling. I was wearing a tee shirt. My shoulders are slumped. When I see that picture it's so clear that *I was very unhappy* and that nobody else seemed to notice. . . . I think that you were very unhappy when you felt your mother was disappointed and when she left."

Richard is quiet. This time the silence is not at all uncomfortable. He is visibly moved and I wait for him to find words. "Yes, I can feel that, but I'm always grown up. I put that aside. I put all those feelings aside." "You don't pay attention to your inner feelings, your little boy feelings," I reflect. "No, I don't," Richard says sadly.

I continue to reflect his unverbalized experience with a good deal of feeling. "And nobody asked you to tell them . . . to say them out loud. That's why it's so hard when I ask you to let me know what you're feeling." Again, Richard is visibly moved. "No, feelings weren't important. We didn't really pay much attention to them."

My use of self-disclosure in this session served as a major aid in helping Richard to begin to open up and to explore his feelings. At the same time, my own vulnerability—to the reemergence of real childhood unhappiness—and emotional availability helped to deepen *my* empathic grasp of Richard's experience.

However, self-disclosure, as I said earlier in this chapter, is a complicated matter. Although the content that I chose to disclose in this instance was more personal than what I revealed to Nancy, the act of disclosure itself did not entail as much experience of vulnerability and sense of risk on my part. I felt that I was failing Nancy, and that her response would repeat my mother's disappointment in me. With Richard, although the emergence of my childhood unhappiness was painful, I felt secure in the relationship and not at all afraid of his reaction to my disclosure. Nancy had a different and more potentially devastating transferential importance for me than Richard did, which increased my vulnerability in disclosing my drifting or my wish for closeness. Also, the content that I was disclosing with Richard was much more ego-syntonic and acceptable. Often the disclosure of the therapist's subjective reactions in the moment of the transference-countertransference is a more vulnerable and risk-laden experience than the revealing of personal content from outside the room.

In any case, the here-and-now disclosure of my imperfect listening to Nancy felt much more dangerous to me. Vulnerability and disclosure are related but not the same thing. The experience of risk and vulnerability is more a factor of the here-and-now relational context, as well as the transference and countertransference, than it is dependent on the content of what is revealed.

Self-disclosure must always be judicious: that is, based upon reflection on, and understanding of, the transferential meaning that it may have for a specific patient and a concern for whether or not it is experienced as optimally responsive within the specific analytic dyad. The important questions are always, Does the disclosure facilitate vulnerability and a deepening of therapeutic process? Does it lead to exploration and further opening or does it limit and impede the process? In addition, two specific caveats related to the intersection of self-disclosure and vulnerability should be considered. The first is that it is essential that there be limits to the use of self-disclosure within any particular analytic dyad, although they may not be codified in technical rules. No advocacy of self-disclosure should encourage an analyst to disclose personal material that he or she does not wish to reveal. We owe our own boundaries and needs for privacy the same respect we accord our patients'. To try to live up to some impossible model of an authentic analyst serves as a poor model for our patients, and detracts from the therapeutic purpose of the relationship. Even if it were to work in the moment, to disregard our own needs and unique personality is as detrimental as neglecting the patient's uniqueness. As we consider what self-disclosure means to our patients, we must consider what it means to us as well. Twin traps await us—to be defensive about our choices, or to rationalize them as theoretically necessary without owning their personal meaning for us as individuals—and it is best to avoid them both. Acceptance of one's choice to disclose or not to disclose, whether at a given time or as a basic stance, is the first step to being open to an exploration of the meaning it has within the relationship and the effect on the therapeutic process.

The second important caveat is that we must remember as well that there are consequences both to self-disclosure and to vulnerability, for the analyst as well as for the patient. Most experienced clinicians are sensitive enough to avoid flooding their patients with their own material, or at least to deal with it as a break in empathy if such flooding begins to occur and the therapy is temporarily derailed. But analysts who begin to experiment with being more vulnerable and self-disclosing may be unprepared to contain the narcissistic injuries that they may incur. More vulnerable means *more vulnerable*—to the pain of narcissistic injury, and to the dangers of shame, regression, or even temporary fragmentation. An analyst who is vulnerable is sometimes going to get hurt. Mild vulnerability means mild hurt. Serious vulnerability means really being open to narcissistic injury along with a regressive increase in selfobject needs.

The following is an illustration of a narcissistic blow disrupting temporarily the analyst's ability to maintain his empathic stance:

> In a group where I had often been open about my own responses and felt quite attached to several members, I frequently lingered at the end of the session as members said good-bye to each other and to me. This is a very close and cohesive group and I enjoy my role in leading it. For a while I taught a class across town immediately following the group, and had to end sessions abruptly on time. Several members became upset with me about this pattern. I handled it well at first, but after people had expressed how they felt about the abruptness, the question of why I was doing it arose. I explained that I had to get to a class at almost the time we ended. There were a few comments about anger at my "lack of organization" in taking on the obligation and the subject

changed. But fifteen minutes later the group felt flat to me. My mind was wandering, and I realized that I had withdrawn emotionally.

As Walt Stone (2001) points out, shifts in the leader's affect and involvement may be clues to something that has been missed in the group, to a selfobject failure. In this case, I had missed the deeper message in the question about why I was leaving. I had felt shamed and wounded by the innuendo in the question, and instead of asking for elaborations of how people were feeling in asking the question, I felt a momentary twinge of annoyance. Once I recalled that moment, I was alert to my own pattern of response to certain injuries. I tend to bypass the sense of being scolded or shamed that I begin to experience. My conscious experience is a mild, occasionally not so mild, annoyance that I dismiss as unimportant. But the result of this self-protective pattern was a disruption in my empathic stance as well as in the vitality of my self-experience and emotional presence.

We invite patients to be open and vulnerable and promise to make an effort to be nurturing or at least empathic and noninjurious. Our patients cannot be expected to make the same promise to us. Analysis is at rock bottom an unequal relationship; it may be a relationship between two vulnerable selves, but it is not an equal one. The analyst is trained, and paid, to take responsibility, and this includes the responsibility, ultimately, to self-right when his selfobject needs are frustrated or when the patient's self-expression injures the analyst's sense of self.

Although the support of empathic supervisors and colleagues is vital to all of us, in the analytic moment we are alone with our patients, and the old warning that "fools rush in" does not come amiss. I believe that analysts must take risks to grow;

I also believe that we owe it to ourselves, and to our patients, to be judicious in these risks and not to disregard our own vulnerability and our responses to it.

CONCLUSION

Judicious self-disclosure is based upon consideration of what is likely to be optimally responsive in a specific moment, and the choice and our underlying motivations for it should always be a subject of analytic exploration and self-reflection. This is as true when we choose to withhold personal content and our emotional responses as it is when we choose to express them. In most of the clinical material presented throughout this book, a background factor in the effectiveness of the sessions is a cocreated relationship between analyst and patient. This same facilitative background may exist in analytic relationships that involve very little self-disclosure. The narrow issue of how much is disclosed is less important than the emotional and relational availability of the analyst. His willingness to accept that analysis is always an experience in which both parties are vulnerable is the key factor in facilitating vulnerability and deepening the therapeutic process.

6

Vulnerable Moments in Couple Therapy[1]

1. Parts of this chapter first appeared in Livingston, M. (1998). Conflict and aggression in couples therapy. *Family Process* 37(3):311–321; and other parts in Livingston, M. (1995). A self psychologist in couplesland: multisubjective approach to transference and countertransference-like phenomena in marital relationships. *Family Process* 34(4):427–439. Reprinted here by permission of *Family Process.*

"I don't know what you mean by 'glory,'" Alice said.

Humpty Dumpy smiled contemptuously, "Of course you don't—till I tell you. I meant, 'There's a nice knock-down argument for you!'"

"But 'glory' doesn't mean a 'nice knockdown argument,'" Alice objected.

"When I use a word," Humpty Dumpty said, "It means just what I choose it to mean—neither more nor less."

"The question is," said Alice, "whether you *can* make words mean so many different things."

"The question is," said Humpty Dumpty, "which is to be master—that's all."

Lewis Carroll, *Through the Looking Glass*

Humpty Dumpty sitting on his wall knew that a fall would shatter him irretrievably. To a self psychologist, such a fall—such fragmentation—symbolizes the loss of self, Humpty's fear of not being a person. The wall is a metaphor for his attempts to protect himself from this loss: he remains on the wall, high above the human condition, where he can experience himself as in charge and invulnerable. Humpty establishes for himself the right and authority to define words and therefore to define reality. Yet he continues to experience himself as brittle and fragmentation-prone. He is afraid both of losing his self and *not* being a person, and of experiencing his vulnerability and thus *being* more fully a person.

Alice, on the other hand, feels like a bewildered little girl. She at first relinquishes her sense of autonomy and selfhood in her quest for a knowing authority, and when she allows herself to challenge Humpty even slightly, he promptly puts her back in her place: Humpty Dumpty is to be *the* recognized and validated self in this relationship. The safe role for Alice is to mirror him and look up to him; this is her way, very different from his, of avoiding confusion, vulnerability, and the struggles of self development.

Eventually Alice develops a broader perspective that allows her to make her way out of the rabbit hole and the endless power struggles she finds enacted there. Recognizing at last that the powerful figures she envisions are nothing but a "pack of cards," she begins to sort out fantasy from reality, and achieves a new level in her search for self. Before she manages this, however, Humpty and she play out a power struggle that they co-construct out of their own fantasies and fears. This is a scenario very familiar to couple therapists, and the one at the root of most marital difficulties. Its core is the question of "to be or not to be"—whether to build barriers against vulnerability to each other, or to risk being more fully human and intimate as two separate developing selves. The encounter that we see between Alice and Humpty is a quiet struggle; she is only just beginning to assert herself, and for the most part she cooperates in maintaining a balance that protects the status quo of both of them. If the relationship were to endure, however, as Alice's self became stronger, or Humpty's loneliness and isolation increased, the balance would shift, creating at the least more awareness of dissatisfaction with the relationship, and possibly an overt and tumultuous power battle. That is when the two of them would be likely to appear in a therapist's office.

A fanciful example, perhaps, but the vicissitudes of vulnerability, aggression, and conflict in couples are very real, and in no other therapeutic modality do the balances between responsiveness and reactiveness, and between self-protection and self-expression, show more clearly.

WORKING WITH COUPLES

The various psychoanalytic approaches to theory have been constructed upon the psychodynamics of individual patients. Furthermore, an analytically oriented psychotherapist develops his professional sense of self and the clinical principles that organize his subjective impressions in a two-person universe. Expanding the focus of analysis from the one-to-one of individual therapy to the treatment of couples gives rise to theoretical and technical complications. Attention to vulnerable moments can ease the transition, however, by providing an organizing framework that clarifies and facilitates the conceptual and practical requirements of couple work.

The triadic world of couple therapy includes by definition a third experiencing presence—a whole additional subjectivity. Both patients bring to the work insistent selfobject needs (to be focused on and understood, for instance) that are not being met at home. Generally they do not have the capacity for self-reflective awareness, or for empathic attunement and decentering, that allows people to put their own needs in abeyance at times to focus upon those of their mates; if they did, they would not in ordinary circumstances need a couple therapist. Couple therapy aims at the development of this capacity, which means nothing less than the transformation of the patients' narcissistic experience, and such radical work requires safety and order, never an easy thing to establish where subjectivities clash.

The intricacies of the overlap between the two subjective worlds of the traditional patient–therapist dyad are complicated enough (Stolorow et al. 1987). Since every individual, according to the intersubjectivists, organizes and understands his perceptions of the world and other people according to his own unique set of "organizing principles," every person's experience of himself and of others has an intrinsic validity. These clashes between contrasting (but equally valid) perceptions often lead to stormy encounters between patients and therapists.

They lead to stormy encounters between spouses, too, and in couple therapy there are *three* people in the room—two of them wounded and narcissistically sensitive mates, who share a joint and sometimes bitter history of frustration and disappointment. Couples appear in our consulting rooms precisely because they have repeatedly failed to receive from each other the empathic responsiveness and safe space they need. They feel wounded by each other and unable to repair the ruptures in their bond, and the protective stances they establish in response create further blocks to communication and intimacy. They also make a methodical therapeutic process difficult.

When in individual analysis a therapist finally succeeds in engaging the needs of a macho man, for example, or a contemptuous woman, his careful preparatory work up to that point provides the patient safety to express the shame and hurt that lie beneath the habitual aggressive stance. In couple therapy, however, things are different. Inevitably, just when that painstakingly crafted moment is reached, there is an outburst from the partner, triggered by the terror that his own necessary system of self-esteem regulation may fail if the balance within the couple shifts. Unless the therapist has tools for dealing with this dynamic, the essential and arduously constructed atmosphere of safety and responsiveness is destroyed, and along with it the hope for a new beginning; instead, chaos and the dread of retraumatization reign (Ornstein 1974). This phenomenon is often a therapist's welcome to couple work, and his own professional identity and self-esteem, based as they have been on his experience and expertise with the relatively orderly individual process of working through, may be dealt a severe blow. Like Alice down the rabbit hole, he feels that he has surely fallen into Wonderland.

Why, then, does a psychotherapist enter the realm of couple therapy? Why venture beyond the relatively systematic dyadic relationship of patient and therapist that builds structure and self-cohesiveness through the repair of microfailures? What draws many of us into a situation where our ability to prevent major breaks in empathy is so drastically diminished? Usually it is the hope of getting the marital venture back on track, since at its best it functions as a powerful source of developmentally needed experience, and can thus be a tremendous opportunity for a mutual reparative process and for the revitalization of two lives. One of the great contributions of self psychology to couple therapy is its focus on the *legitimacy* of the need for these developmental experiences within marriage. But, as I will elaborate shortly, self-psychological couple therapy must stress the understanding of what it feels like to be the *object* of such needs as well as the subject of them.

CONFLICT AND AGGRESSION

Self psychology is sometimes accused of failing to deal with conflict, aggression, and rage. This is a misconception, however; self psychology deals decisively with all three. There are significant departures from the classical point of view, however, and the departures have clear implications for treatment. It is not rage and conflict themselves that are the focus of the self psychologist's therapeutic endeavors. The focus instead is on the vulnerability of the patient's self, in protection of which the rage is enlisted. This vulnerability must be legitimized, expressed, and explored. Self-psychological work with conflict and aggression therefore is not considered a separate category of analytic work, but depends, as self-psychological therapy always does, upon (1) the empathic immersion of the therapist, (2) the provision of a safe environment in which to explore shame and narcissistic vulnerability, (3) the fulfillment of necessary selfobject functions, and (4) the concept of "fundamental conflict."

This stress on empathy and safety, which is characteristic of the self-psychological approach, is sometimes misconstrued as a "be nice" attitude, but this not how a self-psychologically informed therapist sees it. Kohut (1984) defined empathy as "the capacity to think and feel oneself into the inner life of another person" (p. 82). An empathic stance is essentially listening and understanding the unfolding material from the patient's subjective point of view. This is not, as some analysts mistakenly believe, the same thing as avoiding conflict by not introducing ideas that differ from those of the patient (Richards and Richards 1995). Similarly, promoting safety does not mean avoiding conflict and aggression, but rather establishing an atmosphere in which they can come up and be dealt with. And come up they do, triggered by the inevitable breaks in the empathic ties that occur between people, whether they be therapist and patient, spouses, or members of a group.

For reasons that will become clear, issues of conflict and aggression manifest themselves especially clearly in the context of couple work, as do the underlying vulnerabilities that give rise to them, and I will use this modality to illustrate some of the ways that vulnerable moments can be used in the psychotherapy of conflict and rage.

NARCISSISTIC VULNERABILITY AND NARCISSISTIC RAGE

Kohut (1978) understood narcissistic rage as a complex mental state (that is, not reducible to an underlying biological drive). He considered the needs of the self to be primary, and the drives to be parts of the self. Under normal circumstances, in which he included healthy assertive behavior, the drives are smoothly embedded within a cohesive self. However, when the self has lost its cohesiveness, or "fallen apart" in response to overstimulation or narcissistic injury, the drives are not so well integrated. At those times they tend to dominate the functioning of the personality, which may then be experienced by others or by the individual himself as "driven." Narcissistic rage is one possible outcome of such a breakdown (or fragmentation) of the self, and it is the result of injuries to vulnerable grandiosity, or of traumatic disappointments with idealized selfobjects.

Narcissistic needs are not central to all forms of angry, rageful, or aggressive behavior, and narcissistic rage is different from the healthy aggressive or assertive behavior that is the expression of a relatively cohesive sense of self. Stolorow (2000) gives as an example of this a man's protective rage when someone threatens harm to his family, which is not necessarily a result of narcissistic injury. However, within an intimate relationship it is usually narcissistic wounding that provokes aggression and blocks more vulnerable kinds of sharing. That is why a focus on the underlying vulnerability when conflict and aggression appear in treatment—especially in couple treatment—deepens the therapeutic process and can lead to the resumption of arrested development and an enriched relationship.

Narcissistic vulnerability is essentially an unprotected self-state that lies beneath the surface of protective behaviors, and narcissistic rage is a breakdown product—a secondary reaction to injury to a vulnerable self. It is not, in self psychology, considered a "given" component of an instinctual or primary phenomenon, but is seen instead as the effort of a fragmentation-endangered self to protect what cohesion it still maintains. This does not diminish its importance, nor is narcissistic rage disregarded in the self psychologist's clinical approach. As Ornstein and Ornstein (1993) stress, this view gives us "a decisive direction in the treatment process. This direction is expressed in our focus on the *narcissistic matrix,* from which the rage arises. Such a focus serves as a guiding principle in the interpretation of both individual and group aggression" (p. 110). This means that conflict and aggression are no longer seen as an interference or resistance to be handled or removed. Instead, the occurrence of conflict and aggression may be viewed as an opportunity to address underlying issues. The aim of technique thus becomes the deepening of therapeutic process and the resumption of derailed development.

To the extent that rage is a self-protective reaction to narcissistic vulnerability, one goal of therapy is to help patients develop ways of tolerating vulnerability that do not require it.

Furthermore, when vulnerability can be safely exposed, related rage becomes accessible to analytic working through. The therapist's skill in recognizing the empathic breaks that evoke rage creates the sense of safety that allows patients to expose and explore their narcissistic vulnerability. Within this longed-for sense of safety, the underlying vulnerability that is conceived by self psychology to lie at the root of conflict and aggression becomes accessible to analytic working through.

COUPLES AND CONFLICT

Kilian (1993) insists that self psychology is a psychology of conflict after all—conflict over who is to be the "self" and who is to be the "selfobject." And joking aside, that struggle is often the conflict at the heart of marital tensions. Couplehood has been said to be the nearest equivalent in adult life to the early bond between parent and baby (Dicks 1967), and it is similarly fraught with primitive and chaotic emotions. The very nature of the marital attachment suggests that it is an attempt to begin anew, in a manner very similar to the engagement of a transference with an analyst in the treatment setting. Mutual developmental needs, often very early ones, are stimulated and evoked in the marital relationship. The frustration of these needs, and the disappointment that results from it, are common sources of marital discord.

A second significant source of marital conflict has to do with fears about expressing anger or being self-assertive. Many patients learn in childhood that aggression (or other direct expression of their own needs for self-delineation) is sufficiently unwelcome to their caregivers that it threatens necessary selfobject ties. Variations of this "fundamental conflict" (Stolorow et al. 1987, p. 52) are often the underlying source of disturbances in relationships.

In both of these cases, a self psychologist is more likely to search for the fears and disappointments, and the underlying organizing principle that produces them, than for increasingly deeper derivatives of repressed rage. And since marital discord is itself a manifestation of powerful transferences between the individuals involved, it contains within it both the hope of growth and the potential for it, and therefore for a constructive therapeutic process. Many couples' difficulties can be understood as a mutual attempt to heal the deficits of two wounded selves—an attempt that has gone awry, but still holds great promise. A healthy marriage is potentially the most powerful adult relationship there is, with the possible exception of an intensive analysis, for the legitimization and working through of the tension between attachment and self-delineation. One reason for this is its unequaled capacity to encourage vulnerable moments.

Furthermore, the exploration of vulnerability and shared affective experience is especially central in work with couples because it is actually the relationship that is the focus of treatment. There is a potential for reciprocity and sharing between the partners when they are both present that is not often found in other relationships, including the analytic one. The experience of less-than-omnipotent humanness that characterizes vulnerable moments is often felt, at least at first, as a narcissistic blow, but the intense feeling of relatedness between husband and wife, with the help of the couple therapist, can provide the sense of safety and the reinforcement of risk that make it tolerable. In this kind of a supportive selfobject surround new openness is possible, and openness is the antidote to the debilitating sense of shame with which so many patients struggle. In a couple for whom the achievement of intimacy has been a problem, the sharing of vulnerable moments can open the door to a longed-for richness and depth within the marital relationship.

APPROACHES TO COUPLES

Psychoanalytic writers working from other models have ventured into the region of couple therapy: Siegel (1991, 1992) and Scharff and Scharff (1991) from the standpoint of traditional object relations; Sharpe (1990) from what she refers to as a developmental object relations perspective; and Sander (1978, 1985, 1989) from the classical position.

Marion Solomon (1985, 1988, 1989, 1991) has written extensively about working with couples from a self-psychological vantage point. Ringstrom (1994) has written about treating couples from a self-psychological and intersubjective perspective, and in my own previous work on couple therapy, I have also taken a self-psychological approach (Livingston 1995, 1998a). However, none of these writings, including my own, focuses as directly on the issues of emotional availability and on the role of here-and-now shared vulnerability as I intend to do here. David Shaddock (1998) takes an approach that is similar in some respects to the position I am taking here. Shaddock focuses on empathy as what makes relational transformation possible. He stresses the healthy kind of dependency that can make relationships the best place to work out individual problems and develop intimacy out of impasse. This focus on empathy is closely related to my stress on an empathic understanding of each person's vulnerability.

Solomon takes off from a quip of which Kohut (1984) was fond: that "a good marriage [is] one in which only one partner is crazy at a given time" (p. 220); that is, so that when one (the "crazy") partner temporarily needs selfobject support, the other one is available to provide it. Solomon sees a working marriage as one that allows both partners to regress occasionally to childlike dependent states. A wish for unconditional mirroring, or to adore another in an idealizing transference, is not necessarily destructive, as long as the demands that it be met are limited in duration and include some sense of reciprocity. Solomon (1989) sees the partners in a working relationship as exchanging roles; they take turns in meeting each other's needs, without either feeling trapped in an objectifying role that could be experienced as diminishing of their own self. To help a couple develop these capabilities, the therapist must focus "not [on] what either is doing wrong but on how the behaviors and reactions of each may be a defense against narcissistic injury" (Solomon 1991, p. 126).

This approach bears some resemblance to the concept of the vulnerable moment that I am developing. When people are enabled to drop their defenses, particularly contemptuous and shame-related behaviors, and to share their vulnerable selves in a safe and nurturing atmosphere, a softening and reforming of boundaries and an enhancement of self development can ensue. This is true in individual therapy and in psychotherapy groups, and is even more powerfully so within a marriage. But, especially within the intensely concentrated focus of couple therapy, the therapist must never forget that the individual subjective experience of *both* partners has to be safeguarded. When one partner threatens to negate the other's subjective reality, the therapist must intervene in order to protect that person from feeling invalidated. A partner who feels that his unfolding needs are treated as infantile or undesirable is quite likely to give up hope—not only for the treatment, but possibly also for the marriage.

FROM CONFLICT TO VULNERABILITY TO INTIMACY: WORKING THROUGH IN THE INTRACOUPLE TRANSFERENCE–COUNTERTRANSFERENCE

The self-psychological approach to couple therapy is as usual distinct from other psychoanalytic views in its stress on empathic attunement to the subjective experiences and self-states of the members of the couple. This requires that the analyst be sensitive to the narcissistic vulnerabilities of *both* people, and also to the legitimization of the narcissistic needs and selfobject transferences of both of them. The therapist pays special attention to the unfolding of these selfobject transferences *within the couple itself*, and also to the countertransference-like experiences stimulated in the partner who is the recipient of the other's transference demands.

Furthermore, as in individual treatment, the self-psychological approach to conflict and aggression in couple work is based upon the view of rage as a breakdown of the cohesive self that I have outlined above. Work with anger is a special case of the self psychologist's habitual focus upon the state of the self and its vicissitudes. Interpretations are intended to enhance the self-cohesion of both partners, and thus to allow them to relinquish some of their defenses, including aggression. This sets a tone of safety and introspection, and promotes an exploratory process, and it allows as well for vulnerability to emerge. The focus is on the patient's *subjective experience of anger* and what is expressed through it. The task of the therapist is to come to an empathic grasp of the idiosyncratic complexities and personal meanings involved. A self psychologist's interpretive focus always begins from this vantage point within the patient's point of view. It can then shift easily to the broader context of the experience from which the rage arose. In this context, and still within a stance of empathic attunement, it becomes possible to explore the functions that the aggression serves and the roots in childhood vulnerability of these experiences. This exploration of subjective meaning, both in the here and now of the transference (particularly the intracouple transference) and also, eventually, in the "there and then" of genetic roots, leads to a deepening of the therapeutic process. A brief clinical vignette from a group illustrates this principle and parallels a typical marital conflict.

> A man in a group suddenly, and seemingly without reason, became enraged when a woman changed the subject. After the group showed some interest in what he was experiencing, he moved from a loss of control that was frightening both to the group and to himself to a more introspective position. He spoke briefly about how scary his temper felt. He believed that he couldn't expect anyone to grasp how upsetting it was for him to be ignored by this particular woman. He counted on her to care about him and to be attuned to him. He was venturing to express something that he privately took significant pride in. "When you turned away from me at that moment and changed the subject, you crumpled my grandiosity." The entire group felt the poignancy of his injury and he was able to relax. Later in that same session, he connected his crumpled feelings to instances when his wife had said things that made him feel tiny. He began to see how his rage made him feel bigger, although in a frightening manner.

The focus in couple therapy is upon empathic attunement, as it always is in self psychology, and upon the repair of ruptures or breaks in this attunement. But in this case the attunement is important not only between therapist and patients, but also within the couple. The task of the couple therapist is to help the couple to achieve Kohut's (1984) description of a good marriage: "one in which only one partner is crazy at a given time." That way, he went on to say, "They can rise to the challenge of providing the selfobject function that the other's temporarily impaired sense of self needs at a given moment" (p. 220). This means that partners must learn to create enough safety for each other that they can allow themselves, one at a time, to be open and vulnerable.

Initially the couple therapist must create this safety himself, and as it becomes established he can facilitate vulnerable moments by teaching the partners themselves to recognize and foster the atmosphere that has permitted them. Only one partner at a time is allowed to be, as Kohut put it, "crazy," and the other is helped to listen and respond. This experience creates over time an expectation within the partners of responsiveness, and encourages them in turn to expose and explore their reactiveness in a vulnerable but orderly (rather than an attacking or defensive) manner. The therapeutic process may begin with self-protection and blame on both partners' parts, but as the spouses with the therapist's help learn to contain these responses, it becomes safer to risk softening, and being open becomes less threatening.

The sharing of vulnerable moments leads to an increase in intimacy and an enriching of the marital relationship. Sometimes it becomes possible for a couple to transcend the need to take turns in being the empathic provider or the vulnerable nurtured one. At these moments, both partners can share their vulnerability and explore the personal intersubjective meaning of their patterns of relating to each other. It can at times even include a simultaneous experience and acceptance of both separateness and differences on the one hand, and of an underlying basic humanness and alikeness on the other.

PAULA AND VINCE: AN ILLUSTRATION

Both the husband and wife in this vignette have been in individual treatment with me for many turbulent years. Vince was in weekly psychotherapy briefly several years ago, and Paula, after many years of psychotherapy, is currently in a three-times-a-week analysis. This complicates the session presented here and influences Vince's feelings about what is going on.

Paula is an attractive professor of sociology in her mid-forties, well read in self psychology and intersubjectivity. She is a sophisticated patient who, after years of struggle, has developed a good deal of trust in me and in the therapeutic process. Vince is a world-renowned scientist in his early fifties. His ability to grasp concepts and his perceptiveness are exceptional. These abilities are partially offset by a significant degree of skepticism about the value of treatment. He also resents the need for "another man" to help make the marriage work. This is related to the complication of Paula being in analysis with me simultaneously with the couple treatment. Vince has only recently, after much exploration of his reluctance, begun tentatively to look to me for support, and to request a few individual sessions. Paula has been his source of selfobject experience. It is only his yearning for more closeness with her (and for her acceptance) that motivates him to participate in the couple sessions.

Their relationship has been a rollercoaster ride of extreme ups and downs, including a serious separation about eight years ago. Recently they have begun to be more compassionate toward each other, and the periods when both of them feel hopeless about their needs being met, or even understood, have been shorter and less frequent. The following session was the result of a great deal of previous work.

Paula: We've been getting along pretty well. I've been going through my shifts, but I haven't been blaming Vince. What I got in touch with was that (she turns directly toward Vince) I do want something from you. I think that I want you to do with me what I experience that I do with you. This morning you were telling me about an accomplishment . . . and I think you needed me to be excited and to say, "That was great and I'm really proud of you." I think that I need more of that. . . . I've been entertaining the idea that there's something that I get here that I don't get at home. You can't be Marty, but . . . I have moments where it feels like Marty admires me . . . and it feels really good.

Vince: I do have that feeling . . . and I don't express it enough for you to take in. I admire you. I've always admired you. I'm impressed with your growth and development and intelligence. I always have been. I guess that you're asking for more.

Paula: Yes.

Vince: The problem is that I don't express my excitement. I really am excited about you.

Marty: So, part of it is that you need to do some self-searching about what's in the way of expressing it when you're excited. I think the first thing, though, is to feel that it's okay that you're not always perfectly responsive. What's really important is having room for Paula to talk about her disappointment rather than to go away . . . going into that whole chain of events . . . drinking and getting depressed.

Vince: That would be much better.

Marty: You can't always have what you want, but most of the time if somebody cares and understands what you didn't get, it helps it heal.

Paula: I think that for me, on the weekends, I've been expecting you to intuitively know what I need and to give it to me. That happens at moments, but never enough. When that doesn't happen it starts the ache and then asking you for what I need triggers a lot of shame. So, I either get humiliated when I don't ask and then you don't magically figure out what I want, or I feel ashamed if I have to ask. So it puts me in a real bind.

Vince: (Clearly uncomfortable) Mmm-hmm. What would you feel if I told you? How do you feel when I tell you that I really don't like being here, I don't feel like being here?

[This is a good example of Slavin and Kriegman's (1998) concept of conflict of interests, and how it makes it difficult for spouses to be vulnerable with each other. Paula is trying to explore, in a vulnerable way, her need for more mirroring responsiveness. I tried to help her to explore her responses to experiences of selfobject failure in this area. My goal was to help them develop the ability to repair these breaks in their empathic bond and to question some of the painful, repetitive patterns in their interaction. However, Vince also has needs, and for the moment these conflict with Paula's need to be more central. In addition, Vince was probably hurt by Paula's comparison of his response to the one she experienced in her individual session.]

Paula: How do I feel? I hesitate to answer. I guess I'm not shocked, but I guess I want to hear more about what's going on.

Vince: So, you don't have any feeling about it?

Paula: I'm not sure what's going on so it's hard to have a feeling about it.

Vince: (A bit peeved) So when I say that I don't feel like being here, it doesn't affect you? It doesn't trigger a feeling? That's what I'm asking. If there's no feeling that's okay, too. It's just that I'm sitting here saying to myself, "Boy! I'm not really present."

Marty: And you're wondering if it's all right to express that?

Vince: Yeah, I can keep my mouth shut and . . . I'm worried that if I said it, like in a different way, like, "I really don't want to be here," that will really . . . I guess I was trying to say it in a way that would stay engaged, that wouldn't shut you down . . . because you're being very vulnerable here and . . . but I don't feel like being here.

[Vince is aware of a conflict between his need for more positive attention and Paula's need for mirroring. He experiences her need to redefine him to suit her selfobject needs and withdraws. This is an example of the "undertow" inherent in intimate relationships and the need to creatively negotiate these divergent interests and views.]

Marty: Maybe something is going on in response to this particular kind of vulnerability. Because your first response was that it made you feel bad about yourself.

Paula: I can understand why you wouldn't want to be here. (With a warm laugh) Why would you want to stay and feel bad about yourself?

Marty: Paula started off saying that she wanted something . . . and didn't get it. She said, "I get it in therapy." That's not going to make you feel like being here.

Vince: Yeah. My first inclination was to say that it felt good not doing these sessions for two weeks and uncomfortable getting back. But maybe it's the content of what Paula is talking about. Maybe I'm just not in the mood to hear you talk about yourself.

Paula: (Quietly) My worst fear.

Vince: Maybe when you started out by saying that we've been getting along better, that may have made it more impactful when you started talking about my not giving something to you. It might have raised my hopes and then crashed them. I didn't want to hurt you by saying that I'm not here anymore.

Paula: (Smiles warmly) But you had to be honest. I'm glad you did.

Marty: I think it's a big step for Vince to know that these feelings are important to express and that it's potentially dangerous. So he's trying to find a way to express it that's a working way. He's putting it on the table [trying to negotiate the conflict of interest].

Paula: I was really glad that you told me. I like that a lot. When you're in your experience and you share it with me, I like that. That makes me feel closer to you.

Vince: (Later in the session, to Paula) What really scares me is that you're often a bully! You cut me off before. You weren't hearing what I was saying. Now I don't remember what I was saying. This is a problem for me. I feel humiliated.

Marty: What feels humiliating?

Paula: (Sadly) I interrupted him.

Vince: She interrupted and when I tried to persist she intimidated me again harshly. When I was a kid, my mother and father would just drown me out. I didn't stick up for myself. I'd want to zone out.

Marty: It's hard for you to stick up for yourself . . . rather than letting it build up to the point where you're going to not want to be here.

Vince: (To Paula) What you need to say is really important, I acknowledge that. It's very difficult to keep up with you. Now I'm lost. I don't have anything to say.

Marty: What you're saying is very important. At the same time that you see Paula had a real need to cut you off and to express her fear . . . and you're interested in what she's feeling, it also felt humiliating because you repeatedly let yourself get cut off and not count. And then you experience Paula as a bully.

Vince: And then, once I feel bullied, I'm in the shame position. I feel like I'm bad and that I've done something bad to you (to Paula). Cutting you off is being selfish. Holding on to my self becomes something bad, selfish! And then I'm lost. I'm really floundering. My identity is really in trouble.

Marty: You don't know how to hold on to yourself at that point. You're really in trouble.

Vince: I've never understood that as well as I understand it at this moment.

Marty: Yeah, this is exciting.

Vince: Yeah, I feel excited about it.

Marty: It's a real insight . . . about you, and about the interaction between you. That sometimes there is a real problem. You both have a real need to talk at the same time.

It's hard not to feel lost then if Paula is stronger at the moment. [As they both feel understood, by the therapist and by each other, an increased risk of vulnerability is possible. Selfobject needs are more openly expressed and the intersubjective meaning of their interaction becomes available for exploration.]

Vince: I think I really had an insight about it because now I'm happy to be here.

Marty: You're happy to be here because you're excited with your ability to see something.

Paula: (A little later) You two seem to me to feel very connected. I'm feeling a little separate . . . scared.

Marty: So, it's dangerous that Vince and I understand . . .

Paula: I don't get a feeling right now that you're understanding me. You're understanding Vince. You two are very connected. It's really funny. It seems to go back and forth in here. [Again, a conflict of interest emerges for exploration and negotiation within the experience of an increasingly safe selfobject surround.]

Marty: If I'm connected to one of you the other can feel left out. But, also, if one of you has the floor for a while in a meaningful way, then the other one can start to feel a drifting away . . . a sense of "I don't want to be here."

Vince: That's right.

Paula: I think that's true. That's a real problem.

Marty: It is a problem, and it's exciting to be able to see it without yelling and screaming at each other. When you're scared that you aren't being understood at a particular moment, your pressure to come in builds because there's a fear that there isn't room for you and that we aren't understanding you.

Paula: That's true. It's very humiliating to say that. I'm sitting here thinking that I should be a big girl. I shouldn't be feeling this way. They're just working clinically. My grown-up self is saying, "Paula, get a grip."

Marty: You really need to express your fear and your little girl feeling.

Paula: It's there!

Marty: And are we forgetting you? Can you trust that if Vince is exploring for a while for himself, he will come to the point where there's room for you?

Paula: It's easy for me to think of how Vince gets bored and wants the attention. It's harder for me to think of how I do it. But I think you're right. It goes back and forth. It's almost like two hungry kids and nobody can get fed enough.

Marty: Getting fed has to do with attention and understanding. And if Vince was getting fed, you begin to feel like it's never going to be your turn. That's an old familiar feeling.

Paula: Yeah.

Marty: It's a very desperate feeling.

Paula: And a very humiliating feeling. To admit that you're right. It gets very total.

Marty: It's a feeling that's developed over the years. You also developed a survival technique, the ability to make sure that the attention shifts to you.

Paula: (Enthusiastically) Oh yeah.

Marty: Even if it becomes a battle and it's not satisfying.

Paula: You're right. (Lighter) I was thinking of that. I was thinking, Okay, Paula, this is *all right*. You know, this is a good survival technique. I grew up with five brothers. They were all over six feet tall. I had to have a voice! Or else I was nothing.

Marty: So when Vince says that you were being a bully, you don't experience yourself as a bully. You experience yourself as a little kid who's got to fight to survive. [This is a clear example of two very different subjective experiences—an intersubjective disjunction. It is also the beginning of a resolution of that disjunction through a vulnerable sharing of how each spouse's organizing principles and personal meanings interact in the intersubjective context.]

Paula: I'm not going to say that I didn't know I was bulldozing. It's been effective, in some ways, but maybe what I'm hearing is that it's not as effective as I hoped.

Marty: It's effective in alleviating the fear that you have in the moment.

Paula: Yeah, that's true.

Marty: But it's not effective in getting you what you really need.

Paula: What feels sad to me is that I could do something humiliating to myself like that in order to try to get something that's much softer. And I don't know at those moments how to get it any other way, really. And even though I feel like I'm going to get rid of the humiliation, it actually exacerbates the feeling, especially when it's exposed. But if I wasn't doing that, how would I get you to hear me?

Vince: Well, let me see if I get this. What I understand is that when you try to bulldoze, what you're really trying to say is, "I'm frightened that I'm not important . . . that

I'm ignored . . . that I'm not meaningful. That he's all . . . that everything is for him and not for me. And I'm not going to get enough. And I feel humiliated about that. So, I'm going to bang right through here and take it because I want Marty and I want the focus back and he's had it long enough. I'm afraid it will never come back to me ever again." That's what I'm hearing that led you to bulldoze. My guess is that the points you were making were not the critical elements. The critical element was your yelling out, "I'm here and I count!"

Paula: Mmm-hmm.

Vince: So how else could you have said it? You know I think it's ironic. The whole process tonight is like a full circle. I expressed my own jealousies. I said that I'm jealous of what's going on with you and Marty and I'm sitting here and I'm getting bored. And my way of dealing with that is to be a little yelping puppy dog. Maybe that's how I got my parents to pay attention to me again . . . to play the soft side. And I'm hearing that what you needed to do to survive in that moment was to bang through against your big big brothers. So I yelp and you bang. It's really no different. It's like a full circle for me. I see the similarity in our feelings . . . with very different expressions.

Marty: Mmm-hmm. The underlying hurt and fear are the same, yet the behavior is so different.

Paula: Yeah, the way we express it is so different. Yeah.

Marty: When you see that similarity, it's easier to really understand each other.

Paula: Yeah, that was really helpful. It was helpful for me to hear you talking about your own stuff in that way. I guess it always feels good to me when I can make it equal. It's more quid pro quo. Then I can take it in better. [The reciprocal sharing reduces the risk involved in vulnerability.]

Marty: So, you need things to be more equal and it's exciting that Vince is able to take a look at himself.

Paula: Yeah, that's great.

Marty: I also hear that once you were able to give him the space to do that and to be with him, then he really understood what you were saying differently. So there's an equalizing over time that way too. There was room, a little space here, for about ten minutes, where you both were here, both exposing and understanding at the same time.

Paula: Mmm-hmm!

Marty: That's exciting. We started out where not only did you have to take turns, but I had to do something to make it safe for somebody to have a turn. What we evolved to was that I could be quiet and you were both listening and expressing.

Paula: That's right. Tricky, isn't it?

Marty: You have to *get* to that. You often can't. Often we start out with both of you needing to be listened to and nobody is able to listen.

Vince: And I think I'm onto something for myself, too, in the sense of how one responds to being bullied is to be very soft. People back down from being bullied. It's like with dogs. In the park if a big dog gets on top of our little one, she becomes very placid and then they start licking her. And I think that's what I do. When I get bullied, I don't bully back. I tend to be a yelper . . . at least with my parents. I think that that worked.

Marty: You experience yourself as becoming soft . . . not soft and open the way you were doing today.

Vince: No, no, no.

Marty: Like soft and withdrawing?

Vince: No, I think vulnerability. I remember crying a little bit and then they would recognize my softness and calm down. Then it would be safe for me.

Paula: It makes me crazy! In that way I'm very different from your parents. It makes me more sadistic.

Vince: We're different people . . . different operating principles.

Paula: It makes me crazy when you turn over on your back. Then I'll dominate more.

Marty: That's what I was hearing. It works with your parents. It doesn't work with Paula.

Vince: That's right. It doesn't work with Paula.

Marty: And then you stop being soft and you get angry, but in a shut-off kind of way.

Vince: Right, right, right.

Paula: What I respond to is when you match my intensity.

Vince: We are diametrically opposite. We seek opposite solutions to each other's problems. So my suggestion to you is instead of bulldozing to be soft, because my response to your being soft would be to be soft.

Marty: Uh-huh, so Paula's bulldozing sets off a softness in you, but not an openness . . . a sort of surrender. If she wants you to hear her, letting go of bulldozing and being softer would work better. You would be more able to hear her. (Vince agrees enthusiastically.) And what Paula is saying is that what she needs, in order to be able to hear you, is for you to not let it build up into a rage. Instead, to stand up and say, "Well, you did this . . ." (Vince continues to nod his understanding and to interject an occasional "right.") " . . . and it was hurtful," or "You're being a bulldozer now. I need to be listened to too."

Paula: Yes, that's right, without becoming the injured puppy dog.

DISCUSSION

This session illustrates what is possible in couple treatment after a great deal of groundwork. It begins with Paula's expression of her unfulfilled yearning for more of a mirroring selfobject responsiveness from her husband. Vince experiences her description of selfobject failure as a statement of his personal inadequacy. He responds by becoming somewhat depressed and withdrawing emotionally from the session. Having experienced the sessions as a safe-enough place, however, he is able to risk expressing his response. He struggles to do this in a nonattacking manner, and then he explores his own reactions. The therapist's task here was to support simultaneously the vulnerability of both partners. Paula is out on a limb exposing her need for mirroring, while at the same time, Vince is exposing his reaction to being the focus of her sense of selfobject failure. His predicament is quite similar to that of an analyst caught up in a countertransference reaction. He is vulnerable, and needs attentive responsiveness as much as Paula does. The therapist does what he can to legitimize and to be empathically responsive to both sets of needs. This leads to an exploration of the intersubjective space in the marital interaction.

At first, Paula and Vince take turns. With support from the analyst each is able to contribute to a sense of safety that lets the other feel understood and explore his or her responses. Each one in turn also experiences a fear of being left out or devalued. In the end they are both able to be open and vulnerable at the same time. They begin to see how basically similar some of their fears and needs are, even when their outer behaviors are very different.

Shared vulnerability in that sense is what Hagman (1997) calls a mature selfobject experience, or Wolf (1980) the "reciprocal empathic resonance" with selfobjects that develops in mature relationships; both individuals in such moments are expressing their own selfobject needs and fears, with simultaneous awareness of the partner as having a similar self with needs and fears. Shared vulnerable moments can provide in this way an important selfobject experience of twinship, while at the same time providing a mirroring experience that supports self-delineation. The legitimization of self-delineation and attachment at the same time not only ameliorates shame, but also strengthens the marital bond.

The impact of this experience of reciprocal empathic responsiveness was profound—in fact, it has become apparent over time that this session was a significant positive turning point in their relationship. It has led to important changes in the way they relate to each other. The sense of twinship between them fulfills a basic selfobject function in the moment. It also enables an exploration and working through of intersubjective patterns that had been disruptive to their marriage for many years. Vince experienced himself as being bulldozed. At the same time Paula was experiencing a desperate need to "bang through" as she had had to do with her "big big brothers." The exploration of this interaction is a good example of a mature selfobject experience that allows the exploration of underlying vulnerability and organizing principles. It also clearly illustrates the importance, for therapeutic process, of a couple analyst who values, facilitates, and sustains vulnerable moments.

Attention to the patient's subjective experience of his self and selfobject surround is even more significant in a couple session than in individual analysis. The selfobject failures and narcissistic injuries that inevitably occur in therapy are multiplied by the presence of a partner who has his or her own needs and priorities. The therapist's role is not to prevent such occurrences—although he tries, over time, to modify them by helping the partners learn to be more responsive to each other and less reactive—but rather to accept, understand, and interpret conflict and aggression as an expectable reaction to actual or fantasized slights within the transferential context of the relationship and the couple sessions. Angry responses are understood in the subjective context in which the patients experience them, and thus are legitimized, rather than treated as inappropriate distortions. Rather than directing his interpretive activity toward a displacement that needs correction, the self-psychologically oriented couple therapist is more likely to be interested in the question of what it feels like to be angry, or to be gotten angry at.

Anna Ornstein (1991) elaborates upon this point. She suggests that the therapist must be responsive to the patient's experience, which usually includes a dread of potentially disruptive and destructive affect. In other words, she understands the problem of rage to lie in the patient's trouble containing and regulating affect, rather than, for instance, an inability to differentiate past from present. She stresses that the state of the self is always primary. The cohesion of the self (its vigor, aliveness, and capacity to contain and regulate affect) should always be at the forefront of therapeutic consideration. The way the analyst responds in the transference is always dictated by his focus upon the state of the self and the vicissitudes of its fragmentation and cohesion.

Although we write and speak of *conflict* and *aggression* as things in themselves, in the clinical moment a self psychologist can meaningfully consider only the *experience* of conflict (or the conflicted person) or the *experience* of aggression (or the aggressive person). To focus on conflict and aggression per se is at best an experience-distant stance, and at worst an adversarial one. To focus on the patient's experiencing self reminds the therapist of the importance of maintaining an empathic stance even in the face of great provocation, and encourages the exploration of the important idiosyncratic meanings that each person attaches to his own experiences. When couples are in conflict, the source of the conflict often lies in the *subjective personal interpretations* the individual partners put upon what occurs between them. The therapist's role is to be attuned to both of them. He tries to provide interpretations that bridge *both* subjectivities, and support a shared reality within which all parties can feel accepting and accepted. An example of this can be seen in the following session, which also provides a reminder that self psychology is a form of psychoanalysis, and as such relies on a genetic understanding of psychodynamics and the use of interpretation.

THINGS STINK. THINGS STINK WORSE THAN EVER!

The patients are a couple in their late thirties who have been married for twelve years. They have been separated twice and have come for couple treatment in states of crisis several times over the past five years. They remain in treatment for about six months each time, breaking many of the scheduled every-other-week sessions. I have seen them both in occasional individual sessions over the five-year period, and the wife has sporadically been in treatment with a female colleague. They are not an easy couple to work with. The following session occurred after the wife called me after a year's break in treatment.

"Things stink. Things stink worse than ever! That's why I called. We used to fight all the time. Now we don't even do that. I think we've given up. At least I've given up. David will never be able to give me what I need. It's like trying to put a square peg in a round hole."

David sits in silent despair. He wants to defend himself, but he knows from painful experience that attempts to explain only add fuel to the flames of Janet's anger. Sometimes he manages to contain his impulse to respond to what seems to him like an endless flow of devaluation—a litany of his defects—in the hope that Janet will see him as listening.

"He doesn't understand what I'm talking about," Janet says now. "I need someone who can respond to me. Even right now, he's silent and unresponsive. I can't even tell if he's listening or just zoning out—tuning me out like he always does."

David turns to me for help. "If I talk, I'm defensive. If I'm quiet and try to make room for her feelings, then I'm cold and unresponsive. I feel hopeless. If she stopped telling me that I'm no good, then I might be able to be nicer to her. I might not stay away so much."

In response to this plea, I acknowledge how difficult it is for David to listen to what he experiences as devaluation. I note how tough it is not to get defensive, or fight to establish that he is not in fact so lacking. I also comment on how uncomfortably helpless it must feel not to know how to respond. David appears a bit more present and adds, "That's when I zone out. I don't want to zone out, but I don't know what else to do."

I respond, "It sounds like that's the only way you've found to protect yourself from a feeling that could be devastating. It's understandable that you feel a strong pull to zone out."

Janet is impatient with what she experiences as my coddling David. She also feels that *her* need is being forgotten. "He always withdraws. I need someone to step up to the plate and he just doesn't." Realizing that my attentiveness to David may have unbalanced the need to connect empathically with *both* members of the couple, I attempt to reestablish a connection with Janet—to repair the empathic rupture. "I think that my understanding David's need to protect himself may have felt to you like dismissing your need for a response at that moment. What David experiences as criticism is also your attempt at telling us what you need. I can hear how hard it is for you to tell whether he's listening right now or whether he's withdrawn and become unavailable."

Janet softens slightly and continues, "I can't tell if he's here or not. At home he spends so much time on the Internet. He's never with the family. He doesn't try to be what I need."

David's voice is angry and discouraged. "Maybe I would try instead of withdrawing if you were nice to me." "I'm too angry all the time to be nice," Janet replies quickly as the sense of rage increases on both sides of the room. "You *are* always angry," David continues. "You never step up to bat," Janet taunts back. "You withdraw, you go into despair and talk suicide every time I need you to be with me."

David angrily defends. "No, that is not true! I am often there for you." I turn to Janet and speak quietly, trying to cut through the growing gulf of rage and resentment between them. "There's a ring of authenticity in David's voice. He clearly believes that he is sometimes there for you. Is there some way that that rings true for you too?" [This is an example of an intervention intended to bridge an intersubjective gap between spouses.] Janet slows down and for the first time begins to mellow. "Yes, it is true. When something terrible happens we're very together. Like when my mother died. David was very attentive then. He really knew what I was going through. He was right there with me in my pain and he understood how resentful I was about how inadequate and fragile she always was. There was never room for me with her. I always had to take care of her."

The room is quiet now. Janet and David look at each other for a moment. Then Janet continues. She is talking directly to David now, in a thoughtful tone, rather than complaining to me about him. "It happens when I'm angry with *you*—when there's difficulty between us and I need you to listen to me. You're great when I'm troubled about something outside of us. Then you're great and I get what I need."

"You aren't criticizing me then," David says.

"I am an angry bitch sometimes," Janet agrees. "I don't like to be an angry bitch, but I get so angry when you get hurt and talk suicide or zone out."

"You're very angry at David's vulnerability," I clarify. "It blocks your attempt to express what you need or to protest when you don't get your needs met." "It feels like he's being just like my mother at those times," Janet adds.

I continue in an attempt to find a reflection that will balance the needs of both husband and wife. "It's ironic that although you don't want to, you become an angry bitch in response to David's fragility. It really feels impossible to express your anger or demand what you need if he's vulnerable and gets so hurt. Yet at the same time, David can't respond to what you need while this is going on. You see, he's very responsive when he can sense the vulnerable soft part of you (like when your mother died); but when he experiences you as an angry bitch he can't see that part of you, can't respond to your vulnerability." David nods his endorsement. He seems to feel understood and is, for the moment, not hearing all this as about his inadequacy. "It's not you or me," he says. "It's the way things fit together from both of us."

Seeing that David is okay, I turn again to Janet. "It sounds like you've never had anyone who was strong enough to stay with you while you were angry and resentful. You need someone to be able to do that—to really stay and get the message. Then you could get back to that sensitive vulnerable little girl that you cover up so well when you become the angry bitch."

Janet begins to cry, and David is visibly moved also. "That's my real yearning," she says through the tears. "I'm feeling sad now," David relates. "Sad that I'm not strong enough." But just at the wrong moment he can't resist his impulse to go back to his original point in the mistaken hope that at this vulnerable moment Janet will be receptive. He adds, "If only you were nicer to me for a while first, then I wouldn't zone out so much." Janet immediately recoils from the shock. "Maybe if you would step up to bat first I would be nicer," she snaps back as the tears stop and her whole expression changes. She turns to me and complains. "This stinks, he always expects me to change. He never steps up to the plate. I need someone who steps up to bat. I don't know if we belong together. If he worked for me, I would fire him." David slumps in silent despair.

DISCUSSION

This material illustrates a self-psychological approach to conflict and aggression in couple therapy, as well as the occupational hazards I mentioned at the outset. Janet and David finally get through the protective layer of conflict and aggression that had arisen as a result of repeated unmet needs and narcissistic injuries and experience a brief glimpse of intimacy—which, as often happens in marital therapy, is shattered even before the session ends. Still, the rage and conflict between them is not the focus of the therapeutic endeavor, but the underlying vulnerability of the selves involved that needs to be legitimized, expressed, and explored. The working through of the ruptures associated with conflict, and their connection to narcissistic wounds both in childhood and in the present, allows the underlying weaknesses in each self to be gradually ameliorated. In turn, it is the process of shoring up their vulnerable selves that enables the individuals involved to achieve gradually increasing levels of affect regulation. The key issue is not the management of conflict and rage. It is the strengthening of capacities for affect regulation, containment, and self-cohesion that enables a deepening of intimacy and the facilitation of a therapeutic process.

The session clearly illustrates the therapist's efforts to maintain a balanced empathic responsiveness to both partners. Empathic breaks inevitably occur, both between the spouses and also between each of them and the therapist. When they happen, the therapist tries to understand and eventually interpret the resulting injuries from the perspective of each spouse's subjective experience. It is the personal meanings that an experience has for each patient, along with the underlying yearnings and vulnerabilities touched upon, that need to be understood and worked through. Janet's angry-bitch self needs to be grasped and reflected as an understandable response that protects her when her needs are not met. When this is understood, her more vulnerable yearnings can tentatively surface in search of acceptance. David's self-protectiveness must also be accepted and understood as a response to the steady devaluation he experiences. For a brief time, both subjective vulnerabilities were balanced and supported. This was a vulnerable moment in which both partners felt nurtured and understood, and began to touch a deep underlying connection with each other.

The intimacy, unfortunately, was only momentary. Janet needed to be accepted just where she was at the moment, but David, responding from his own subjective experience, was unable to understand that, and saw the situation as an opportunity to have his needs take a more primary position. This is a very common temptation in couples when one partner senses vulnerability in a spouse who has been unavailable for a long time, and David could not resist it. The resulting empathic break quickly triggered a regression back to the conflict that had begun the session. When it can be tolerated, the repeated working through of painful triggers like this one forms a rupture and repair sequence that gradually leads to a firming of self structure in both partners.

THE INTRACOUPLE TRANSFERENCE AND COUNTERTRANSFERENCE

Intricate transference and countertransference-like experiences occur in the triadic context of couple therapy as they do in individual therapy, and they must also be understood multisubjectively. The partners each have their own separate subjective experiences of the treatment and of the therapist, and an important aspect of them is the unfolding of developmental needs and transferences toward the therapist. Both patients rely upon the therapist to enhance their capacity for self-cohesion and their self-esteem. But an even more significant aspect of the self-psychological approach to couple treatment is the way it legitimizes the partners' developmental needs *for each other.* In addition to the expected unfolding of transference needs toward the therapist, transferential responses (which include the expression of selfobject needs) also unfold within the patients toward each other. This means that the spouses experience not only their own transferential needs, but also a host of other subjective experiences in response to their partner's transferences to them as selfobject. I call this characteristic phenomenon—the responses to transferential demands within the couple—*countertransference-like experiences,* because they parallel in some respects the analyst's experience of countertransference. The couple therapist must be ever alert to the complexities of this situation. It is not enough to be sensitive to, and supportive of, the patient who is struggling to express his or her demands for self-sustaining responsiveness. In addition, the therapist must also maintain an empathic sensitivity to the partner's experience *of being the object of these demands.*

As in individual therapy, transferences reflecting selfobject needs can develop and unfold in an atmosphere of safety, and thus become available to exploration and eventual working through. These transferences, as Kohut (1971) has made clear, depend upon the analyst's ability to provide a sense of safety through acceptance, empathic attunement, and the disciplined effort to do nothing to interfere with their development. Working through them centers upon the repair of the inevitable ruptures in the empathic bond. Repeated selfobject experiences with the therapist lead a couple to expect an empathic responsiveness to their needs; that is, a selfobject relationship becomes established (Bacal 1994). In couple therapy, however, selfobject transferences also arise between the two spouses, and these are ultimately more important than those attached to the analyst. Within these transferences and, if possible, within the newly established reciprocal selfobject relationship between husband and wife, vulnerable moments and interpretive clarifications can be mutative.

Treatment therefore focuses on the patients' needs for mirroring and other narcissistic supplies *from their partners* rather than from the therapist, and on their experiences of empathic failures *with each other*. These reciprocal needs give rise to intense transference–countertransference interactions within the couple. In many couples, the inevitable moments when these intense needs are frustrated, as well as the fears involved in responding to the other, are often the source of the conflict and aggression that bring them to therapy in the first place.

Kohut (1971) discussed at some length the nature of analysts' responses to being the object of transferential demands; countertransference in this sense includes, but is not limited to, the analyst's subjective experiences in response to the unfolding transference. If he is being used to fulfill an archaic mirroring function, for example—that is, the patient needs him to listen intently and provide an audience for the expression of infantile grandiosity—he may be required to refrain from any expression of his own thoughts and feelings. It is not necessarily easy being the recipient of a selfobject transference, and many analysts experience boredom and sluggishness when being used as a function (as the provider of archaic selfobject experience) rather than being related to as a person. The success of treatment depends upon the analyst's ability to process and contain such responses so that they are not enacted. Enactments of countertransference experiences can hinder therapeutic process, while an informed understanding of them can enhance it.

As difficult as this can be at times, at least analysts are trained to process and contain responses to patients' transferential demands. They have the experience of a personal analysis to put complex feelings into context. They have supervisors and other colleagues with whom they can discuss countertransference responses, and they have, at least theoretically, a clear grasp of the value of such restraint. The partners in couple treatment have not generally studied for marriage the way an analyst studies for analysis, and they are not prepared for the intense selfobject demands that their partners place upon them. It is threatening to be faced with demands for empathic responsiveness, and to decenter from their own feelings sufficiently to be able to provide it is a formidable undertaking. The partner who has to listen responsively for any length of time will need the therapist's attention, understanding, and support at least as much as the partner who has taken the risk of speaking. The therapist must attune to both patients' experiences at the same time—their differing experiences of vulnerability (at feeling needs and at being needed) in particular. This is a complex task.

However, the main emphasis in couple treatment is on the working through of the partners' transferences *toward each other.* It is thus no surprise that, even more than neophyte analysts, partners need help in learning to cope constructively with the interplay of their transferential and countertransferential experiences, or that some of the help they need is analogous to the help that beginning therapists need from supervisors. Certain understandings about, and techniques for coping with, countertransference can enable this process, and can be taught to the couple. The use of the term *countertransference* or other technical terms is probably not helpful for most couples. But it *is* important to alert them to what is happening. They have deep underlying needs of each other. Some of these needs are fulfillable, and some may not be. The couple has to know that these needs must be aired and accepted, although not necessarily fulfilled, and that this is not always easy. In other words, the partners are encouraged not only to express their own selfobject needs, but also to play selfobject roles, and to allow their partners to express their needs and disappointments as well as their narcissistic hurts. At the same time, the therapist helps them to express, in turn, their responses to the transferences (their countertransferences).

The above interaction between Paula and Vince illustrates this point. Vince was trying to listen responsively to Paula, who seemed to be vulnerably sharing her need for a more mirroring response from him. However, providing her with that experience (being the object of her selfobject transference) did not meet his own selfobject needs at that moment. He felt belittled by her invidious comparison to the "empathic" therapist, and also as though he as a person with his own needs was not included in the discussion. His attention and desire to participate faded until he was able to risk asking that attention be paid to *his* experience (that is, to his countertransference-like response to being treated, for the moment, as an archaic selfobject). Once he felt that this experience was understood and legitimized, he felt more vital, and was more able and willing to alternate in providing and seeking selfobject satisfactions.

It can help to explain in very simple terms what selfobject needs and wishes are; such a clarification can help partners in their exploration of the experience of having to respond to each other's needs. Couple therapy is not a heavily cognitive process. But it is possible to respect and use the couple's ability to make use of cognitive material in order to increase their tolerance for intense experience with, and of, each other.

For instance, Racker's (1968) concept of concordant and complementary countertransferences can be as useful to couples as it is to analysts. The therapeutic exploration of the triggers of the couple's repetitive interlocking patterns is facilitated by the recognition that sometimes a listener identifies with the speaker's self (concordant identification) and at other times with the speaker's objects or significant others (complementary identification). A straightforward example of the application of Racker's concept occurred in the following session:

> Mary was telling her husband Jake about an incident at work. She was extremely upset with an employee who had been repeatedly late and irresponsible. She was exploring how disturbing it was to her when she depended on him and he failed to come through. Jake had been listening empathically, and reflecting his understanding of Mary's frantic attempts to get the employee to fulfill her expectations. He made several comments that clearly conveyed support and "withness." (In Racker's terms, he was making a concordant identification; he was identified with Mary and could experience vicariously what it was like for her to feel let down by someone she counted on.) Mary began to calm down. She experienced Jake as providing the selfobject experience that she needed at the moment, and as she became less frantic she began to be able to sort out her strong reactions to her employee. She pinpointed the event that really set her off. "I really lost it when he lied to me. That is a real trigger when someone lies to me." Jake's manner changed abruptly. "You don't really know he was lying. You could have the facts wrong." Mary immediately became frantic once again and began to go round in circles about how awful this employee was. Then she fell silent and moved toward the far end of the couch she and Jake were sitting on together. Jake was bewildered. "I don't get it. I've been very supporting and caring with you and now without any reason you're clamming up and moving away from me."

Of course, my focus shifted to Jake's experience at that point. "Can you tell Mary what you're feeling right now?" "I feel left. I feel that I really tried to be supportive and I was really with you. I felt close and good. Now I feel discouraged." "You're right, Jake," Mary replied. "You were really there for me. I'm not sure what happened." "I think I know what happened," I said. "You really felt Jake was with you." "Yes," she continued. "He was on my side and then suddenly he wasn't. I really need you to be on my side. That is so important when something goes wrong."

"You were really identified with Mary until she focused on the lying," I said to Jake, whose puzzlement subsided. "She says that to me sometimes. I hate it when she thinks I'm lying." Then turning to Mary, "I need you to trust me . . . to know that I'm always honest with you." "At the point that Mary made lying the issue it became tough for you to identify with her," I went on. "Of course, because of some of your own experiences and how important it is to have Mary trust you, at that moment your identification switched to the person being accused of lying." (That is, in Racker's terms, it switched to a complementary identification.) Mary reinforced the point. "I can see how it happened, but when you identify with the enemy I don't feel you're on my side." Jake got it and his expression changed to sadness and compassion. They sat quietly for a moment, then he reached for her hand and she reached back.

Teaching partners to tolerate their countertransferential responses, and helping them become able to provide containment and safety for each other must be done with a great deal of sensitivity to both individuals' vulnerabilities. Encouragement and reinforcement are needed, and the therapist must be very careful to avoid implying that one of the partners has failed or done something wrong. The emphasis must be always on how understandable their reactions are, and how difficult this work is. The achievement of intimacy in a relationship takes a lot of processing, a lot of tolerance of painful and anxiety-provoking feelings, and a lot of just plain hard work. The participants need mirroring, respect, and at times praise for the struggles they endure. When such work can be done with both members of the couple, so that the willingness to express and the willingness to listen are simultaneously enhanced in both, risks will be taken, and some very deep vulnerabilities may be uncovered. These, too, can be shared by the couple with the therapist's sensitive support, and, when necessary, active protectiveness. As always, the hardest part of couple work is protecting one partner's vulnerability without losing sight of the other's.

They need the therapist to validate the experience that to allow feelings to be expressed, and to listen to them, can be frightening. This is especially true when a partner's subjective experience of the feelings contradicts his own view of himself, or in some way evokes shame. This is another opportunity for what Lichtenberg and colleagues (1992) have called "trying on the attributes." But couples need to make some room for the expression of this kind of feeling, for both partners. The therapist can support them in this effort by acknowledging how difficult making that room for a partner's feelings can be. The therapist must always be aware of the complexities of the multisubjective situation, and of the vulnerabilities and needs of both partners, shifting as necessary from support of the speaker's risk-taking to an exploration of the listener's discomfort, to allow both to develop tolerance for both experiences. This is not an easy feat, and failures occur. However, breaks in empathy and their repair are an unavoidable and a necessary part in the process, as they are in other self-psychological therapies.

RESPONSIVENESS, REACTIVENESS, AND VULNERABILITY

What Bacal (1998b) has called the balance of reactiveness and responsiveness is more important in couple therapy than in any other therapeutic modality, because the sessions directly influence the basic relationship, which is the focus of the treatment. For a relationship to be growth-enhancing, partners must learn to balance reactiveness and responsiveness in the way they listen to and interact with each other. Many couples enter treatment precisely because of their failure to achieve this balance.

"Responsiveness" is a mode of listening and responding from an empathic sense of the speaker's subjective experience. It requires that the listener decenter, to some extent, from his or her own subjective and emotional reactions. Partners need to develop the capacity to be empathic and responsive toward each other. The leader sets an example of this attitude in his attempt to be sensitive to both patients' subjective experiences, especially at times of heightened vulnerability. He interprets and explains each partner's needs and behavior to the other when necessary, and as the couple begins to understand these processes, an empathic surround is established. Within this safe space each patient's uniqueness and selfobject needs can unfold. The empathic bonds established with the leader and between the partners allow arrested development to resume.

"Reactiveness," in contrast, is a mode of listening and reacting that is limited to the listener's own subjective and emotional perspective; it is an expression of how the speaker's expression impacts upon the listener.

As the partners follow the therapist's example, they begin to develop the capacity to be what Bacal (1998b) has called "responsive," as opposed to "reactive." They become capable of providing selfobject experiences for each other (listening empathically, for example, or allowing each other to express anger without reacting with anger of their own). Often the development of such abilities at the right time is a developmental achievement that suits the needs of both the listener and the person expressing himself. However, the couples analyst must always be attending to both partners. While one member of the couple is listening to the other's expression of need or hurt, the therapist must be sure to be attuned to the listener as well as to the person talking. It is very important to pick up stifled feelings and their importance, and to indicate, even if only nonverbally, attention to and understanding of *both* patients. Holding both partners in this manner is difficult. The wish of both partners to be attended to at the same time, by the therapist and by each other, is a primary source of conflict, and the fact that this can't always be managed is frequently what produces the empathic ruptures that Kohut considered central to working through.

The couple therapist also must help his patients learn to balance reactiveness and responsiveness, since without this balance there is no safety for the vulnerable expression of need. The therapist sets an example of responsiveness in his attempt to be sensitive to each patient's subjective experiences and especially to their vulnerability. He also interprets or explains, when necessary, one patient's needs and behavior to the partner. As these reactions become expected and comprehensible, an empathic surround can be established. Couples begin to count on a responsiveness from the therapist and from each other. It is largely within this sense of a safe space that each patient's uniqueness and selfobject needs can unfold and arrested development can be resumed.

However, the unbalanced expectation of rigidly consistent responsiveness is not a desirable outcome. Reactiveness is just as important as responsiveness in a well-functioning couple. It must be encouraged and respected, and the therapist must be ever alert to the presence of the fundamental conflict. Encouraging a couple to be consistently empathic toward each other is not only unrealistic, but is frequently a traumatic repetition of a childhood experience for many people who were forced, as children, to put aside their own needs and reactions in order not to threaten a parent. Suppressed wishes for fulfillment revive in marriage, and when they do, couples may become enmeshed in struggles over whose feelings and needs will be central and whose will be submerged. They are trapped in mutually incompatible demands for responsiveness and equally mutually incompatible patterns of reactiveness.

Each partner in turn, therefore, must be supported in developing the double ability to express needs and reactions, *and* to postpone expressing them. Partners often find it stressful to decenter from their own subjective experience in order to provide empathic support for each other. It is the analyst's empathic attunement to this stress that enables them to tolerate the decentering. In the learning process, both partners must develop the confident expectation that the therapist understands and appreciates the difficulty that the balance between reactiveness and responsiveness poses for them. They must be able to expect that the therapist will, in time if not immediately, be responsive to them, as well as to the partner. It is this trust that enables a patient to make a healthy choice to contain the impulse to reactivity. Otherwise the containing behavior is submission, and re-creates the childhood sacrifice of self-delineation to appease a caregiver.

SAM AND MARIA

This was an atypical session. Sam, a business executive in his mid-forties, was on an important conference call and couldn't leave work in time for their appointment. Maria, a designer, and I spent most of the session waiting for Sam and wondering what was detaining him. When he finally arrived, fifteen minutes remained out of the usual sixty-minute hour. The time pressure created some intense work in a short time. I was more active than usual; the time frame was short, and I had a sense that the couple needed help in avoiding an escalating spiral of frustration and anger with each other. This session illustrates the use of educational interventions, even though I would not usually make so many of them in so brief a period of time. They are intended to help couples learn to be responsive rather than just reactive to each other, and to encourage them to risk being more vulnerable. (This couple has been in treatment together for several years. A couple new to therapy and without established trust in and alliance with the analyst would probably not respond well to the intensified approach portrayed here, and the therapist would then need to be more patient.)

After greeting each other, the couple settles down and Sam begins the session:

Sam: So, what shall we talk about?

Maria: Well, what's going on for me . . . what I think of is that things have been good. No major fights, but I start to pull back a little bit from being more intimate with you, and then I start getting grumpy. I think that I pull back a little bit and disconnect from you and then I start to . . .

Sam: I notice you getting grumpy and you get this look on your face, like you're deep in thought about something and I ask you and sometimes . . .

Maria: That was just last night, when I came home. I went out with the group and you were home and I remember feeling estranged from you . . . and I felt it in the morning too . . . not from you. I shouldn't say that. *I* felt that way.

Sam: I don't know what went on. You came home and I was watching TV. So what about your seeing me home threw you off balance? You seemed surprised.

Maria: I felt like I had done something wrong.

Sam: Like what? You felt that you had done something wrong? Or did you feel that I had done something wrong?

Maria: That I did.

Sam: What? Because you went out with the group? Big deal! You told me you were going. I encourage you to go out with the group. I only get upset when I don't know. When I cook dinner. I think it's nice that you go out. You shouldn't feel obligated to rush home, and if you go out you shouldn't feel guilty. I was happy that I could get home early and relax.

Maria: That leads me to a realization that I've been angry with you. I was angry that you were home, and I was angry the next morning when you were in the bathroom.

Sam: I had the sensation that you came home, you saw me home, it threw you off balance, and you were really annoyed that I was home. I felt like you were going to put me through an inquisition.

Marty: What did it mean? If you were angry, it must have had some meaning to you.

Maria: Well, it threw me off. He was supposed to come home later than me. I wouldn't have stayed out. It made me disoriented, like I had done something wrong.

Marty: So the anger maybe covers a feeling that you did something wrong?

Maria: Yes, the anger at him. I felt mad at him.

Marty: So that might be a protection?

Maria: Right.

Marty: What did you feel you did wrong?

Maria: I went out when I didn't really have to . . . and . . . I left you . . . I didn't put you first, and I didn't call when Alice didn't come with us. I was afraid that Sam would see Alice and then say, "Wasn't my wife supposed to be with Alice?" That's the extent that I was . . .

Marty: You were afraid that Sam would think you were hiding something?

Maria: Yes.

Sam: Let me ask you a question. When you saw me home at a time I wasn't supposed to be, did you think *I* was hiding something?

Maria: No, I was angry because you screwed me up.

Sam: (Incredulous) I screwed you up? I screwed you up? Why? How?

Maria: Yes! I went out . . .

Sam: Stop right there! You went out. What is this thing about you going out and feeling bad about it?

Maria: I don't want to leave you home by yourself.

Marty: So, in some way, you're feeling that you screwed up, and it's his fault that you screwed up.

Maria: Yes.

Sam: Oh great! The old no-win scenario.

Maria: Yes, I screwed up and it's his fault, because he gave me the wrong information.

Marty: So, the important thing is that you felt you didn't do your job of being home. In some way you felt that you screwed up, that you didn't play your role.

Maria: Yes, I screwed up.

Marty: So one thing that happens when you feel you screwed up is that you get angry.

Maria: Yes, I cover it up. He gave me the wrong information.

Marty: So, how can you do your job?

Maria: Yes, how can I do my job? I can only do it if I have the right information.

Sam: (Sarcastically, after a long pause) Next time I'll stay out at a bar. I'll tell the guys there that I can't go home before eleven.

Marty: Sam, we really have to slow down and try to understand her reactions. It's not "rational." To understand it we've got to understand some assumptions that she's making. (A pause, then to Maria) I hear an assumption that it's your job not to leave him alone for a minute missing you. If he misses you, if he might be lonely, then you screwed up. If you had a good reason for it, it would be all right.

Maria: He would never say that . . . that he was lonely or anything.

Marty: (Softly) This is all your fears and thoughts?

Maria: Something I'm putting on it, right, yes.

Marty: I don't hear Sam being angry that you came home later.

Maria: (Softly) No, he never would.

Marty: It has something to do with your assuming that you have a job and that if you fail that job then you're not going to be special. Nobody is going to love you anymore. So, if he throws you a curveball, how can you do your job?

Maria: Like I got caught unprepared. Yeah, like I got caught unprepared.

Marty: (After a long pause) What are you feeling, Sam?

Sam: I don't like to throw you a curve ball, but my feeling is, Okay, great! I have to be checked in at work all the time so that my boss knows where I am. Now I have to do the same thing at home. I don't want to do that.

Marty: (Playfully) Don't!

Sam: I'm not going to.

Marty: I don't really hear any need for you to do that. I just hear a need for Maria to have room to explore. It's an interesting set of rules that she's stuck living by. The rules make her uncomfortable, and I think that if she can feel free to look at it with us . . . You see, I think it's terrific that she could say she gets angry at you without either of you making a big deal out of it. Just, "Oh, that sounds interesting. What made you angry? What's that about?" Then we can begin to discuss the idea that she has a belief system that she has a job to do. That she had to be home before you.

Sam: That phrase, "Isn't it interesting." Didn't we have a big fight about that?

Maria: Not a big fight, a little fight.

Marty: Because you used that phrase?

Sam: My response to Maria getting angry at me . . . I don't even remember what it was about . . . because I think it was a stupid argument and it was getting heated at one point. I don't even remember what it was about.

Maria: It was about the noise in the car.

Sam: I said, "You're having a reaction to my upset about the noise." I said, "You know, you're having a reaction to something. You're having your own feeling about it." I said, "Why couldn't you hold yourself back for a minute instead of lashing out at me and use that phrase that Marty uses? You could say, "It's interesting that I'm feeling that." And then I said that we could at least look at it in a rational manner, instead of having a fight over nothing.

Marty: (Thoughtfully, after a long pause) That's a good point, except I wouldn't emphasize the rational. It's like, "Let's take a step back and look at it, look at what's going on." But if you feel a pressure to be too rational, we wouldn't be able to get to some of these feelings.

Sam: Well, it would keep us from feeling that we've got this gallon of gasoline and now let's just throw a match on it!

Marty: So it's less passionate in a way, one step removed.

Sam: Then at least we could understand what's really going on, rather than just going with the flow and escalating the fight.

Marty: I think of it as an exploring attitude rather than "Let's fight." (Turning to Maria) But you didn't like his saying it.

Maria: I got annoyed when you started bitching about the car again. I wanted to shove something down your throat. Which never works. What I wanted to shove down your throat was that when I'm being irrational, I'm asked to look at it and to get my act together, but when you're being irrational it's appropriate. It's a "real thing" that you really have to deal with.

Sam: First of all, where do you come up with irrational? Who says it's irrational? If you're angry about something, you're feeling something. To tell me that my hearing something, sensing something, feeling something, is irrational . . . that I'm being irrational . . . that's totally judgmental.

Maria: No! It's the complaining.

Marty: (Gently) He's right in a sense.

Sam: You hear it as a complaint.

Maria: And you hear me as complaining a lot and you don't want to hear it.

Sam: Sometimes I do and sometimes I hear it as an observation.

Maria: Okay, but when you hear it as a complaint and you get frustrated and annoyed and you basically ask me to shut up and stop complaining, I want you to . . .

Sam: No, no, no, I don't ask you to stop complaining. I ask you to stop and desist, which I guess means shut up, and do something about it.

Maria: Well?

Sam: So, I'm doing something about it.

Marty: You're both frustrated now. I think Sam is right on target in saying that at those times it's a good idea to step back and explore what's going on.

Maria: (Tentatively) Okay.

Marty: What I hear you (to Maria) trying to say, and you feel like you're fighting a losing battle to get it heard (Maria laughs), is that when you're emotional Sam essentially says that you should explore what's going on.

Maria: Yes.

Marty: And when Sam is emotional and you react to it, then Sam is saying that you should explore your reaction to it.

Maria: Yes! That's exactly what I'm saying.

Marty: So, in some way (to Sam) it sounds like she's always the one to do the exploring. And you're right that the exploring needs doing. It's just that she's feeling that it's a little too one-sided.

Sam: Well, you're the one having the reaction. When the shoe fits . . . I was having a reaction to the car and I took the step to alleviate what was making me a little nuts. I made an appointment with the mechanic to look at it.

Marty: See, some part of it is constructive. You do take those steps . . . and in some way you do explore. But, what Maria is experiencing is that you maneuver in some way so that she is always the one with the problem, the one who needs to explore.

Sam: Perhaps it's because in this example she's having a

reaction to something that I said or felt. Then it becomes her problem. I can't control that. If you want me to not have a feeling and not say anything, I can do that, but then all we're doing is doing everything that led up to our coming to therapy.

Marty: Let's take the part that I like about what you're saying. (Turning to Maria) If you want *him* to be the one who needs to explore, then you have to sometimes not react. You have to be able to say, "I see that you're upset, let's explore it." As soon as you say, "I see that you're upset *and I'm angry about it, or and you should . . .*" now you've got the ball again.

Maria: Oh. I see that. I understand that. Right.

Marty: You always end up on the hot seat, you're always the crazy one.

Maria: Yes.

Marty: But there's a part that you contribute to the pattern.

Maria: Okay, so when he was bitchy about the car, if I calmly said, "Hey Sam, let's look at this," we could have explored it.

Sam: Yes, we could have. You didn't even have to get into a mode of calming me down. I wasn't bitching. That was *your* take on it.

Marty: Even now, when you call it bitching, you're having your reaction and labeling and you're going to allow Sam to see you as the target. Somehow if you want him to become the focus you have to calmly be *interested*. "Hey Sam, you seem upset, what are you feeling?"

Maria: Yeah, I'm not doing that at all.

Marty: You haven't been able to do that.

Maria: I haven't been able to do that.

Marty: Whereas Sam can do that all too well.

Maria: I get too hooked in.

Marty: Hooked in a way that it becomes your problem. So then Sam can't explore *his* feeling, because you're the one who is louder and noisier at that point. And then you end up feeling that you're always the crazy one.

Maria: Right, and then I always have to do the work. I'm always the one who needs to change.

Marty: See, for Sam to have room to be a little more crazy at times and then need to explore it, you have to be more in his role . . . staying calm and really being sincerely interested in him and in his feelings.

Sam: (To Maria) I *really* want you to be more interested in my feelings and not take the focus all the time, but I think it would be very uncomfortable taking more of your role.

Marty: It sounds like there's been a real cooperation here to keep Sam as the rational strong one and Maria as the one with all the irrationality and problems. Although it's scary and uncomfortable to question these roles, I hear you sensing it can lead to getting some things that you really want from each other.

Maria: This is really meaningful to me.

DISCUSSION

This is how couples learn to balance the capacity for empathic responsiveness with the right to express their own reactiveness.

In this session Sam and Maria are learning to make room for each other's vulnerability and for an exploration of the personal meanings underlying their reactiveness. Each person's unique subjectivity and efforts at self-delineation is encouraged and validated. This kind of exploration within the intersubjective matrix allows them to begin to see their contributions to the cocreated patterns between them.

I was monitoring the self-states of both patients throughout the session. When Maria began to explore the more vulnerable underpinnings of her angry attacking behavior, Sam got sarcastic. I noted this as a sign that he was feeling threatened, and tried to slow him down and help him to contain his reactiveness *for the moment* in order to allow Maria to explore the assumptions underlying *her* reactiveness. This is an example of Kohut's point that only one person can be crazy at a time if the relationship is going to work. The intervention is effective, and Maria moves to looking at her own fears and thoughts rather than blaming Sam.

It was then possible to go back to Sam (who by then was feeling as if he was expected to be submissive and behave according to Maria's needs). Instead, I encouraged him *not* to give up his own needs (for self-delineation and separateness) in order to be responsive to his wife. We worked toward Sam's being able to balance his own reactions and needs with an ability to support Maria's exploration.

There is an interesting demonstration too of a process of identification in Sam, who has taken in the therapist's modeling of the idea of stepping back and gaining some perspective. The phrase "That's interesting" is something that Sam has picked up from me. It is not fully his at this point, but he is playing with it constructively. In other words, he has taken upon himself a function that the therapist serves during the sessions, and carried it into his outside life. Sam's introduction of the phrase developed into a fight that was explored in the session and that led ultimately to a very meaningful understanding of how they both contribute to the roles they play in the marriage. By the end they had each begun to have an inkling not only of their involvement in maintaining the pattern, but also that it does not really meet their needs.

CONCLUSION

The multisubjective context of couple therapy always involves three individual perspectives. While the therapist brings his own organizing principles and subjective sense of reality to the situation, it is essential that he not privilege them; he must not play judge, or imagine that he has some access to an undistorted "reality" that his patients do not. All subjective positions must be considered valid, and none elevated to the level of concrete reality. Only when the therapist consistently encourages this multisubjective attitude does a couples session become a safe enough place for both partners that the transferences and archaic narcissistic wishes that feel dangerous to them can unfold and be worked through. The process of gradually negotiating a view of reality that embraces and supports the needs of all three vulnerable participants is essential to the transformation of marital conflict into mutuality and a growth-enhancing relationship.

7

Vulnerable Moments in Group Therapy[1]

1. This material first appeared in Livingston, M. (1999). Vulnerability, tenderness, and the experience of selfobject relationship: a self-psychological view of deepening curative process in group psychotherapy. *International Journal of Group Psychotherapy* 49(1):1–21, and is reprinted here by permission of Guilford Press.

Winnicott's (1953) concept of an "intermediate" space in which judgments about logic and reality are suspended and playfulness and exploration are encouraged is a metaphor that captures the attitudes needed to encourage the emergence of vulnerability in all therapeutic modalities. (I see the creation of that play space as underlying the therapeutic process, and consider that it may be the common element in some otherwise diverse psychoanalytic approaches.) But just as the vicissitudes of intracouple selfobject transferences and countertransference-like responses are perhaps most central in work with couples, the need to create an intermediate space or play space is the focus of many of the leader's interventions in the self-psychological approach to groups. The special importance of this concept in the group setting reflects the propensity of groups to recreate, relive, and restructure early family patterns. This re-creation within a safe play space can provide an opportunity for a new developmental experience, a resumption of arrested development. A therapy situation comprising six or eight people who are not committed to each other in the way a spouse or therapist is can provide an opportunity to heal the wounds of past experiences when self-revelation and expression went awry.

At the same time, though, it also increases the risks of revealing oneself and raises fears of the repetition of childhood trauma. These fears must be legitimized and explored as an essential part of the analytic process. The creation of a play space makes these processes possible and safe.

Freud (1914) used the term *spielraum*, or "play space," as a metaphor for the analytic atmosphere that allows the unfolding of a transferential process, and Meares (1990) has suggested that this metaphor underlies the therapeutic process itself. Certainly Winnicott (1953) considered play a serious matter—both developmentally and interpersonally—that encouraged investigations of the boundaries of reality and fantasy and of self and other. Kohut (1984) felt that play, in its spirit of freedom, curiosity, and exploration, was necessary to the "growth of a healthy self" (p. 70). The nonjudgmental atmosphere of play in the clinical situation also invites the emergence of the vulnerable self, and nowhere is this more apparent than in work with groups, as I will show shortly.

Some self psychologists (although we are in the minority) have focused on the application of Kohut's ideas to group. Harwood and Pines (1998) have compiled a book entitled *Self Experiences in Groups*, which is the first book devoted to self psychology and group. I am currently editing a two-volume issue of *Group* (the journal of the Eastern Group Psychotherapy Society) that will also be devoted to recent work in the application of self psychology and intersubjectivity to group psychotherapy. These recent publications and a number of articles reflect a growing interest in a self-psychological approach to group.

As in any other psychoanalytic therapy, effective work with psychoanalytic groups requires a progressive deepening of therapeutic process. And as in any other self-psychological therapy, it is the sustained empathic immersion of the analyst, and the legitimization of early needs and wishes, that allows the selfobject bonds by means of which this deepening occurs. But in self-psychological group therapy, selfobject bonds are possible not only with the leader, but also among the group members themselves. By its nature, therefore, group therapy enables a complex and multidimensional exploration of members' self experiences and therefore of their underlying narcissistic vulnerabilities; it is an environment where a clinical emphasis on the recognition and use of vulnerable moments is especially fruitful. The presence of multiple subjectivities guarantees a rich source of self experiences and of potential selfobject bonds. Occasional ruptures of these bonds cannot be avoided in any therapy, but within groups they are especially sure to occur with some frequency; no participant, including the leader, can always be perfectly empathically attuned to everyone, and the presence of more than one patient guarantees that conflicting needs will exist within the group. There is no way that everyone's selfobject needs can be perfectly met at the same time. However, in groups as well as in individual and couple work, the repair of such ruptures is an important part of the therapeutic process. The rupture-and-repair sequence in an atmosphere of empathic understanding creates enough of a sense of safety (Shapiro 1991) to allow new vulnerabilities to be exposed, and new selfobject bonds to be created. Ruptures and repairs occur repeatedly, and in fact one of the advantages of the group setting is that it provides more opportunities of this kind than one-to-one therapy does. The repetition of this sequence encourages the process to deepen and unfold further as new underlying vulnerabilities and personal meanings are exposed and explored.

The clinical usefulness of vulnerability is enhanced in group process by the fact that vulnerable moments are contagious. A person's willingness to risk the exposure of his fears and wishes is often very moving to others; in groups this can result in a deepening of affective involvement, and the acceptance of a wider range of human feelings and needs, in the group as a whole. But if such moments are to fulfill their potential, they must be nurtured. The group leader must recognize them and focus on them when they occur, and protect them while they deepen, lest the group interaction dissipate these moments too quickly.

Vulnerable moments, and the working through of barriers to them, create a great deal of intensity and tension. One group member's vulnerability stimulates affective reaction in most of the other members. It can vary in intensity and in form, but often the feeling of pain or need that is opening up in the overtly vulnerable individual stirs a concordant identification in the others, who reexperience painful feelings and memories of their own. If they can tolerate these feelings until an opportunity arises to express them, the group "contagion" will work in favor of the process, and the engagement is facilitated for everyone involved. However, group members sufficiently uncomfortable with their own reactions may self-protectively (and reflexively) cut off their own emerging vulnerability by changing the subject, joking, or demanding attention. Members who identify with and care about the vulnerable individual may experience a strong natural impulse to comfort, advise, or otherwise resolve prematurely the developing tension in themselves and in the group. Moreover, group members at times make complementary identifications, and experience the reaction that the vulnerable patient's partner (spouse or parent, for example) would have. This gives rise to a pressure for enactment with the vulnerable patient as both people's repetitive protective patterns engage. This provides important "grist for the mill," but if acted upon it interferes with the unfolding and exploration of vulnerability and selfobject yearnings. Analyzed and worked through, it becomes part of a healing rupture-and-repair sequence. Again, this is valuable, but it distracts from the vulnerable moment. It is important to note as well that the group leader himself is at times susceptible to the same kinds of reactiveness. The ability to sense his own vulnerable and self-protective impulses and contain them is crucial to the deepening of vulnerable moments and allowing them to play their role in furthering the analytic process. For all of these reasons vulnerable moments must be actively protected.

Patients enter any psychotherapy, as Ornstein (1974) has said, with "hope and dread"—the dread that the selfobject failures and humiliations of childhood will be repeated, but, at the same time, the hope that new kinds of selfobject responsiveness and connection may yet be possible. These wishes and fears can be especially intense in the group setting, and are often experienced by patients as a re-creation of their original families. The presence of "siblings" who demand a share of the leader's attention tends to promote regression and an even more archaic sense of selfobject need than the individual setting. For many patients it revives yearnings for attention, acceptance, and belonging that have been held in abeyance for years. At the same time, the group setting triggers fears that the shame, rejection, and abandonment experienced in the original family may be repeated. The hope that this "family" will be different, and the dread that it will not, adds an extra dimension to the hope and dread that accompany all psychotherapy.

Vulnerable moments occur when a sense of the danger of narcissistic injury coexists with the wish for new selfobject experiences, or, more precisely, when people are willing to risk narcissistic injury out of the hope of new selfobject experiences, which may include validation, affect regulation, connection, or an affirmation of basic humanness. These moments are the seizing of an opportunity to try for the tenderness, empathic responsiveness, and nurturing that have been secretly yearned for beneath a protective shell—but at the cost of exposure.

Exposure, and the vulnerability that goes with it, is a multifaceted state of affairs. I have pointed out previously that the therapeutic process depends on the patient's willingness to take risks—to allow specific human needs, fears, and foibles to show—to give up the wish never to be vulnerable. The particular phenomena that I am calling vulnerable moments are experiences of acute vulnerability that endure only briefly. However, with practice, familiarity, and positive experiences, the courage to *allow* oneself to remain vulnerable (in the sense of open) in intimate relationships can become a consistent personal quality. The capacity to allow, and at times to express, vulnerability of this kind is an important aspect of a strong sense of self and the freedom to build fulfilling relationships. Group therapy, with its guaranteed presence of other subjectivities, is a good arena for developing this capacity.

Since the tolerance of vulnerability both facilitates growth and is a result of it, one of the goals of treatment is to enhance it. It is the shared aspects of vulnerability that give it its clinical power, and for this reason too it is particularly effective in group therapy. The experience of our less-than-omnipotent humanness in vulnerable moments is often felt as a narcissistic blow. It carries with it a great deal of pain and grieving. If protective barriers are to be lowered or softened, even for brief moments, the individual must expect to obtain something of value in return. A group can provide this, in intimacy and a sense of belonging. Intense experiences of selfobject relatedness among group members (as well as with the leader) provide both the safety and the reinforcement for risking such openness. A safe group, like a safe marriage, can detoxify shame.

VULNERABILITY IN GROUP PROCESS

The technical issues specific to groups arise from the presence of more than one patient, and they relate very specifically to the question of vulnerability. The need for the leader to be aware, not only of the risk-taking of individual members but also of the reactions to it of the other members of the group, is as acute as it is in couple therapy, and more complex. While the relationships among group members may not be as intense as the relationship between spouses, the presence of many other people makes for complications in both content and process that do not exist in work in smaller units. When the focus is on one member of the group for a while, especially if the leader is being protective of that member's vulnerable space, very intense experiences of one kind or another may be elicited in other group members.

As I described earlier, these intense reactions can take several forms. Not only do members react with either concordant or complementary identifications, the group leader's focus on one person's emerging vulnerability also can stimulate strong feelings of jealousy, abandonment, or other early childhood experiences. Often such emotional reactions are masked by strongly judgmental responses.

> In a recent workshop, I was concentrating on helping one young man stay a bit longer with his feeling of wanting more attention from the women in the group. Another patient

broke in to criticize what I was doing: "This is not what we're here for! This should be taken up in his individual therapy. I came for a group experience, not to watch Jim work with you. You aren't any better than all those other leaders I told you about." This outburst forced a shift in my attention. I explained to Bob that "what makes it a group experience is that now you have the opportunity to explore your experience in response to what's going on. You feel that I'm letting you down, and also that what's going on is triggering some strong feelings in you. Can you say more about what you were experiencing as I worked with Jim?" "I was uncomfortable," Bob replied. "A pressure built up like I was going to explode." I asked him to say more about the pressure. "There's nothing to say," he responded angrily. "I just felt upset that you and Marge were so attentive to Jim for so long." "It sounds like Marge's response to Jim was an important part of what you're reacting to," I underlined. "She doesn't seem to appreciate me," Bob said. "And that really hurts," I added, focusing once again on the emerging vulnerability and narcissistic injury. "Can you tell Marge more directly what that's like for you?"

The leader must always gauge when one patient's vulnerable expression can remain the focus of the other group members and when another person's reactiveness demands attention and the focus must shift. Sensitivity to this issue is an important part of the therapist's attempt to provide a responsive safety. Other members' reactions disrupt the therapist's intention to provide safety for emerging vulnerability, but they also can provide valuable material themselves. In this example the need for a shift was obvious; Bob's response could not be ignored. However, the leader needs to maintain an alertness to the more subtle reactions that are going on at all times. If they are not addressed, they may erupt in judgmental attacks or in serious withdrawal. Obviously, the need to be empathically tuned in to each member, and to respond to the multiple subjective experiences taking place at once, is one of the difficulties of working psychoanalytically in groups.

It is obviously impossible for the leader to be perfectly attuned to so many subjectivities all at the same time, but he can and must always consider how any intervention directed to one member of the group may affect the others. This is not to say that the leader has to be self-conscious, or to plan all his responses cautiously. Spontaneity, authenticity, humanity, and emotional availability are all essential to the process. What it does mean is that it is often desirable to reflect upon optimal responsiveness after the fact of a response. A leader may respond spontaneously with a deep empathic attunement to one person in the group, and only later be able to deal with another member's reaction to the interaction. Optimal responsiveness to one member may be experienced as empathic rupture by another member. When this occurs, and it often does, the leader must be sensitive to all members of the group, and empathically respond to the experience of rupture. Perhaps a brief example will be helpful here:

> This group is one that I co-lead with a female analyst. The contrasting advantages and complexities of coleadership are discussed elsewhere (see, for example, L. Livingston 2001). It is interesting to note, though, that in this example the presence of a female coleader served two important functions. First, it provided Carla, one of the patients, with a safe selfobject connection at a time when her connection with me was threatened. Second, the presence of a male/female

pair also provided an opportunity for the re-creation of a new healing version of Carla's early family experience.

Ted was leaving group after five years of intense involvement. In the process of saying good-bye he expressed both a good deal of excitement at "going on to new things," and sadness at leaving important ties. At one point he talked directly to me about how much working with me had meant to him. I responded warmly, and I let him know that I too had felt that our work was very meaningful and that I would miss hearing about how his life developed. We were both tearful as the group ended.

In the next week's session I noticed that Carla was removed and distant from me. It had taken us several months of work to develop enough of a bond for her to feel safe in a group with me, so I was concerned with the shift. When I asked her about it, she said she didn't know why she was scared, but that she had been having thoughts about a time when she was about 12. She told us that her father noticed her developing breasts and commented that she was becoming a woman. She was terrified, and her mother took her father into the next room and told him never to do that again. She recalled that as the one time she could remember her mother effectively protecting her from her father's inconsistent and inappropriate responses.

Later in the group she commented that she wished my co-therapist would talk to me about what was appropriate for a leader to express in a group. With some support from my cotherapist, Carla was able to clarify that she felt I had acted like a member of the group, not like a leader. When I had responded to Ted's saying good-bye she experienced me as out of control, and the group became unsafe. We were able to explore and repair this empathic rupture over a few sessions and it became a constructive part of the working-through process for her. However, it's a good example of the impossibility of choosing responses that will be optimal for everyone in the group. It's the transferential, subjective, and personal meaning that an interaction has for each person that determines the effect of any particular response. Often the leader must approximate things as best he can at the time and then pick them up and work them through after the fact.

The leader must "hold" each patient sufficiently that he or she does not feel too left out, too overstimulated, or too stifled. Empathic ruptures, when they do occur, provide opportunities for the repair and exploration of the wounded patient's narcissistic vulnerability. They make the repetitive dimension of the transference available for analytic exploration (Stolorow et al. 1987). Still, ruptures of traumatic intensity are to be avoided as much as possible, and this requires attention from the leader.

The maintenance of Bacal's (1998b) balance between responsiveness and reactiveness is also an important aspect of group leadership, as it is in parallel ways for the couple therapist. Patients in a group, like partners in a marriage, have to learn both how to be empathically responsive to each other, and how to risk expressing their own reactions. Sometimes this latter need runs counter to the group's need for responsiveness and safety, as it does in some childhood families. When original caregivers respond to a child's self-delineation unsupportively, by withdrawing or becoming hostile, a "fundamental conflict," as Stolorow and colleagues (1987, p. 52) have called it, is enduringly established, and an organizing principle is formed that assumes an inherent conflict between attachment needs and self-delineation.

It is essential that the group leader be alert to this conflict, which can be especially intense in groups. In a previous work (Livingston 1998b) I used a television drama "Harvest of Fire," a Hallmark Hall of Fame Presentation on April 21, 1996) to illustrate the power of this fundamental conflict in groups and its destructive potential when not addressed. In this drama, there has been a series of barn burnings in an Amish community. The arson endangers human life as well as livestock, and poses a serious threat to the economic and emotional survival of the community. The close-knit Amish community stresses conformity with group values to maintain cohesion and stability. When one member of the group expresses a need for self-delineation by building his barn with a window shaped differently from the norm in order to let in more sunlight, the elders react by invoking a shunning. No one in the community, including his own son, is supposed to acknowledge him until he submits to the group's need for conformity. The son is torn. He has strong loyalties to the elders and to the group, but this is his father. He finds ways to compromise until the girl he relies on for validation and support is forbidden by her mother to see him anymore. That's when his rage erupts and the barns burn. The investigator, an outsider, like a group leader counterpart, tries to attune to all the group members in order to understand what is happening. After several empathic failures (which of course are inevitable in entering a culture so unknown to her), she wins their trust. Eventually, the boy comes forward and the community rallies in support. They stand up for him as he faces the sheriff, and the implication is that he will be rehabilitated within a caring community as wounds are healed on all sides.

As this example shows, groups have the power both to insist on conformity at the expense of self-delineation, and to support cohesion and twinship needs at the same time as individual needs are recognized and legitimized. Similarly, therapy group members must not be encouraged to be always responsive to each other at the expense of the expression of their own feelings and reactions. The value of group cohesion and stability must not be overstressed at the expense of the individuals who make up the group. This is even more essential in a therapy group than it is in a community because the purpose of group treatment is always the development of the individual patients within it. As in life, reactiveness in groups is just as important as responsiveness. It must be encouraged and respected—and vulnerable patients' needs for support and protection in the face of this reactiveness must be respected as well.

The conditions and composition of groups influences the therapeutic process and experiences of vulnerability among their members. The group leader's sensitivity to these issues conveys to the members his analytic stance and may even determine whether a particular group will be viable or not. One such factor is the specifics of the composition of the group. For example, the sense of safety in a group is especially crucial when the leader's focus is on newly emerging vulnerability, and this requires that the leader be sensitive to contemptuous and masochistic responses in a group. Narcissistically vulnerable people frequently respond to vulnerability in others in these ways, and, whether overt or subtly expressed, these attitudes can quickly suppress a group's willingness to lower defensive barriers (Livingston 1975). To assure safety for the group as a whole it is essential to screen out, at least in the beginning, prospective members whose characterological patterns seriously inhibit group process. Patients who at times protect their own vulnerability with contempt, for example, can contribute to a good group atmosphere despite their occasional shaming of other members; the leader and the group learn to perceive and relate to the vulnerability that underlies the behavior, and this can lead to very poignant moments that enhance the group process. However, the presence of people who are characteristically distant, contemptuous, or judging can seriously inhibit other members' willingness to open themselves to the danger of ridicule and shame. These patients need individual work before they are introduced into a group. Conversely, people who are extremely vulnerable or fragmentation-prone may also require individual treatment before they begin group work, as they put too great a burden on the other members to contain their own reactions, and thus prevent them from opening up their own vulnerability.

One advantage of psychotherapy groups is the possibility of knowing and being known by different people, and in this regard the self-psychological approach itself has some implications for forming groups and for establishing combinations of people who function well together. Groups ideally offer a balanced provision of "sameness" and "difference." A certain amount of difference allows members to risk being known by an other, and when this risk is navigated successfully, the tolerance of vulnerability is greatly enhanced and shame is reduced. It is important as well that each member not feel too alone—that there is another available who can provide some sense of likeness, or twinship. When there are significant variations in culture, age, or protective patterns, it is important to remember this need for twinship. Short-term homogeneous groups often move to deeper material more quickly and they provide necessary twinship experiences. However, in my experience, therapeutic process and opportunities for vulnerability in a long-term psychoanalytic psychotherapy group are best served by a counterbalance of difference.

I prefer to work in groups of five to eight, as larger groups make intimacy more difficult. The length of meetings also influences the leader's ability to facilitate and sustain vulnerable moments. The usual 90-minute group is sufficient when the continuity of weekly sessions over a long period provides the group with a sense of "enough" time. A longer time, though, or even an occasional double or extra session, can often lead to increased vulnerability and important deepening.

The leader's focus on emerging vulnerability, and the creation of safety for it, is essential for the development of the group process, as well as for the facilitation and optimal use of vulnerable moments, which must be protected and fostered when they occur. The leader tries at all times to maintain empathic immersion in each patient's inner experience, particularly in the fluctuations of their self-states, which creates an intensity and a support for these moments.

Attunement to the multisubjective context of six or eight separate patients is clearly a challenge. It is helpful for the leader to have substantial knowledge of each patient from individual sessions, and patients need to be prepared for group over a period of time—ideally a year or two, but at least several months. This period of preparation allows a bond to be established so that when the impossible task of attuning to everybody leads to empathic failure there is some trust to fall back on while the rupture is explored and repaired. Preparatory sessions allow the leader to have some idea of how each patient is likely to organize the happenings in the group. Understanding the patient's usual transferential patterns, especially the typical response to selfobject failures, gives the leader an edge in picking up as much as possible of what is going on in the here and now of the group, and how each patient is likely to organize and give personal meaning to it. Experienced group leaders have often expressed the opinion that a leader is doing well if he can pick up about 35 percent of what is going on—but we try to be on top of things, if not as they happen then soon after.

Further support for vulnerable moments can be developed by slowing down the process, and focusing upon emerging material that is related to the patient's self-state. Changes in affect and self-state show themselves subtly, in changes in voice tone or emotionality and in other nonverbal cues. The leader's attunement to these cues focuses the group directly on the exploration of underlying self-states, and also demonstrates to the group the importance of such a focus. The moment-to-moment fluctuations in self-experience, which frequently go unnoticed, provide important openings for exploration of changes in affect and self-esteem, as well as cohesion and fragmentation-proneness, vitalization and depletion, and other dimensions of self-experience. As I have said, the tension between vulnerability and self-protectiveness is another one of these dimensions.

> A group was talking about making room for emotional reactions, including anger. Almost everyone entered into the discussion, but I noticed that Mike, who had at first been quite active, had become quiet. I briefly saw a thoughtful look on his face, but it was fleeting, and he then came back into the discussion more actively. When there was a pause in the talk, I asked what he had been experiencing. This simple intervention led to an opening up of Mike's fear of one of the women in the group. When she got angry she triggered a feeling in him of being back with his crazy mother

> and grandmother. "I'm like a deer that smells a lion. I hear Tanya talking about getting angry and I want to run. Any slight scent of her anger and I want to run."

The concept of "state sharing" (Lachmann and Beebe 1993, Stern 1983) is another tool the leader can use to recognize and support vulnerable moments in group situations. The leader's emotional availability (Orange 1995), and his willingness to feel and use his own vulnerability, sensitizes him to subtle cues. Self-reflective awareness of his own inner experience at times provides a finer-tuned awareness of emerging vulnerability in his patients than the most astute observation of external behaviors or words. Invitation or inquiry at such points may bring out a *shared* vulnerability and deepen the group's empathic understanding of the member involved.

The poignancy of a vulnerable moment for observing others is based on this sharing and the commonality of human experience at this basic level. Superficially, we all have different behavior patterns and responses, and we develop our own styles of striving and self-protection, but we all have losses to mourn and parental failures to come to terms with.

> Marge was talking in group about how difficult it was for her as a mother to stay in touch with her love for her young-adult son while he separates from her and builds his own family. She feels discarded, hurt, and angry, and has to struggle to remember the young boy she loved so much. She also talked about how hard it is for her to allow people to be so important to her when they might abandon her. Audrey began to cry. She spoke briefly of how she had made her parents unimportant following some early disappoint-

ments, and how she still doesn't feel as close to them as she would like. Many people in the group were teary-eyed, including me. The sense of early loss touched all of us.

The mourning of these losses is an essential part of the working-through process in any analytic context. In group the other members share in this process much the way a family comes together at times of loss to grieve together and begin to heal. This is an aspect of group therapy that makes it a valuable addition to individual work; an analyst is less likely than group members to participate openly in this process.

The leader's alertness to, and attitude toward, subtle signs of vulnerability is an important force in how and whether the therapeutic process deepens. Experienced leaders sense when a group member is moving toward a vulnerable moment, and after a while, the group members also learn to recognize and be responsive to these moments. It is not at all unusual for a group experienced in the leader's emphasis on vulnerability to sit silently with a careful attentiveness while one of its members struggles to be more in touch with his affective experience.

Group work also sheds further light on Orange's (1995) comment about the importance of the therapist's emotional availability as "an underlying and often overlooked element in the success or failure of therapeutic relationships" (p. 125). Orange understands the analyst's emotional availability not as any type of interpretation or intervention, but rather as a nonspecific readiness to respond that can take many forms. Just as the selfobject transferences between the partners are as important in couple work as the ones between the partners and the therapist, so the emotional availability that group members learn to offer each other is as important as the emotional availability that the leader offers. Patients come to expect it and to count on it, and it contributes greatly to a sense of safety and to the emergence of vulnerable moments.

However, vulnerability is never an entirely comfortable self-state, and emotional availability in addition means the willingness to be touched by our patients' emotional struggles. Leaders (often with the active cooperation of other group members) sometimes abort the development of vulnerable moments. This is generally an unwitting process, triggered by the ordinary human reaction of avoiding certain kinds of discomfort, but staying with an experience a little longer than comfort levels dictate is often key to opening up or deepening vulnerability. More than any other simple guideline for technique, staying with an affective experience a little longer than either the patient *or the leader* is comfortable with will often lead to a significant deepening of vulnerability and with it the therapeutic process. This is as difficult a lesson for beginning therapists to digest as it is for group members, because as my patient Roz (Chapter 3) so poignantly complained of her own struggles to allow vulnerability, it is counterintuitive.

Similarly, allowing a patient to get off the hook is sometimes mistaken by inexperienced group leaders for an empathic response. Sometimes it is, but often the optimally responsive, and thus most empathically attuned, intervention is to empathize with the forward edge of the patient's courage to go further. Pushing a patient without sensitivity to his or her fears of humiliation or falling apart can be a major, and traumatic, break in empathy, but an attentive encouragement can be fruitful. The guideline in matters of timing is the therapist's sense of empathic "withness" and emotional availability. It is an experience of attunement and an intuitive sense of when to push and when to back off. As all therapeutic skills do, this one develops over time and with experience, both in the analyst's growth in general and in the relationship with a particular patient and group. It is an experience-near attunement, and not a matter of objective or experience-distant observation. Self-reflection, and alertness to the tendency that we all share to cooperate in shying away from these moments, is essential to the sense of timing. Clearly, a real understanding of the patient's terrors is equally important at these times.

In all these ways, the group leader's focus on patients' self-experience and narcissistic vulnerability enhances the deepening of therapeutic process. From a self-psychological vantage point, this means that, through the analyst's empathic immersion in the patient's subjective view of the world, earlier and earlier forms of the unique patterns and beliefs that organize this view, including selfobject yearnings (along with fears of retraumatization), are experienced and become available for interpretation. Vulnerability is the more therapeutically accessible end of the self-state continuum whose other end is self-protectiveness.

MOMENTS IN A GROUP: AN ILLUSTRATION

This session illustrates some of the attitudes and interventions that enhance the emergence of vulnerable moments in a group, and the leader's consistent focus on affect, shifts in self-state, and emerging vulnerability. It also illustrates the importance of the patients' cooperation in helping the leader to fine-tune his empathic grasp of the material presented.

This is an experienced group of seven members, most of whom have been together for upward of five years, and most have been in individual treatment as well. Roz (see Chapter 3), who is the focus of most of this session, is the newest member of the group. She has been in the group for two years, and over the past several months has often held the center of attention. She relates a lot of the details of her everyday struggles, and speaks with a good deal of urgency. She shows a degree of insight, but not much affect.

Two weeks ago, however, she had spoken with considerable anger about her mother's pushing her "fast forward button" whenever she tried to express any real feeling. "She obliterates me every time I talk to her." I had asked her to slow down and to try to tell me what she was experiencing at that moment. She spoke about a feeling of not getting enough, and of being afraid of losing the group's attention. "Then I go on fast forward. Now I do it to myself." That was the background for this session.

Two patients are absent today and two are rather quiet through the session. The focus shifts back and forth between Roz and Tony, a 50-year-old business executive. Tony often supports Roz, and identifies with her struggles. He joined the group four years ago, and until recently has tended to bring himself in only through the presentation of concrete issues. In the last year or so he has developed a much more introspective attitude, and has contributed a great deal to the group's process.

Tony begins the group by talking about that very shift. He feels frustrated. Since he no longer needs to come in with emergencies, he doesn't have any "stuff" to bring in. "I have a lot of stuff going on in my life that I would like to talk about. Instead we get into something that's in the moment. It's meaningful, but it's not about what's going on in my life. I can't figure out how to bring it in. So I don't." I reflect, "What I hear is that there's something valuable in being involved in what goes on, but at the same time there's something important that . . ." Tony, feeling heard, continues: "All the stuff in my life." Now, more on target I add, "that you want to bring in, that you want us to know about, to know what's going on in your life." Tony responds excitedly, "Yeah, yeah! That! And I can't organize it well enough to deliver it in a simple fashion."

Roz adds a resounding "Yeah!" and Alice, a sensitive and supportive expectant mother, adds, "I think I really understand what you're saying. Several of us have talked about that before. It's like having some uneasiness or restlessness . . . or a lot of things . . . and if you can't frame it neatly . . . you feel like you're going to take a lot of time with it." Tony now adds still another, "Yeah! That's right." Alice continues with a more serious tone, "Because you need a lot of time and it feels awkward to bring it in. You feel like, How long are people going to be able to stay with me on this? Tony nods a strong assent and adds, "It's like being on stage and I don't have my material." Alice continues the active sharing of these experiences, "No music, the lights are not on properly, it's really hard. It's torture to have to perform, to compete for space."

Roz is an active third in the interaction. "It really is tough. It's like having to improv. That's really hard in group. I can do it in individual, but not in here." Tony, still excited with the sense of being understood and not alone with his struggle, takes it a step further. "It's very hard to get the space to improvise in group. In individual you can go on and on if you need to, but in group it's totally different. It's very scary." Alice agrees roundly, "*Very* scary."

"What is it that's very scary about it?" I ask. The mood is deepening, and Tony responds quietly, "You'll lose people. I felt it even then when I was speaking earlier. I felt that I started talking about something and then I felt, 'I'm losing it. I'm not sure exactly what I'm talking about.' Then I found something and everybody came back again. That's the scary feeling. 'I'm losing it. I have nothing to say.'" "I'm losing it," Alice joins in supportively. Tony adds, "Yeah, like I don't know where I'm going with this . . ." Alice completes his thought: " . . . but I know I need something. I really do want something." Tony picks up the thought, "Right, a meaningful need." Then turning toward me, "It's your job to help me figure out what it is I'm trying to do or to say. . . . I mean, it's not like you don't do it. You do. It's just . . ." Alice, again right on Tony's wavelength, joins in. "He does it when you . . ." Tony picks it back up enthusiastically: " . . . when it looks like you're really dying. Then he says, 'This is what's going on.'" Seeing an opening, and also really beginning to feel Tony's need, I underline, "So there are times when I respond in the way you need (and then after a brief pause) but there are other times . . ." Tony smiles and finishes my sentence playfully: ". . . when you let me hang out there. 'Let him hang for a while; see what he comes up with.'"

The group is silent for a moment. Then Alice thoughtfully comments, "I think that's a universal group feeling, that feeling about hanging in the wind." The group seems to drift for a while and then I try to bring them back to a further exploration of their unmet needs. "So, when you say that it's my job, that I do something sometimes and not often enough, what is it that I do?" Tony reflects inwardly for a moment and then offers some clarification. "Well, you get to the bottom of the situation and you go, 'Okay, this is what's going on. This is what it seems like you need. 'And then I go 'Yeah!' . . . and then the whole thing takes on a different lucidity." Feeling close to Tony, and getting a clearer sense of what he wants, I reflect, "So sometimes you need some help in getting a sense of what you really need." Tony continues, "Like where am I going? You help to organize . . . sometimes we're going on and on and you come in with a thing . . . what's really happening . . . and we go 'Yeah, that's what it is.' There are times when I have very little tolerance for you not doing that. I feel impatient . . . like, 'Get to the bottom of this thing,' especially when it's other people going on and on."

Several members talk about wishing that I would do more organizing. Roz, in an excited-little-girl tone, expresses a building sentiment, "Wouldn't it be great if Marty knew what we needed to talk about and brought us in at just the right time? Like an orchestra conductor. Like, 'Roz, you talked about this in your individual session. Do you want to talk about it now?'" Tony agrees that that might feel good, that he would like more direction. Then he turns to me and adds, "That's not your style. You aren't that directive." "No, I guess I'm not," I say with a laugh, but I feel that we're on the same wavelength and continue, "Your wishes are very important to explore. That's more important than a lot of content. What seems important to me right now is getting a clear sense of what you *miss*." Then, turning to the group, "Tony is pretty clear that he wants me to get a sense of what he missed, what needs weren't met or aren't being met now, and to spell it out because he has trouble doing that without help." Then, turning back to Tony, "Sometimes I can do that. More important is our understanding your experience of really missing a coach [this is Tony's word from previous sessions].

"That's something I've missed my entire life," Tony responds. He is thinking hard. "That feeling of wanting a parental person to know. People would go, 'What's wrong?' and I couldn't say." I reflect back to him, "Sometimes you need someone to recognize from your facial expression or just looking at you . . . to recognize what you're feeling and to help you put it into words." He continues softly, "I remember there was a point in my life, like 11 or 12 . . . I pouted for two days, three days, to see if anybody fucking noticed. *I'm not talking! For three days!* What's going on? Then I went over to my aunt's house. I never thought of her as taking care of me, but she's real down to earth. So she looked at me and right away she goes, 'What's bothering you?' I was so stunned that I couldn't tell her. I had to make it that something was bothering me right then. I couldn't tell her 'Like three days ago someone hurt my feelings.' I couldn't do that. I felt stupid, so I said 'Nothing' and then there was nothing to say." "At least she asked," Alice says in a caring tone. "Yes, and I couldn't tell her," Tony repeats. Seeking further clarification, I tentatively reflect, "It still felt good that she asked. That was like a first step." Tony helps me to fine-tune my understanding. "Yes, but the sadness is stronger than any good feeling. The sadness is that I really wanted my parents . . . it was too far removed already . . . it was family, but it was removed. I couldn't feel the same connection to her even though she was someone I could have connected to." Now more on target, I respond, "You really needed your *mother* to know." Tony relaxes and confirms my understanding with a simple but meaningful "Yeah."

After a brief pause, Roz responds to the sense of sadness in the room. "I don't know what makes me sadder—that I want that so badly and didn't get it, or that I can't do it myself for others. I can't see past my own shit and see the other person's feeling that doesn't have to do with me. I'm really missing something—the capacity to read people's feelings." Alice questions this. "I don't think that's it. I don't think the capacity isn't there. It's exactly what you said. You get so anxious about what it has to do with you or about not being right." Roz continues, "I have to somehow guess the right feeling." Again Alice tries to shift the focus more to Roz's inner experience. "You have to go into your own feelings first before you can take in someone else's." "If I do that then I'll never see you," Roz persists with a growing sense of urgency. Alice, trying to be reassuring, replies, "Maybe not right away, but if you keep reflecting . . ." Roz is not reassured. Her anxiety mounts. "It seems to me that taking a wild guess at what you're feeling is the quickest way of getting what you're feeling. If the goal is trying to read Mark [her husband], for instance . . ."

I try to find out what her growing urgency is about. "What do you mean by 'read'?" I ask. "What I meant is getting it right," Roz replies. "Let me see if I'm getting this," I say. "Getting the right words or the right label seems important in order to reach some feeling of safety. That's different from understanding or trying to feel into what Mark is experiencing."

I sense that Tony seems to be more attuned to Roz at the moment than I am, so I back off and let the group work. Tony proceeds, "The reason you can't do that is because there's something going on inside of you. You want to look at Mark without paying attention to what's inside of you. You're afraid of the answer if you look in. You're somehow afraid that it's your fault." Roz begins to feel understood and to slow down. "The thing is that at that moment I get confused. I get stuck. I have a lot in my life that's stuck. It's about not wanting to go down here [pointing to her gut] . . . and straining to get there [pointing to her head]."

Speaking directly to Roz I suggest, "It sounds like the first thing you have to do is say to yourself, 'Hey, look at me. I'm scared. All I can think about right now is how am I going to stop him from being angry with me . . . or thinking badly about me.'" "Right," she responds, "and what I do, Marty, is that I've learned to 'inquire' of my feelings, but I'll say 'Now *why* am I feeling scared?'" I reflect, "It's a test question, and if you can get the right answer . . ."

"It doesn't occur to me to ask, 'What is my feeling,' . . . not 'Why is my feeling.'" She proceeds. "Can I solve this thing? Can I change his feeling about me? Sometimes in desperation I go to my breathing. It's the most basic thing I can do . . . to notice my breathing." I reflect encouragingly, "The most basic thing you can do is to notice things about your experience, even something so simple or basic as your breathing."

Then after a pause in which it's clear that Roz's feeling state is shifting, I ask, "And what are you experiencing right now? What can you notice at the moment?" "There isn't time for that," she replies attempting to hide her smile. Sensing that she's really working with me and trying to get her to stay a moment longer with her experience, I continue. "You're afraid that there won't be time. That's an experience. You're experiencing a feeling that there isn't going to be enough time." Alice adds, "We're all terrified of whatever we'll experience if we slow down. Like a fear of being criticized or rejected."

"Whatever is going on inside is the scariest thing there is," Roz says with conviction. "It's not where I want to be. If I notice it moment to moment, I never want to be there." "What is there at this moment?" I ask. "A choppy dangerous ocean that I can't control," she says after a moment of thought. "I'm on a little boat and I can't control anything." "Stay with that for a moment," I say with a touch of excitement in my voice. "See what you can notice about it."

"I notice that I can't control it. I can't name it. It really feels like a rough surf." Then after a long pause, "I have a real urge to get away from this." "To get away from . . . ?" I ask. "To get away from the rough surf," she says. After a pause I suggest, "Try to get more of a sense of that rough surf." "It's really a huge ocean. I'll never . . . I'll never . . . I don't want to be a tiny craft on the huge ocean. No shore . . . no place to go. I don't want to be here right now." "You don't want to be in that little craft," I say understandingly, yet my tone encourages her to go on. "I just don't have anything to say about it, Marty. It's just too . . .

it's just forever. It's never going to . . . it's too powerful." "Stay with it. See what else you can notice," I urge. "Very alone. I'll never master the Atlantic Ocean. I'm a little life raft in the middle of it. It just feels infinite." She sighs deeply. "No land . . . no rescue. I don't want to do this."

"You must think that there's some way of getting around it," Alice interjects. Roz continues, "Yes, I'm really holding out. I'm not going to have to do this." "What are you not going to have to do?" I ask. "I'm not going to be alone on this ocean forever. Somebody is going to make it all right. Some cruise ship is going to come along and say, 'You don't have to be alone anymore.' Someone is going to take care of me and I won't have these feelings."

"That's a real wish . . . a real need for somebody to come and take care of you," I restate, wanting to legitimize her yearning. Roz sighs. Tears come to her eyes. "It's even more than a wish." "It's something that you really need," I say tenderly. Her fearfulness becomes an open sobbing momentarily and then she continues, "It's got to happen. If I stare long enough at that horizon, it's going to appear. It's got to. It's much more than a wish . . . or even a need. It feels like no one understands. It's got to happen or I *am* going to die . . . or want to die." "You just can't bear the time when it's not happening," I reflect.

Roz sighs once again and then becomes angry. "How can they not see me? I can't give up. How can they not see me here?" She cries for a while and then continues. "Because if I face that, then I have to go 'Oh, I'm invisible . . ." and since I can't be that . . . I'm just going to stay here going 'You're going to see me!'" I start to reflect, "You really have a terror that . . ." but she completes my interpretation before I can formulate it. "If they don't see me, that means I must be invisible. What would I do? I don't know what to do if they don't see me." I try to keep her from retreating from the intensity of her experience a moment longer and to include the others more at this point. "Before you jump to what to do, I think what's important right now is that we're getting a deep sense of how awful it feels not to be seen. Like Tony feeling no one knew that he didn't talk for three days." Roz responds tearfully, "Exactly." I continue very gently, "So what does it feel like not to be seen? You start to feel that you're invisible . . . that there's something about you." "Yeah," she replies, "only I just don't quite go there. I'm still stuck in my . . . I don't want to go there . . . having to conclude that this boat is not coming and in the next moment I'm invisible."

After a while Tony begins to work with feelings that have been set off in him by Roz's vulnerability. "It seems to me more about the primary experience in yourself that you were having. To me that's the thing. . . . I had a thought that there are only a couple of primary experiences that we have and that's one of them. It's like something you try to always run away from and not experience. By running away from it or whatever . . . it was really inspirational for me to see that. We're always running away from our 'thing.' That was your 'thing' and I was trying to see what was my self experience that if I just let myself be . . . What would happen? What could I come up with . . . and I can see that it's going to be different at different times. If I'm feeling good and connected and whole, it's going to be one thing, but when I'm not, then my self experience is pretty much always similar. It's like I'm nothing . . . no sense of entitlement. Like I'm not entitled to live. That's the feeling that I'm running away from most of the time . . . feeling 'that.' It's like I know nothing . . . I can do nothing."

"You believe you have no worth," I reflect. Tony continues, "No worth . . . no worth . . . and then I have to go 'Let's see if

I can convince myself that I have worth.' Oh look, I just did that. Okay, I have some worth. But there's a tape telling me that I have no worth, no value . . . just like Roz believing that she's invisible." The others join in a bit in a shift to talking about and summing up what has gone on somewhat intellectually. Perhaps it is a process of consolidating or maybe just a way of lessening the intensity prior to ending. Then I make my usual closing remark, "It's time to stop there for now."

DISCUSSION

This session illustrates "deepening" in a group from the self-psychological perspective—the emotional exploration of underlying longings for certain selfobject experiences, and how it feels when they are not met. There was also a deepening of the elucidation of "the continuing influence of organizing principles and imagery that crystallized out of the patient's early formative experiences" (Stolorow et al. 1987, p. 36). This process is particularly clear in Tony's exploration of his desire for help from the leader. He begins with a surface wish for coaching and assistance in bringing his life experiences into the group. From there he moves to the exploration of deeper yearnings for mirroring, for his mother to know his hurt, and for help in organizing and expressing his feelings. Both Tony and Roz clarify, with increasing emotional involvement, some of their shameful beliefs about themselves. As the process unfolds, we see an exploration of their "search for antidotes . . . [to these] crushing organizing principles" (Orange et al. 1997, p. 66).

The most important theoretical attitude promoting this deepening is the basic self-psychological one of sustained immersion in the patient's subjective experience, along with the spirit of empathic inquiry. The way this works in practice is evident in the several times that I tentatively reflected what I understood to be Tony or Roz's experiences, and they corrected or fine-tuned my impression. Each time this sequence occurred it represented a minor break in our empathic connection, and an attempt to repair the break through a deepening of my understanding. This process in a responsive context created a sense of safety that allowed both of them to share more of their vulnerable selves.

This session also demonstrates how a leader can focus on self-state experience, and how this approach can get built into the group process. Frequent inquiries into the patients' moment-to-moment inner experience, along with attempts to slow them (especially Roz) down enough to attend to them, were an important part of deepening the process.

Probably the most significant factor of all, however, is the development of bonds—selfobject relationships—among the members of the group over many sessions as they share these vulnerable moments. It is the confident expectation of the emotional availability and responsiveness of both the leader and the other group members that makes interpretation meaningful and allows each individual to risk and to grow.

8

Dreams: The Royal Road to the Emergence of the Vulnerable Self

> Each of us has something to offer to anyone who shares a dream. Care must be taken not to offer too much, or too little, or to become too enamored of our offering. It is the dreamer who should remain in charge of his dream images. To him belongs the excitement of seeing the images come to life as connections are made to waking life. When this happens the truths they convey become apparent and, along with them, the healing that comes from knowing the truth.
>
> M. Ullman, 1987

Analysts, going back to Freud (1900), have always considered dreams to be the "royal road to the unconscious." Intersubjectivists Stolorow and Atwood (1992) state, "There is probably no psychological product that is less fettered or more spontaneous than the dream. As human subjectivity in purest culture, the dream constitutes a *royal road to the prereflective unconscious*—to the organizing principles and dominant leitmotivs that unconsciously pattern and thematize a person's psychological life" (p. 275, emphasis original). I agree that dreams are "human subjectivity in purest culture," and as such they do more than allow access to prereflective organizing principles; they are also facilitators of vulnerability—the royal road to the emergence of the vulnerable self.

DREAMS AND THE FACILITATION OF VULNERABILITY

This therapy session centered around a dream and the work with it. It illustrates clearly both the patient's struggle to allow her vulnerable self to emerge and the analyst's attempt to focus and facilitate this emergence. Here and in other dream examples I will re-create as much of the session in which they were presented as possible, as my purpose is to explore the clinical use of the dream within the analytic session, rather than an analysis of the meaning of the dream itself. The dreamer in this instance was the patient Roz, whose efforts to free her vulnerable self from self-imposed restraints were illustrated in Chapter 3. This dream addresses the same issue.

Roz begins the session with the comment that her father "seems to be coming up all over the place," and then relates the following dream: "I was walking up a back staircase. It was outside the house. Debbie [her daughter] had a puppy on a leash. He walked over the edge and fell to his death. I identified with Debbie and was all upset. She isn't upset. She asks me, 'What did he mean to you?' I realized that what she meant was 'He was mean to you. Why are you crying?' We went back and forth. She made me question my reaction."

After a brief thoughtful pause, she continues with a good deal of excitement. "I wake up like I had a big cue card, 'Wake up! Let go of something!' I think to myself, 'You can let go of your father or of the puppy, but think about it for a second before hurtling into despair. Ask yourself whether the surface story is the real story. . . . What does it really mean?' It was really obvious that Debbie was a stand-in for me . . . that I'm sending a film to myself."

Trying to attune to the affect, and to Roz's sense of struggle as well as her excitement, I ask, "A film about why it's so hard to let go, about what it really means to let go?" As I hope, Roz begins to clarify for me. "What Dad really means. . . . Letting go of my father is sad, but I ask myself, 'Why are you holding on to this? It's about the symbol not the fact. What he meant to me . . . even though he was mean to me."

"So, what are your thoughts about what the dog meant?" I'm trying to encourage her to explore a bit further. "Well," she replies, "A puppy is a brand new dog. You never question the relationship between a child and a puppy. It's about unconditional love . . . protection . . . it's innocent."

I repeat in a querying tone, "Innocent?" Roz explains, "Well, I didn't understand when Debbie said he was mean to me. I had a flash about him being mean . . . about him not liking me, . . . but he was innocent. A puppy hasn't formed his own values and discriminations yet . . . hasn't formed its loyalties yet. It's a one-way street."

"Flesh that out," I suggest, supporting her venture into deeper thought and affect, and she continues, "It's unlike even a baby . . . There's no impurity. He wants to play and eat and have fun. It's not about the other person. It could be anyone . . . and you don't begrudge him that. There's no relationship. You love the puppy, but it doesn't really connect, imprint, to *you.*

"I must have had this feeling as a child with my father. Surely, I felt that Dad . . . he loved us, *but I wasn't really sure it was me.* He didn't really see me. He still doesn't see me . . . doesn't see me as different from Joan [her sister]. He could never hear something and say, 'Roz wouldn't do that, Joanie might.' I don't think he ever goes there.

"So., if that's true, then every encounter was an effort to imprint myself on him. *'This is me! 'You are going to remember this about me.'* It was never about winning the argument. It was about him remembering me. A good example of this kind of struggle was an argument Mark and I had about Kazan being given a lifetime achievement award. I think it's outrageous that Hollywood would give that award to someone who was so outrageous. He really hurt his peers. Then Mark, as I was making this speech—he felt swallowed by my emotion pitch—he rises above it. He gets haughty. He feels steamrollered. I wouldn't have a back and forth with him. I stake out my territory. So he elevated himself. That's how he defends.

"I felt as if I was being lumped in with the ultra-liberals, what Mark calls the irrational left, and the specificity of *me* was being erased. I've seen Mark's father do that to him. My father doesn't do that when he argues with me. He's surprisingly open-minded when he's arguing. If you make a good rational argument with my father, he's capable of granting you that point. He's God . . . he decides. With Mark, though, something different happens, especially if there's a witness.

"I get contemptuous. We both use tools that our fathers used on us. I was behaving like my father . . . except that I was emotional about it. There was a button that got pushed. Not being allowed to mix emotional outrage and rationality pushes my button. I have to be rational to argue with my father. I can't be emotional . . . not with Mark either. He's afraid of being swallowed. His reaction is, 'I'm going to drown.' So he climbs on a chair. Then I feel stifled by a prohibition against having strong emotions in an argument. He's up on the chair, being God like my father. It makes me nuts. I'm not just emotional! I'm still rational. I don't like having to take that off, to prohibit that part of me, in order to be respected. I don't really care about whether or not Elia Kazan gets an award. I just want room for my position, for my emotion."

I want to encourage her not to dismiss her feeling, and also I'm playing metaphorically with a phrase from the dream. I add, "But it meant something. He was *mean* to people." Roz pauses and then explores. "I'm playing the role of the unforgiving one. You make choices and have to live with them. Yet, I always want a clean slate for me. There seems to be a purpose here . . . like I was separating myself from Kazan . . . by being his judge. But there also is a difference between forgiving and forgetting. *There has to be a bookmark.* You can forgive, but giving him the award means forgetting. Mark argues for absolution and I argue that it *must not be forgotten.*"

I want Roz to explore in an experience-near, rather than an intellectually distant way, so I continue to use the language of the dream. "So how does this relate to the puppy dog and its meanness?" Roz is puzzled momentarily as her affect deepens and her language becomes a bit unclear. "I don't know . . . unless Kazan is also my father. He was mean. He betrayed people. He destroyed people. I can allow him to live in peace . . . I can even have sympathy for his pain. But like my father—and it's about myself, too—I guess it's saying it about my father." Once again, I ask her to "flesh it out."

She continues, "Caring about a connection with my father is all about forgiving but not forgetting. I struggle . . . I can't combine the access to love and compassion while seeing that it happened. *A crime was committed.* Probably, if I felt more of the crime I would feel more love . . . so it trickles. I can't really forgive."

"So, you need to remember the puppy's meanness," I underline. "Yes," she agrees, "I have to remember what it means to me, but I don't want to be judging of an innocent puppy. It seems unfair . . . uneven." Now I hone in on what I sense is the main issue being worked through at the moment: "So, it's hard to stay with what it means to you."

Roz, follows my lead, staying emotionally connected to the dream imagery and beginning to touch the deeply conflicted feelings surrounding her self experience and the difficulty she has in accepting and expressing a sense of personal (as opposed to "objective") meaning. "I was blocked from crying . . . on the verge of emotion. Debbie said, 'Wait before you go there.' It's hard for me to go there. I can tell you the facts, but I don't stay there long enough to know what it really means to me. I could probably find out if I just stayed a little bit longer."

[Patients who fear letting go of rationality often need encouragement to stay with an exploration or a feeling a bit longer than their comfort level dictates. My repeated returns to the dream and the personal meaning of its imagery is in the service of keeping her in an *affective* experience, as well as staying experience-near myself. My encouraging her to stay with her experience, at the same time staying safely with her through my empathic attunement and emotional availability, allows her vulnerable self to emerge tentatively.]

She is silent. I remain silent too. Sometimes an intense quiet is the best way to help a patient to stay in her experience. Roz eventually breaks the silence. "I didn't trust my father's love. There's a big piece of me that doesn't believe in my father's love for me. *I have to earn it every day.* I don't trust. I feel that if I didn't come up with the goods, he would say, 'Take her away.' There was always a higher standard than his love for me . . . a cold moral position. That was more important than the irrational ties to me. He loved physics and the rational world. He was cold about it. Like when he, a Holocaust survivor, said that he would have voted to let the Nazis march in Skokie. Something was far greater than his own self and pain. I wanted to scream at him, 'The Nazis almost killed you and you're going to—because you believe it's right—let them march?' He's in love with his cold logical geometry. He loved that more than he loved me. I never saw him take an emotional position."

Roz is portraying her father vividly enough for me to sense deeply what she must have felt as a child, but still, she is describing him and skirting her own experience. I try to move her closer to it. "So, what does it feel like to be the daughter?" She responds poignantly, yet still she describes, and fails to express her inner experience. "At every turn my needs, my preferences, are overridden. I'm told they don't matter." "What does it feel like?" I ask, focused and somewhat stubborn.

My persistence is fruitful. Roz responds with tears in her eyes. "Shameful, like I have this dirty stuff in me. It doesn't occur to me that it should be honored. I never insisted . . . I hide it . . . at the same time desperately scrambling to matter on the rational side . . . trying to be seen on rational ground and hiding, cutting short, any emotion and feeling."

As the session ends, I say to her, "What we've been trying to do is stay with *your* experience, stay with your feelings a little bit longer . . . in the face of how tough that can be." Roz pauses briefly before replying, "When I stay with the feeling, the feeling is desperate." I am very touched and feel a bit teary myself; I simply reflect, "Desperate." We sit quietly together for a while. Then, both aware that it is time, we stand and say good-bye.

DREAMS: A SELF-PSYCHOLOGICAL FRAMEWORK[1]

Dreams have been seen as disguised messages that require an expert interpreter since Joseph interpreted the Pharaoh's dream as a prophecy of seven years of prosperity followed by seven years of famine, and probably long before. After Freud, dream messages were no longer seen as mystical or spiritual, but the belief that they are disguised communications (arising in the unconscious) and that they need decoding or interpretation by an expert, remained.

The search for hidden meaning and truth, often considered to be the spirit of psychoanalysis, is exciting and fascinating. However, this chapter is not about dream interpretation in that sense. I will demonstrate instead how the self-psychological approach to the clinical use of dreams facilitates the therapeutic process by fostering the sharing of vulnerability. The sharing of dreams—the dreams themselves, the fact of sharing them, and the way they are responded to—provides an opportunity for the kind of playful metaphorical communication between dreamer and other that can encourage vulnerability, facilitate the therapeutic process, and enhance relationships. This is as true in couple and group work as it is in individual psychotherapy. I will discuss and illustrate the clinical use of dreams in all of these modalities, and demonstrate several different approaches to self-psychological dream work that can be used to support, in various circumstances, the emerging vulnerable self.

---

1. A portion of this material first appeared in Livingston, M. (1998). Dreams, the understanding-explaining sequence, and the facilitation of therapeutic process. In *Progress In Self Psychology*, vol. 14, ed. A. Goldberg, pp. 125–145. Hillsdale, NJ: Analytic Press, and is reprinted here by permission of Analytic Press.

Classical procedure stresses the uncovering of meaning through the analysis of discrete dream elements. It provides valuable information as the analyst tries to understand the patient and the vicissitudes of the transference. But there are other possible kinds of responses to the reporting of a dream, and the classical approach may not always be the best choice.

My training, in the 1960s, was in classical dream analysis. We were taught to ask for associations to the elements in a dream, the intent being to search out the disguised multiple meanings. Some experienced analysts seemed to be able, solely from dream content and associative material, to delineate the transference, its genetic roots, and often what to expect in the following sessions. They adapted their technique to each unique situation, and their clinical work benefited from their stepping back to grasp the unfolding dynamics. However, my own clinical experience was disappointing. I felt that although the detailed investigation of separate dream elements was a wonderful teaching technique, it did not fit well into the flow of the actual therapeutic process. Asking for associations to discrete elements of dream material led to a search for latent content that felt experience-distant to me. It yielded insight without sufficient affective involvement. Stolorow (1978) has described this as a "molecular" view, and suggests that asking for associations to "molar" themes leads to additional meaningful material. I found that self-psychological work with dreams integrated in a more satisfactory way with the flow of the process.

The self-psychological approach to dreams, as to everything else, stresses empathic attunement and the need to remain close to the patient's subjective experience (that is, to remain experience-near). Fosshage (1987) for example, states, "The primary dream interpretive task from the vantage point of this model is to remain with, as closely as possible, the phenomenology of the dream; to understand the meanings of the particular images and experiences as they are presented in the dream itself" (p. 31). Self psychologists approach dream images as expressions of affective reactions or thematic experiences (Stolorow 1978), rather than solely as the product of disguise. This helps them to sustain their empathic immersion in the patient's experience of the dream, and also to discern the dream's connection to the patient's sense of self. Empathic attunement, where dreams are concerned, is the analyst's immersion in the patient's experience as opposed to a theory-based speculation about meaning. The analyst's responses to dream material are best guided by the sense of how the patient experiences the dream.

My own particular clinical interest in dreams, however, is less in interpretation, self-psychological or otherwise, than in their contribution to therapeutic process, and their facilitation of the search for the optimal responsiveness to patients' emerging vulnerability that furthers the unfolding of selfobject transferences. I will outline some key concepts here that inform this interest and provide helpful clinical guidelines.

Kohut (1977) accepted that many dreams were usefully understood in the traditional manner as disguised representations of latent drives, wishes, and conflicts. However, he believed that free association was not useful with some dreams, and did not lead to meaningful hidden layers. He thought that these dreams and their associative elaboration were attempts, through the use of imagery, to express and to bind the nonverbal tensions of traumatic states of overstimulation or self-fragmentation. He called dreams of this kind "self-state dreams" (p. 109), because he saw in them healthy sectors of the psyche reacting with anxiety to a disturbing change in the condition of the self.

Recent writers (for instance, Tolpin 1983, 1989) have expanded this concept. Kohut's self-state dreams portrayed specifically a fragmenting self. His successors do not feel that self-state dreams reflect only the extreme states of disturbance that Kohut described, and so they include in that category other dreams about the self and its experiences with selfobjects. Greenberg (1987), for example, postulates that "all dreams are self-state dreams, sometimes with evidence of failure (fragmentation), but other times with evidence of integration so that one can see the construction of new coping mechanisms, which is actually what structures are" (p. 102). Ornstein (1987) takes a similar view. He sees *all* dreams as self-state dreams in the broad sense that "the dream is always about the self; that is, the dream always presents various aspects of self-experience to the dreamer's attention" (p. 101).

This approach gives rise to two important deviations from the classical model. Fosshage (1987) points out the first difference: that an expert decoder is no longer required. He considers that dreams serve a synthetic or organizing function in the development, regulation and restoration of psychic structure—that they are not primarily preservers of sleep, and so there is no "theoretical necessity to posit the ubiquitous operation of disguise and transformation of latent into manifest content" (Fosshage 1983, p. 652; also see Stolorow and Atwood [1992] for a similar view). Fosshage, in fact, eschews the manifest/latent dichotomy altogether (personal communication). The dream is the best possible expression of itself and not necessarily a disguise for something else. Thus, instead of being an authority on interpretation of hidden meanings, the analyst is an "amplifier of images"—a facilitator and elucidator of the patterns of meanings manifested in the dream imagery.

The second essential difference distinguishing the self-psychological approach, as ever, is that the self psychologist's orienting principle (Tolpin 1983) is to focus always upon the vicissitudes of the self. This means that associative material is not understood in terms of infantile drives and prohibitions, or interacting forces of id, ego, and superego. The essential conflict, when conflict is involved, is considered to be between the self and its selfobjects.

THE UNDERSTANDING/EXPLAINING SEQUENCE IN INTERPRETIVE INTERVENTION

In spite of these two differences, however, work with dreams in self psychology is still an interpretive process. Kohut's (1984) idea of the process of interpretation in self-psychological analysis, which he described as countless repetitions of a "basic therapeutic unit of understanding and explaining" (p. 209) applies to work with dreams as much as it does to other analytic material. But if the patient is to feel sufficiently understood to allow his vulnerability to increase, the analyst must allow empathic attunement to guide the unfolding and timing of the interpretive process. Experience-distant interpretative statements are often, even when accurate, experienced by the patient as a rupture of the empathic bond. Vulnerability and the unfolding of selfobject transferences are optimized for many patients when the analyst remains very close to what they are experiencing at the moment. All good analysts, of course, cultivate this sense of empathic timing; Kohut, however, viewed it as an explicit and central part of the interpretive process. He identified a first step in the interpretive process that he called the "understanding phase"—a necessary predecessor of the explanatory aspect any interpretation, and one that is key to the facilitation of vulnerability in general, and to work with dreams in particular. Because the dream is already an unfettered creative product the dreamer is more likely to feel vulnerable in exposing it than he might with other material. Thus, an ill-timed explanation or depth interpretation is likely to be experienced as an experience-distant and unempathic observation and be disruptive rather than helpful.

In the understanding phase the analyst "verbalizes to the patient that he has grasped what the patient feels; he describes the patient's inner state to the patient, thus demonstrating to him that he has been 'understood,' that is, that another person has been able to experience, at least in approximation, what he himself experienced" (Kohut 1984, p. 177).

The recognition of the importance of a prolonged period of this specific kind of understanding (that is, empathic understanding) as a part of interpretive work was a significant contribution that extended classical ideas about the listening that precedes deep interpreting. Kohut never wanted to be misunderstood as suggesting that empathy itself was the curative factor in psychoanalytic work, and he emphasized repeatedly that "analysis cures by giving explanations (the second phase in the understanding/explaining sequence) on the level of interpretation" (p. 532). But the two are intimately connected. They are two facets of a single interpretive process.

Complex factors within the intersubjective context of the session determine whether "understanding" or "explaining" is called for at any given moment, and the analyst must be sensitive to them. Among them are the patient's current experience of the analyst, and his experience at the moment of his everyday life. But probably the most crucial element to be considered in the analyst's choice about whether at any given time to stress understanding or explaining in his responses is his sense of the patient's current self-state, including its inner sense of cohesiveness and safety and how he might expect his choice to impact upon it. This means that the analyst's choice to understand or to explain depends on which will best foster *tolerable* vulnerability, as opposed to either traumatic vulnerability and fragmentation, or reactive defensiveness.

All this is true as well of the analyst's response to a patient's dreams. Work with dreams is a variant of interpretive activity, and as such can be imagined to move through a merger-like phase of understanding to an explaining phase. It is important to bear in mind that Kohut considered understanding an interpretive activity. It is a planned intervention aimed at creating the safety necessary for the unfolding of transference, the toleration of vulnerability, and the resumption of arrested development, and to Kohut's way of thinking, a *phase* of interpretation. In fact, although Kohut never neglected the corresponding phase of explaining (perhaps to maintain his tie with mainstream analysis and its emphasis on insight), I have seen a good deal of development in some patients without ever making the move to explicit explanation, which in some people provokes disturbances in the work and in their self-state, or a compliant and usually intellectual and superficial agreement. This sense of understanding as a relatively archaic selfobject need is illustrated in the metaphorical play in the clinical material to follow. The analyst's response to dreams enhances intrinsic dream functions through illumination and affirmation.

Kohut (1984) pointed out that for many patients (I would add especially for ones who do not yet tolerate well the experience of vulnerability) the understanding phase of treatment may last for a very long time. Some patients fear that they will be overwhelmed by other people's intensity, or by their own inner experience—such people often need a prolonged period of the selfobject experience of understanding before they can tolerate and make use of explanations.

Eventually, however, the explanatory phase offers a different emotional, as well as cognitive, experience. The intensity of the patient's experience of an archaic bond lessens as the analyst moves from understanding to explaining. The empathic bond between patient and analyst is retained, but on a more mature level. One selfobject experience is replaced by another; that is, merger with the selfobject (during the understanding phase) is replaced by the experience of empathic resonance (through explanatory interpretations). But protracted periods of understanding may be necessary first, in analytic work in general as well as in dream work, to help very fearful patients tolerate the vulnerability of analytic exposure and exploration.

Ideally, the patient experiences this selfobject availability as an opportunity to play creatively with dream (and other) material, as a child can "play" creatively and without judgment in the "intermediate space" that he and a sufficiently available mother cocreate (Winnicott 1953). The analyst's response to the dream facilitates an unfolding process that carries over from the work with the dream itself to other aspects of the analysis. The following clinical material illustrates how these considerations apply to the use of dreams in analytic work, and also the value of a prolonged understanding phase with certain patients.

MRS. A. AND THE UNDERSTANDING PHASE

At the time that these dreams were reported, Mrs. A., the "nondifficult" patient from Chapter 4, had been in treatment four times a week for several years. The dreams were presented shortly after the sessions reported in Chapter 4. She had formed a rather intense idealizing transference in which the analyst was seen as a source of safety and protection as she tentatively approached a deeper experience of her yearnings and fears.

Sessions included long silences; she was sometimes very

anxious, and withdrew from her subjective experience. Often after one of these uncomfortable silences, she would report on the large assortment of physical and mental devices that automatically come into play to help her to regulate her affective experience. These developed at a very early stage of childhood, and protected her from the terror that her feelings will lead to abandonment. She feared that alone with her intensity she would be overwhelmed, and no longer exist. Kohut (1984) describes a similar fear of disintegration that he links to a loss of humanness and of all selfobject experience. It was probably my empathic grasp of these terrors, although I did not think clearly about it in those terms at the time, that led me to restrict my interpretive activity with Mrs. A. to a prolonged period of understanding. When my response was particularly well attuned, when she felt deeply understood, she would remain silent for several minutes, as if she needed time to for assimilation. At other times, her silence reflected a terror of allowing any further expression. In both situations, I learned to be respectful of her need for the silences (although it is not easy for me to rely heavily on nonverbal cues to understand what is happening between us)..It seemed essential to match her pace and to assume that, when she feels safe enough, the protection will be less necessary.

Mrs. A. brings a small bouquet of flowers with her from a fundraising luncheon she organized. She places the flowers on the window sill and lies down on the couch without any comment beyond a simple hello on her part and a thank you on mine. After a brief (for her) silence, she relates that she has been very aware of having missed the session the previous day, because she had to be at the luncheon.

Mrs. A.: Somehow being back here feels like everything that was here last week is back, although I can't remember what it was. I almost wish it wasn't here because I'll begin to feel it and to remember it, and then next week you'll be away on vacation. Maybe I'm just edgy. Things come up here and then I leave or I bury them. I'm scared that they'll be more conscious and you won't be here. So I get busy at work and it swallows me up. It doesn't just swallow me. I have a need for those feelings to get swallowed. I think I'm afraid I'll be alone with something. I don't want to be alone with it. . . . I dreamed something. There were images. I was real small. I was just there at the center of something and going away from me as far as I could imagine was ice. It was almost like being inside an ice cube. There was nothing else. Just ice.

Marty: What did you feel?

Mrs. A.: What I felt was incredibly lonely.

Marty: Frozen and alone?

Mrs. A.: No, I wasn't really frozen, just everything around me was. [This is an important correction, and once she corrects me I realize she has often spoken of how intensely she feels and experiences but dares not express it in an unresponsive world. Before I can respond, she continues.] Then there was another one. It was sort of the same, but not ice. I looked like I had a body, but my head was the shape of a long diamond. It began changing from looking like a tiny bird's mouth—pulsing, opening, and closing—then to a flower. There is a flower that looks like that. It kept alternating between a flower and a bird's head—but it was my head.

Marty: What did you feel?

Mrs. A.: The same kind of alone feeling. Like a hopeless feeling in the moving—in the pulsing. It's an endless kind of unsatisfiedness, a sense that something wouldn't be—a yearning for something and it not being there. It felt like trying for such a long time and yet still not totally giving up.

Marty: You weren't giving up, yet you felt hopeless.

Mrs. A.: Yes, and I think the ice dream came second. It sort of followed the other one. It wasn't really giving up. Giving up would be like dying, it's the feeling of isolation—of staying there within this frozen environment.

Marty: It sounds as if the sense of living in a frozen world followed from the bird's not being fed for *so* long.

I am feeling very connected to her sense of aloneness and to her long struggle to find a semblance of responsiveness in a world that she experiences as so totally unempathic and cold. The imagery in the dreams clearly illuminates her subjective sense of the world in which she grew up. My aim, through a restrained but emotionally very available stance, is to allow her to play in an "intermediate" space. I make no attempt to offer any explanation of the dream, or to reconstruct its genetic roots for her in any detail. However, I do give some inward thought as to whether the self and the selfobject surround she expresses include her experience of me in the transference. I have sometimes been concerned that my restraint is experienced by her as detachment even though I don't feel it that way.

My decision to maintain this prolonged understanding phase in response to Mrs. A.'s dreams is an intuitive one, and in retrospect, I think that it was connected to the way I understood her silences, and to the metaphorical and vulnerable nature of the material itself. Metaphor is often the poetic language of a narcissistically wounded and sensitive self, and it can call forth a tender responsiveness that is difficult to express in ordinary language. Responding within the patient's metaphor seems to me to be a very natural way of conveying what Kohut considered to be understanding.

Therefore, my interpretive response about the bird's not being fed for so long is deeply felt, and I hope that my patient will experience it as empathically attuned and responsive. When it triggers an extremely long silence, I am not sure. I have learned though, as I mentioned earlier, that sometimes Mrs. A.'s silences have to do with her feeling free to take time to assimilate her experience of me as a new object. To take time for what she needs without having to respond to my need for feedback appears to be an important step in her self-development. So I restrain my inquiry for what seems to me a long time and then ask, "What are you experiencing now?"

Mrs. A.: Well, for a moment I had a feeling of . . . I don't even want to talk about it. I wanted to just feel it. For the moment I had such a terrific feeling. It was like a feeling of . . . wanting is not exactly right. It had wanting in it. It was a full good feeling that had wanting in it—vibrant—lush. I must have had it for two seconds and then I thought, "Nobody should want that much." I wouldn't have even said it if you didn't ask. I put words on it like greedy, unnecessary. That two-second feeling has to be gotten rid of and made smaller. It has to be made less of all the things it is—less round, less lush, less everything.

Marty: As if it were dangerous.

Mrs. A.: And shameful, too. You're not supposed to admit it. (Then after a long pause) I took the flowers home because I couldn't bear to leave them. They seemed representative—so opposite to the iced feeling. The flowers are so varied, such a contrast to the ice-cube feeling of a lonely desolate place. It means something to me. I took them home and put them in glasses. I took a whole bunch of them so they wouldn't die. I wanted to bring some here, too. Then when I say that I feel sappy, I wish I didn't. Some part of me wants to not make it a big deal, and it is a big deal. I feel it's a big deal and to feel that too much, to get too close to that, becomes difficult. It's like somebody is going to know. (After a long pause) I really feel like there's a whole life inside me that I have to hide.

Marty: You feel you have to hide it because there was never any support for it in that ice world.

Mrs. A.: It feels like it would overwhelm, like the nature of it would overwhelm someone. I would overwhelm and I can't overwhelm. I would be too much.

This session clearly shows the role of the dream (and the analyst's response to it) in the amplification of affective experience and vulnerability. No attempt was made to search for and decode hidden meanings or latent content. The manifest dream, and the whole session as an associative elaboration of it, provides a rich illumination of the patient's self-state and the organizational principles that color the subjective experience of her selfobject surround.

The conflict for Mrs. A. that appears, to a self psychologist, most central in the dream is the one that Stolorow and his associates (1987) have called the "fundamental conflict": between pursuing the development of her own inner core with its intensity of yearning, and a fear that this would be damaging to selfobject ties. Her fear is that the people serving these essential functions would withdraw into cold unresponsiveness, leaving her in her dreaded world of ice.

Another session about two months later further illustrates these principles. It demonstrates how the development of metaphorical communication between analyst and patient helps to amplify affective meanings and furthers the creation of the intermediate space. The session begins with a long silence broken by the analyst's inquiry:

Marty: What's doing today?

Mrs. A.: (Thoughtfully) I don't know. I don't feel anxious. I don't have anything to say, though. I'm comfortable with it. I feel sort of open, just right this minute I don't feel any need to talk.

Marty: Did you have any dreams over the weekend?

Mrs. A.: Yeah, I did, but I can't tell you what they were. I had a weird dream, I think. I think it was about a turkey—about some kind of animal. I was making a turkey and there was something in it—a person or a table—something ridiculous. I don't really remember. It was a bizarre sort of dream.

Marty: What do you think of if you think of the turkey?

Mrs. A.: I don't even know if it was a turkey.

Marty: It doesn't matter. Any piece can be a point to associate to. It doesn't have to be in order or formed.

[Looking at this material in retrospect, I think I was not very well attuned. My request for a dream may have been in response to my wish for one more dream for this chapter. Then, not knowing where else to go (and committed to working even with the fragment reported) I asked for her association and proceeded to educate her about the usefulness of my request. It plays back to me as experience-distant and not empathically attuned.]

Mrs. A.: (Responding to my informative intervention rather emotionally) I'm not comfortable with that. I'm afraid you meant it like "shrink games." My sister used to come home from therapy and "test" me. I felt like she was playing games with me. She would ask me to say the first thing I thought of in response to a test word and then she would imply that she knew something about me. It feels like you're asking me to respond and then you'll know something and you won't tell me.

Marty: So when I ask you to share something that's not fully formed—something you don't know the meaning of—that feels risky.

The empathic rupture was not as clear to me in the session as it is now. However, I seem to have intuitively self-righted at this point and returned to an empathic recognition that she experienced my intervention as dangerous. It is clear, again in retrospect, that my distance from her experience and my less-than-optimal empathic responsiveness had begun a shift in the transference. What Stolorow and Atwood (1992) refer to as the "repetitive dimension" of the transference had begun to take over the foreground of her experience. I was behaving like her sister and re-creating a selfobject failure through my experience-distant attempt at working with the dream. My responsiveness to her experience of danger was sufficient to repair the empathic break and restore the protective idealizing transference that has been facilitating the flow of analytic material.

In response to my reflection of her experience of riskiness, therefore, she continues:

Mrs. A.: Yeah, I'm not uncomfortable with you, so I didn't really feel frightened. However, the thought of that kind of situation triggers a sense in me that I have to get ready to defend. It feels sad how incredibly restricting that is. Then I hear a voice saying, "That's okay, restricted is better than the fear of that other—that other, whatever it is." I tell myself I can lift the restriction when I want to, that I'm in charge, but I think that's a myth. There's always some reason why I can't right now. So, I wonder what it is that I'm afraid someone will know about me. What will my unrestricted telling say about me? What will it mean about me? (Following a long pause she continues again) I know the answer to that. At least I know the first thing that comes into my mind. It isn't what I'd come up with if I think it out.

Marty: There is a value in your first response.

Mrs. A.: They'll know that I don't belong . . . that I'm different from them. It's all about being adopted and not theirs. What I would automatically say will be different—unacceptable. It will reveal my true blood roots in some kind of awful way. I couldn't know that as a little child. I don't think a baby is born knowing she has to do that. It didn't come from some inborn trait. There must have been cues that I picked up . . . cues to blend in, to fit, not to stand out. The sad part is the restricting. I didn't have to make anything thing up. Restricted is the right word. I kept it narrow. There's an expansiveness that I inherited. I learned to hide it but I know it's there. I've restricted a lot. That's painful.

At this point I go back to the metaphorical language of the

dream. With a sense of sadness I comment: "It's hard now to know what's inside the turkey." My response triggers another of those long silences. I cannot be sure whether she experiences it as attuned and playfully returning to a shared metaphor or as unattuned and returning to the dream after she chose not to work with it. After a long silence, similar to the one described in the first session discussed, I ask: "What are you experiencing now?" She responds with, for her, an unusual amount of affect: "I'm experiencing a kind of regretful feeling, like a sad, reflective feeling. You were good to couch it that way. I was amused. It led me to those kind of thoughts—sort of sad thoughts—reflective about what hasn't been but also, . . . I do know what is in the turkey."

After leaving some room to see if she would go further on her own I offer: "One association you had was that it might have been a person in the turkey." She responds, "Yeah, and when I say I do know, I don't want to apologize for what's in it. The person is hidden the way stuffing is hidden. My expansiveness is hidden like stuffing in a turkey. I've always made very good stuffing recipes. They're not white bread recipes. Some people like them and some people don't. They think they aren't traditional enough—not what they would expect. I always like to cook stuffing."

I end the session at that point and as Mrs. A. gets up from the couch she exclaims with glee, "I never knew I was making a statement with my stuffing."

This session provides a good example of the analyst's restrained responsiveness helping to set up a metaphorical, playful, communication and an ambiance similar to Winnicott's description of an intermediate area of experience. This metaphorical communication is one approach to providing a prolonged understanding phase (especially in response to dream material). The choice to take this approach was rooted in a self-psychological understanding of this particular patient's self-state. It's a deceptively simple approach to working with dreams. It relies heavily on Kohut's (1977) discovery of the self-state dream, as well as on his description of the understanding/explaining sequence of interpretive process.

Every patient–therapist dyad has to discover its own optimal responses. In working with a patient who did not have Mrs. A.'s history of disintegration terror, or one who seems to be ready for the explaining phase of interpretation, I would respond differently than I did in these sessions with Mrs. A. The following case material is an example, and sheds some light on the other side of the understanding/explaining sequence.

MISS B. AND KOHUT'S EXPLAINING PHASE

Miss B. has been in treatment three times a week for several years. She is an active and lively woman in her late thirties who has had several serious relationships, each lasting two or three years. Her inability to be sure she is making the right choice repeatedly interferes with her making a lasting commitment. She recently left a relationship that was close and emotionally very satisfying because she yearned for a partner she could idealize. She felt that the man with whom she was living was not motivated to succeed in the world in the way she needed a partner to be. She also was uncomfortable with the recognition that she did not feel proud of him when he accompanied her to functions with her colleagues. She is currently dating a highly educated and successful man who she feels *can* fulfill the yearning she has for an idealizable partner, and her uneasiness in this relationship is that this man is not as emotionally supportive and accepting as the previous one. He tends to become withdrawn and judgmental when he is disappointed.

Like Mrs. A., Miss B. has formed an intense idealizing transference, in which the analyst is seen as a source of safety. However, her need for protection is not as central as Mrs. A.'s. She needs help in organizing her experiences *after* they occur, rather than in regulating them *before* they occur. As opposed to Mrs. A., who overregulates to ward off her terror of being overwhelmed, Miss B. allows herself a good deal of intensity and then is at times overwhelmed and confused by it. However, she is not terrified by the confusion and flood of her feelings to the same degree as Mrs. A., and she has not had to develop the elaborate system of cautious self-regulation that Mrs. A. has to avoid the flow of her feelings. On the contrary, she tends to go with her impulses, sometimes in pursuit of realistic dreams, but sometimes following fantasies that are less than fully thought out. She doesn't like this sensation of confusion and the inability to organize and control her world, and seems ready and eager to join the analyst in stepping back and making sense of her experiences. These are indication that an explaining-phase kind of responsiveness is called for, as opposed to the prolonged understanding that was optimally responsive to Mrs. A.

Miss B. does not resort to Mrs. A.'s long silences, and sessions with her are usually quite lively. It takes some conscious restraint to keep myself out of conversational interactions that although pleasurable, seem to remain focused on reality concerns in a superficial or theoretical manner. In recent months this restraint has enabled me to be more analytic in my responses, and at my suggestion Miss B. has begun to use the couch. She has become increasingly interested in exploring dream material and her own internal fluctuations, instead of simply evaluating her partners. The struggle to further this shift is evident in the session that follows.

She begins the session with a dream. "I had three 'early on' dates [by which she means that each date was with a different man and early in a new relationship]. They were all pleasant. I liked all three men very much. The details are muddy on the first two. They're strangers, no one I knew or I can connect to anyone I know. The third one I do remember. He wasn't extremely handsome, but good looking—tall and athletic. We stayed in a hotel for two nights. We weren't sexual yet, but we were clearly attracted to each other. We shared a sense of humor."

She continues without a pause, "On waking, it was a little bit disturbing. What I saw is that there are a number of types of men that can generate an excitement in me. Like 'maybe this is the one.' There were three back-to-back and I felt confused because any of them could have been a potential partner."

Therapist: Mm-hmm.

Miss B.: The confusion was that it could have been any of them and I could make a commitment and make a go of it. Each man was different—had different qualities, posed a different challenge—but all of them could be a good partner. That's what I feel with Joe and Tom. They pose different challenges, but I'm drawn to both of them. Probably the third person is the man I've never met. I guess the confusion came up because last night Joe again seemed like a possibility. He seemed like a man I could really build with. He keeps coming back and trying. He gets overwhelmed and withdraws, but he comes back. He isn't totally rejecting me out of hand. It was okay that we didn't make love last night. He was really tired. I was okay with it because I was getting enough of being cared about and loved. So it feels again like progress for me to realize that I wanted more, but I felt good about what the evening did contain. I'm still appreciative of what went on between us. So, I'm feeling once again reassured that there is potential. I had felt rejected and he came over to repair what I felt. I appreciate that. Then I started looking at his résumé and being afraid that I don't have enough to offer. At the same time, I know that I have a tremendous amount to offer him. For example, he had a difficult day yesterday and I had a lot to offer talking to him without having to fix it. I was really able to offer him something that he could take in, but somehow I get scared that I'm not going to be enough and that triggers that whole rejection thing.

T: So the dream seems to suggest that you could let go of searching for "the one" and always being the one doing the evaluating. You could choose one man, decide that he's okay and make it work, but then you get concerned with questioning whether you're good enough, whether you have something to offer him.

Miss B.: Yes, then I could be the one who feels rejected. I feel like we're at a turning point. There's still a lot of stuff that hasn't been hammered out. Would he be willing to stay? There are still some uncertainties. I'm aware that, right now, I want you to make it all better, to tell me that everything is going to be all right. Also, I want reassurance that I'm handling it okay so far. I'm having my rejected feelings and my regular feelings about being inadequate and feeling a disproportionate reaction to the sense of being rejected. However, I'm still getting back together with him and both of us are working together. I can see that the button is still a big one and that I can still make decisions to leave, to decide that he isn't the right one for me.

T: You switch to an evaluating position.

Miss B.: Yes, I get away from all my feelings of not being good enough. I'm so hell-bent not to repeat what I experienced with Donald (an earlier relationship). Being criticized and thrown away was devastating. It's going to take me a long time to know that Joe is not Donald. [Miss B. had been in the habit of looking at an office clock a few minutes before the end of the session, but several of my patients were becoming too focused on the time, and I had moved the clock since her last session to a less intrusive place behind the couch. At this point she looks for the clock and is surprised not to find it, although we had talked in a previous session about the idea of my moving it. She laughs and exclaims: You moved the clock! Is it about time to stop now?

T: (Laughing with her) It sounds like you want to make sure not to be rejected without being prepared first.

Miss B.: I want to be sure that I'm ready, that I won't suddenly be thrown out. It was so painful with Donald. I really fell apart, shattered when he saw me that way. I don't want that to ever happen again and Joe has access to those buttons.

T: It's really scary to begin to attach to a man, to need a man.

Miss B.: With Tom I wasn't scared. I was the one who could leave. I'm really developing a sense of what he must have experienced in our relationship. I feel really sad that I contributed to him being hurt by my going away the way I did.

T: By your evaluating him?

Miss B.: Yeah, that's where my going away came from. I feel real bad about it.

T: And with Joe you're afraid that he's going to be evaluating.

Miss B.: Yes, both of us are evaluators. I'm scared that he's going to have more of the power because I'm more attached. That it will be unbalanced. Is it time to stop now?

T: Yes.

Miss B.: (With glee) I wish I could come five times a week. Gee, I wonder why I thought five and not four. I've been thinking of adding a session and coming four times.

T: It sounds like you were expressing a wish.

Miss B.: Yes, I wish that I could come *every* day.

Working with this patient and her selfobject needs is clearly different from working with Mrs. A. The addition, the content of the session, and the dream itself are also different. It would be grossly out of tune for the analyst to respond only in metaphor and not move to an explanatory phase. Mrs. A. needs a quietly responsive holding environment that can be expressed in metaphorical play with her own dream symbolism. That is the kind of empathic surround in which she can allow herself to feel vulnerable. In contrast, Miss B. needs a relatively active partner to search out and clarify the organizing principles that are increasingly clear in her dreams and in the content of the sessions. She is clearly beginning to be able to reflect on the patterns that organize all her self/selfobject relationships. She would likely experience a prolonged "understanding-only" response to her dreams as an abandonment. She needs the sense of a more actively contributing, even if separate, responsiveness.

These patterns have to be explained (illuminated and explored) on three levels. Most easily accessible with this patient at this particular moment is the connection between the dream, the content of her associations, and her struggle to develop a committed love relationship. Because it is closest to the patient's experience it is the level to which I directed most of my interventions (at least in terms of their overt content).

I was also, however, very aware that a very similar pattern is also being worked through in the here and now of the transference. Miss B. is in the process of deepening her involvement in treatment and with me. Her fears of attachment and of possible evaluation and rejection are also manifest in the transference. I did not assume that I was represented in the dream directly, although it is possible that the third man is an expression of the transference. I do, however, believe that the dream expresses the patterns that organize the patient's self/selfobject relationships, and thus probably include the transference at times.

With that tentative hypothesis in mind, I noted to myself how much of what she was saying seemed to relate to her interaction with me. She seemed to be gradually allowing herself to form a selfobject bond with me while occasionally expressing some fears of lapses in my interest or imbalances in our relationship. I addressed our interaction "between the lines," rather than overtly, because I felt that to make the intersubjective situation the central focus right then would interfere with the excitement and flow that is evolving naturally. I chose to join with her in the work of clarifying the patterns that are up front for her at the moment, and to let the selfobject dimension of the transference unfold in the background, although I am also of course concerned with facilitating this unfolding in a subtle manner.

The third level of explanation, which is not manifest in this session, is the genetic level. Miss B. holds to an idealized perception of her parents. Only recently has she begun to recall feeling misunderstood and unappreciated (as she did especially following the births of her sisters). There have also been some hints of anger and disappointment in this regard. Most of the time, however, when I inquire into the genetic roots of her dreams or the content of sessions, her responses, though cooperative, lack the lively flow present here. Therefore, I choose to leave this third level of explanations for a later time. The unfolding of the clinical material must provide the cues about when to make earlier self/selfobject patterns more central.

ON SHARING DREAMS

The defenses available in dreaming are limited, in comparison to the defensive armory available in waking life. Dreaming is a vulnerable state, and a person in sharing a dream relinquishes a degree of control and self-protection, and presents a vulnerable part of himself. The recounting of a dream is by definition an exposure and a sharing of the dreamer's vulnerability, and as always, the sharing of vulnerability is a profound force for deepening therapeutic process. Dream content itself does not always relate directly to conflicts around emotional expression and vulnerability (although often it does, as Kohut's concept of self-state dreams makes clear), and it would be unidirectional and simplistic to approach all dreams by focusing on vulnerability and the barriers to it. Still, attention to issues of vulnerability in dreams is always appropriate, since dream-sharing is in itself an act that makes the dreamer vulnerable.

To encourage the reporting of dreams is by definition an encouragement of vulnerability. The dreamer is taking one risk in sharing the obvious content of the dream, and a further one in exposing the dream to the partner's associations and subjective understanding (or misunderstanding). A good deal of control is relinquished, and the dreamer knows that he may be sharing more than he bargained for once the dream is related.

The self-psychological approach is more encouraging of the shared use of dreams than some other approaches, since the manifest content of the dream is seen as a communicative expression in itself, and not a disguised representation of latent content. This allows patients to play with dreams without the heightened self-consciousness they might experience if the therapist (or a partner, or a member of a group) were making interpretations of hidden sexual and aggressive motivation, and allows them at least some control of the vulnerability they undertake in the sharing of the dream.

Dreams are an offering of the dreamer's vulnerable self, and they provide an excellent opportunity for the development of playful and metaphorical communication, whether it be between therapist and patient, between the two partners in a couple, or among the members of a group. For all of these reasons, work with dreams seems to call for the kind of *spielraum,* or play space, that I mentioned briefly in connection with groups. The shared quality of dream work makes it as valuable in group and couple settings as it is in individual therapy, and the concept of play space encourages both a sense of safety in processing dreams, and an appreciation of their metaphorical power. This deepens the therapeutic process in all the participants, and also the intimacy of the relationships among them. This kind of work with dreams is one way that first the therapist, and eventually the patients, can provide an empathically attuned responsiveness for each other.

DREAMS IN COUPLE THERAPY[2]

Surprisingly little has been written on the use of dreams in couple therapy. Working with patients' dreams is a "time-honored technique [that] has been one of the mainstays of psychoanalytic technique, used both in psychoanalysis and psychoanalytically oriented psychotherapy" (Goldberg 1974, p. 75). Ullman and Zimmerman (1979) have called the family "the natural setting for dream appreciation. . . . After all, the sore spots and unresolved feelings pictured so extravagantly in our dreams are most frequently linked to the family" (p. 148).

Still, I found only three papers directly related to the use of dreams in couple treatment (Fielding 1966, Goldberg 1974, Perlmutter and Babineau 1983), and three more that addressed other couple-focused uses of dreams: Nell (1975) wrote about using dreams in couples groups. Ullman and Zimmerman (1979) focused on a family that shared their dreams with one of the authors, and Calogeras (1977) reported on a couple who shared their dreams with each other without being in conjoint treatment.

---

2. Parts of this section will be appearing in Livingston, M. (2001). Couples in the play space: self psychology, dreams, and couples therapy, *Journal of Couple Therapy*, volume 10, numbers 3/4, and are reprinted here by permission of The Haworth Press, Inc.

Nell, Calogeras, and Perlmutter and Babineau stress the value of dreams in bringing unconscious material to the surface. Nell approaches dreams from a Jungian perspective that stresses interpretation of dreams on the subjective level. On the objective level the manifest content is taken to mean simply what it seems to mean. That is, as Nell (1975) says, "Black paint is simply taken as black paint" (p. 7). On the subjective level, however, which is seen as more confronting and much more important, "Every part of the dream, be it a person or just paint, is symbolic of a part of the dreamer's personality" (p. 7). Nell describes this as "a method of confrontation that forces the dreamer to take responsibility for the content of the dream right away" (p. 8). This sounds like a powerful approach if the timing is careful enough and the process is not taken as routine.

The couple that Calogeras (1977) studied shared their dreams in an attempt to understand each other's unconscious communications. He reports that the couple developed an ability to converse using a "dream-language." Each partner seemed to be able to "identify with the contents of the other's dream to the extent that they could take their spouse's dream and associate to it as if it were their own" (p. 79). This paper is a fascinating illustration of how much one particular couple was able to accomplish, with minimal guidance from the wife's analyst and without conjoint sessions.

Perlmutter and Babineau (1983), who worked with couples in treatment, stress the use of dreams to access the patients' unconscious, but they also emphasize an interpersonal dimension. They focus upon the patterns of unconscious relatedness manifest in dreams and in both patients' associations and affective reactions to them. The authors use dreams to explore these patterns, and view them as a communication between the partners.

Three of the papers move away from the traditional stress on the interpretation of unconscious content. Fielding (1966), like Calogeras, focuses on dreams as a form of communication. However, he places less stress on the unconscious. He sees the dream as a tool "in helping to change the communication of a quarreling couple into a communication aimed at discovery, examination and understanding of the other spouse" (p. 81). Ullman and Zimmerman (1979) are even less concerned with unconscious content. They talk about dream metaphors helping the family they observed to "objectify . . . unacceptable emotions so that they can be talked about and even laughed about as absurdly human, and thereby help create deeper, more loving relationships" (p. 149). This notion seems to be akin to the concept of working with dreams in a play space to which the self-psychological approach has led me.

Goldberg (1974) feels that the most important question about a dream is not its unconscious content, but "How can the dream be used to enhance communication and closeness between the couple?" (p. 80) This, he feels, is best accomplished if the emphasis is on the couple helping each other, not on an authority making interpretations. In fact, he suggests that couples be educated "not to feel that every dream has to be interpreted and to realize that talking about a dream, sharing reactions, feelings, and associating to it, is in itself an enlightening and valuable process without the need to guess at the dream's meaning" (p. 81). He also points out that the therapist must make important decisions about which couples can profit from the sharing of dreams and when to encourage this. The "prevailing climate" of the sessions and the couple's relationship is the key to such matters of timing. There must be an atmosphere of cooperation rather than excessive competitiveness between the partners and with the therapist. The partners must be genuinely working together, and interested in helping each other. In self-psychological terms, to encourage dream sharing is to encourage vulnerability, and thus it requires a certain amount of safety. Goldberg's work leads very smoothly into a self-psychological approach, where one major emphasis is on the couple's developing the capacity to provide a self-sustaining and development enhancing responsiveness to each other. (The other balancing concept is the need to support reactiveness.)

Dreams in couple sessions can arise to convey an essential truth; they are metaphorical communications, word pictures, that convey their messages at a depth that ordinary language cannot always reach. Stolorow and Atwood (1992) emphasize the function of fantasy in situations where powerful affective experiences have failed to evoke adequate validating responses. Sometimes other attempts at conveying important emotional experiences from the past, or from within the couple's relationship, have failed to evoke a "good-enough" response from the partner. At these times, a dream may be a more effective form of communication. Stolorow and Atwood stress the self-restorative and intrapsychic aspect of fantasy in providing the needed validation. "In such instances, the concrete sensorimotor images of the fantasy dramatize and reify the person's emotional experience, conferring upon it a sense of validity and reality that otherwise would be absent" (p. 61). It is a small step from that understanding to the appreciation of the potential interpersonal function of telling of a dream to one's partner in the hope that he or she can empathically resonate with the dreamer's experience. That is to say, the dream can dramatize and reify the experience for the listener as well.

As unconscious dream material unfolds, the self psychologist explores, and seeks to increase, the couple's awareness of a different content than classical dream theory pursues. The

Freudian unconscious consists of deeper and deeper derivatives of sexual and aggressive urges and conflicts. In contrast, the content that the self psychologist seeks to illuminate, and bring into awareness, consists of the vicissitudes of the self and its selfobjects. If conflict is present in the dream and its associations, the couple is encouraged to explore it. However, the conflict is most often understood as one between the dreamer and the people whom he sees as the source of needed developmental experiences (his selfobjects).

Like several of the writers mentioned above, self psychologists in general have moved away from an emphasis on the interpretation of unconscious content and toward the valuing of the communicative value of the manifest dream. Many self psychologists consider dreams a communication about the state of the self. Ornstein (1987), for example, states, "The dream is always about the self; that is, the dream always presents various aspects of self-experience to the dreamer's attention" (p. 101). In working with a couple, this communication can often be understood as an attempt to be understood by the dreamer's partner as well as by the analyst.

Dreamer and listeners are encouraged to associate to the dream as a whole and to its parts; this serves to amplify the affect involved, and leads to an exploration of the personal meanings of the metaphors provided by the dream. Listeners are encouraged to remain experience-near—that is, to stay with material that is close to the patient's awareness—and to respond from that perspective within their subjective experience of the moment.

This responsiveness serves to amplify and validate the affective communication contained within the dream, and thus can be viewed as what Kohut (1971) referred to as a selfobject experience: that is, an experience that contributes to the development, restoration, or maintenance of a person's sense of self. In other words, it is an experience that helps in the maintenance of self-esteem, self-cohesion, or self-delineation. In many relationships, the core problem is the couple's inability to sufficiently provide such experiences for each other. As we have seen in an earlier chapter, one primary task of the couple analyst is to enable the partners to take turns in providing for each other's selfobject needs. Working with dreams is an opportunity for the couple to develop this capacity for empathy and responsiveness to each other.

As we have seen, the self-psychological approach to dreams demands the therapist's empathic attunement to each patient's unique subjectivity, and exploration in an atmosphere of safety. The therapist's empathic immersion in both patients' subjective experience models for the couple how to listen to each other; because the dreamer who offers a dream is vulnerable, it is important that the therapist encourage the dreamer's partner to provide nonjudgmental support.

A dream presented in a couple session provides the opportunity for metaphorical communication within a play space. The intimacy and sharing of this kind of communication can enhance therapeutic process in the individuals as well as in the relationship. At this point an illustration can serve as an image that might communicate more poignantly than additional words.

OPENING THE WINDOW TOGETHER: AN ILLUSTRATION

The following session illustrates the value of working with dreams in couple treatment. After ten years of twice-a-week individual therapy, Maria has just begun to question her closeness with her father. Jack, as she calls him, was the center of the universe for her during her childhood and early adolescence. She remembers waiting anxiously every evening for him to come home from work. Her mother sat at the kitchen window staring out in a way that Maria understood to be fear that Jack would not return. She remembers sitting in another room looking out the window also. She didn't want mother to know that she was frightened, too. She felt that it would probably be too much for her mother to handle and that she would fall apart crying. No one in the dark, depressed house of her childhood could bring any sense of life into the room—except Jack. To Maria he was the sun and the stars. Only recently has she related that he often expected her to sleep in his bed while her mother slept in another room. In the last few months of therapy, the window to the ambivalent love, dependence, and terror of this relationship has just begun to open.

Maria and her husband, Sam, were good friends for several years before they became romantically involved. In sharp contrast to her first husband, who had been physically and emotionally abusive, Sam was a solid friend who could be counted on. He was very supportive when Maria's father became ill and required a great deal of care. Shortly following Jack's death, Maria and Sam found themselves intensely attracted to each other. Sex was frequent and exciting and remained that way into the early years of their marriage. Gradually that changed. They remained loving and caring, but the intimacy and excitement faded.

Sam was not interested in treatment for himself, but he was aware that Maria was unhappy and that the marriage was suffering. He gradually developed a good degree of trust in me. This trust developed through incidental contacts in my waiting room, on the phone when I returned Maria's calls, and through Maria's talking about how I had helped her to understand her contribution to arguments. He readily agreed to couple therapy when she suggested it, but wanted to work with me. I often refer a patient in ongoing treatment with me to another couple therapist, but in this case I decided to see them together, at first for a consultation, and then on a regular weekly basis. I knew that Sam was not interested in treatment, but that he was looking to me as a friend and ally who could help with the burdened and helpless feelings that lay just underneath the surface. A referral in the face of this already established selfobject transference would, I thought, be experienced as a betrayal and a rejection, and would probably deter him from working with another therapist. I also felt that Maria understood that I would now need to be empathically attuned to Sam as well as to her, and that at times that might feel like an abandonment of our connection. She felt that I was often attuned to Sam when she talked about their relationship and that she had been able to protest and feel heard at those times. On balance it seemed valuable to proceed with the couple work together.

We have been working on a weekly basis for several years, over which time their relationship has deepened. They have worked through many arguments, and have learned to repair narcissistic injuries as they are triggered in the moment. For Maria, this has also led to the uncovering of a great deal of genetic material, and acute feelings of vulnerability. Sam, on the other hand, reveals little of his childhood. This has been true not only in regard to the sessions, but also at home with Maria. In this couple Maria has always been the identified patient. It is always *her* feelings that are explored, and always *her* childhood that is recalled. Sam never gets his chance to be "crazy," as Kohut has famously put it, or to have Maria rise to the challenge of providing the selfobject responsiveness that he needs. We have done a good deal of work in exploring their cooperation in keeping Sam in the supportive and responsive role and Maria in the reactive and emotional one. Although Maria wants Sam to be more expressive and needing, she is frightened whenever he begins to express his feelings. She has seen how regularly she interrupts and reassumes center stage. Sam has also begun to see his stake in remaining the rational and undemanding one, who does not have to experiencing his own vulnerability. At the same time, he is increasingly aware that, like Humpty Dumpty on his wall, he is lonely, and he feels that he is missing out. He has started to insist on more space for his feelings and needs.

In this session we can see some loosening of Sam's reticence to open up his fantasy life and his childhood memories. However, the focus is on Maria's struggle to open the window to her childhood memories, and the haunting effect they are having on her relationship with Sam. The sharing of a dream conveyed Maria's frightening experience within the relationship in a way that words alone could not.

Maria has been having flashbacks at night for several weeks, and has been unable to tell Sam about them. She is afraid that he will be repelled by her feelings and experiences, and also that he will be deeply offended by her confusion of him with her father. She lies in bed terrified whenever Sam moves near her. She remembers that this is what she felt with her father. Just as she did as a child, she pretends that she is sleeping, and never says anything to anybody about the experience. She does not know what actually happened with her father.

Maria begins to talk about being frightened at night, and she remembers a dream. She has never shared dreams in the couple sessions because they feel too private to her, and often shameful. We have explored her fears about this several times, and I encourage her to share this dream. Sam adds, "I told you that I want you to share all this stuff with me. I want to help. What can I do to help?" "I need you to be strong enough to hear about what you trigger in me and not get mad. At least not go away, even if you are mad. I love you and I really want to be close to you." Sam responds firmly and reassuringly, "I'm upset, but I can stay. Tell me the dream!"

Maria is visibly scared, yet enthusiastic. She leans toward Sam and stretches her arms out with fingers wide in a menacing gesture. "There's a man. His hands are blue and white like a chess board. He has gloves on and pushes his hands toward my face. The gloves are like plastic. His face . . . I hope it wasn't Sam's face. His face was like plastic. His skin was plastic. That's how I knew. I knew he was a serial killer. I could tell by the gloves and the plastic skin. Maybe the face was Sam's."

I asked what plastic called to mind. "It's fake. Like molded and solid. Not moving. It's dead." "The man didn't seem alive," I reflect. Maria says, "He had a big smile on, artificial almost painted on like a clown. It was scary." Trying to encourage her to go further I inquire, "It was scary because it wasn't real?" "Yes, because it was fake and not alive." "And you connected it with Sam," I underlined, hoping to focus on her experience of the interpersonal aspect of the dream and to bring it into the room.

Turning to Sam, Maria continued. "Something is going on at night. You keep sleeping on top of me. Maybe it's because I haven't wanted to have sex for weeks. Maybe I would feel differently if we were awake and if a light was on. What pushes a button for me is the half-awake quality. Like it isn't out in the open. You want to make love, but it isn't out there. It's hidden. If I push you away, then right away I want to be closer. It's confusing, very confusing. It isn't that I don't want to be closer to you. I love you and I really want to be closer. Just sometimes at night I get these creepy feelings, like something isn't right or something bad is going to happen. I haven't been able to tell you, but this is going on every night."

Sam is clearly moved. He says that he can feel the terror in the dream and is upset that Maria hasn't been able to talk about her confusion and fear. Afraid that he is angry and hiding it, she asks him to say more about what he is really feeling. "It reminds me of a time when I was a kid," Sam says. "I was at a circus and was supposed to be having fun, but the clown's face terrified me. I hated the clown." Then he adds, "So, what are you telling me with the dream? What does it mean?"

Maria eagerly answers. "It tells how scared I am when you're all over me at night. The serial killer is all over me and I'm cornered. I think I'm reliving something and the only thing that's going to stop it is having sex. And I don't know if I'm talking about you, Sam, my husband, or if I'm talking about my father. The dream feels good in some way. It was really scary, but it feels good that something is letting out what I feel. It's like there's a window that's getting opened. I feel scared. There could be lots of memories. It feels surreal. It's good to feel that you can understand and not be mad at me."

Sam, feeling very close to Maria, is responsive and gets a bit playful. "I can see how scared you are and that sometimes you see me as Jack. Besides growing more hair and being taller so I won't look like Jack, what else can I do to help?" Maria says she wants to be more open about her wish to make love, and would like them to choose a time when they are both awake and alert, not in the middle of the night. I take the opportunity to add that it would be helpful to Maria, and also important for Sam himself, if he could be more open about his feelings and needs. I underline how good they both seemed to feel when he shared his childhood recollection of being scared by the clown.

I also point out how new, and maybe a bit frightening, that sort of sharing seems to be. "Maybe you might tell us some of your dreams."

"I would if I remembered dreams. I don't remember dreams, but I did have a nightmare last night. I don't know what it was about though." "Just talk about whatever piece of experience you can," I say, and add, trying to be encouraging, "It doesn't need to be a whole story or anything like that." Sam continues with some enthusiasm, "I don't know what it was about, but I woke up with my heart pounding. I can't remember this dream, but I once remember waking up from a dream that bugs were all over me." Maria, clearly enjoying the sharing, responds, "It's really weird that we both had nightmares at the same time." Sam enthusiastically elaborates, "Once we had bugs, cigarette beetles to be exact, all over the country house. They came from your dried flowers." "So, maybe the bugs came from my dream," Maria speculates playfully. "Maybe my fears are affecting you." All three of us laugh at this point.

I ask Maria if she has any thought about what Sam's dream might be saying. "It could be my dream. That's the way I feel at night . . . cornered. I could dream about being covered with bugs. It's weird. Maybe Sam can tell how I feel." Sam continues the playful exploration. "I also was wondering if there might be a connection between your anxieties at work recently and these fears."

Maria is surprised at Sam's making associative connections, since she sees him as tending to be concrete. She is delighted and finds his association very meaningful. "I have been unhappy and scared at work. I haven't been willing to look at what goes on, yet I keep being scared that something dreadful will happen. I keep talking about the sky falling and that I'll lose the whole business. I keep crying wolf and you don't believe me that something is wrong. It's like no one knew how scared I was with my father. I wouldn't tell anyone. I didn't want to look and I didn't want my mother or my aunt to look. I didn't want them to take my father away from me. In a similar way, I was afraid that if I looked at my business it would be so dangerous that I would have to give up the business."

I reframe her perception of danger. "Being in business and not looking at the expenses and cash flow can be really dangerous. Looking, you'll spot some dangers with a small 'd' and can deal with them. Not looking really builds up your fears and leads to a real danger." Maria continued, "And with my father, I was scared I'd lose him. My aunt once said I shouldn't be sleeping in his bed." I speak to protect the little girl that Maria had been. "Your aunt and your mother didn't look enough. It shouldn't have been up to you. They should have stopped you from sleeping in his bed."

A little later in the session, Sam, very thoughtfully and with a note of sadness, concludes, 'The real problem is that Maria hasn't been happy in her business or at home for a long time." Maria becomes tearful and adds, "And I don't want to talk about the unhappy. I don't think anyone wants to know about the unhappy so I don't want to look at the unhappy. I just talk about being scared." "You were really unhappy as a child with your father," I add, making the now quite experience-near connection.

"Yes," Maria responds. "I was very unhappy and I didn't want anyone to know. My father needed me to be happy and cheerful, not depressed like my mother. I ended up taking drugs to get away from feeling so unhappy." "It didn't feel like you could talk to anyone about how unhappy you were," I underline.

Contrasting the old experience with the new one available with me in treatment, and increasingly also with Sam, I add, "It's exciting that all this is coming up now and that Sam can play a strong role in looking at it with you."

As the session ends, we walk to the door and I am caught up in the excitement of the new experience, but Maria brings me back to the reality of the lengthy working-through process to come. "I just want to get out of here. Since you said that about my being unhappy as a girl, it all started getting blurry. Now I'm feeling faint." As they leave, I try to balance my enthusiasm with a comment more attuned to Maria's experience in the moment. "It's really hard and scary to look at how unhappy you were and to share it with us. It sounds like it can be overwhelming."

DISCUSSION

Maria had not been able to tell Sam the extent of her fears, especially as they attached to him and to their sexual relationship. The dream images and her associative elaboration conveyed much more than could be communicated with words alone.

Staying experience-near and amplifying the imagery, rather than making an experience-distant interpretation, helped to create a play space for Maria and, eventually, for Sam. Each was able to provide some much-needed responsiveness to the other, and to have the chance for some reactiveness as well. Because it's so easy for Sam to provide selfobject responsiveness at the expense of his own self-expression (and as a protection against frightening vulnerability), it was important to encourage him to react with his own associations and even with his own dream.

It was new for Sam to enter the play space as a player rather than as a provider of safety. This dimension of the relationship will need to be expanded over time.

The work with this dream illustrates a focus on the expression of self-state experience and interpersonal aspects of the relationship itself, rather than on the uncovering of unconscious material or intrapsychic conflict. However, it clearly leads to the illumination of connections to genetic material as well.

DREAMS IN GROUPS[3]

Self-psychological group psychotherapy, with its stress on empathy and safety, is another ideal venue for the shared vulnerability of creative play with dreams. The use of dreams in group psychotherapy has been studied from different theoretical perspectives, and Kieffer (1996), in a paper on the use of dream interpretation to resolve developmental impasses in a group, provides an extensive review of this literature. There is an extensive literature also on the self-psychological approach to group psychotherapy. However, I could not find any articles that focus specifically upon work with dreams in groups from the self-psychological perspective, and I would like to begin to address that void.

The group context uniquely complicates and uniquely enhances the use of dreams to facilitate vulnerability and deepen

---

3. Portions of this section are adapted from Livingston, M. (2001). Self psychology, dreams and group psychotherapy: working in the playspace. *Group* 25(1), and are reprinted here by permission of Kluwer Academic/Plenum Press.

the therapeutic process. Psychoanalytic ideas and techniques of working with dreams developed in the context of dyadic relationships, and the working through of dream material—especially the classical approach to dreams as the royal road to the unconscious—requires a particular kind of safety, and an attention to detail, that are most likely found in the traditional one-to-one situation. The group setting does not lend itself to an uninterrupted unfolding of the dreamer's process, or to in-depth exploration of his associations to each dream element. Furthermore, the other members all have their own reactions to the dream material, and these are often as much a function of the listeners' own archaic processes as the original dream was of the dreamer's.

Notwithstanding, the self-psychological approach to dreams lends itself extremely well to the facilitation of vulnerable moments and the furtherance of therapeutic process in the group setting. Although the reactiveness of the other group members would be disruptive to the kind of orderly dream analysis that might unfold in a one-to-one setting, it can be of great value in other styles of work with dreams, deepening the therapeutic experience for the entire group, including the dreamer, as I will demonstrate in the clinical material that follows.

The analyst's habitual striving to respond in an experience-near way to the subjective expressions of the group members sets the stage for the group to accept and explore dream material. Since self psychology views a dream as the best possible expression of a communication about the state of the self and its relationship to its selfobjects, not as a code that must be broken, the leader is freed from the task of obtaining associations and uncovering repressed content. Instead, he can use the play space already created by his empathic attunement and attention to safety, and the work with dreams further enhances the therapeutic ambiance. Working with dreams in the manner suggested here carries over to the group's functioning in general. It contributes to the deepening and illumination of affect, the exploration of personal meaning, and the facilitation of vulnerable moments.

Even within any one school of analysis, however, there are many ways of working with dreams, and work on the edge of vulnerability requires great specificity. There is no one absolute approach to dreams, any more than there can be an absolute approach treatment as a whole. To some degree, each leader and each group create their style anew with every dream presented. With that limitation clearly in mind, I will present a clinical example of one style of working with dreams in the play space of a therapy group.

ON ROACHES AND OTHER HIDDEN THINGS: AN ILLUSTRATION

The group in this session is the same one that served as an illustration of a focus on vulnerability in the deepening of group process in Chapter 7, although the participants are not identical. Roz and Tony participated in both examples. Maria and Marilyn were absent from the earlier session, presented in Chapter 7, which took place about a year before this one. This group has been together for several years, and a great deal of trust has developed, both in the therapist and among the members. It includes three women and two men (one of whom was away on this day), ranging in age from the early forties to the mid-fifties. They work well together, and can be confronting as well as empathically responsive to each other. This session demonstrates how work with dreams was introduced in a group that had not brought in any dreams for a long time. It also illustrates some of the early interventions of the leader in guiding the group's creative play with dream material.

A general atmosphere of openness and intimate sharing exists in this group, but I had become increasingly aware that the members of this particular group seemed to save dreams for their individual sessions. I felt it was time to address this as a therapeutic issue, and encouraged the group to bring dreams into the group context as well, and the following session resulted. I was aware, as I often am, that my interest in writing about sessions in detail has some impact on the intersubjective context. Many patients recognize my note-taking or recording as a reflection of intense interest, which has significant transferential meaning to them and which deepens and enhances the work. Some experience it as a provision, and an indication of their importance. Others experience it as an intrusion of my needs into the session, and sometimes even a reenactment of childhood abuse. I try to anticipate these personal meanings when I select the patients and groups I focus on (or at least to be sensitive to resulting selfobject failures when I fail in this anticipation). In most cases the ruptures that occur are nontraumatic and a useful part of the process. In the following session, my need for an example was clearly experienced as an intrusion by Maria, and I have tried to take this into account in my discussion of the session.

The session began with some social chatting and then settled down into a brief silence, which is characteristic of this group's style of centering and seeing what comes up. I broke the silence, perhaps a bit impulsively, with my planned remark about the absence of dreams. Roz responded quickly with the laughing comment that she didn't think that it would be all right to want that much focused attention. "I didn't know that we could. I never bring dreams to group because I won't be able to stay with it long enough to get through to the feelings." I told her that it's okay to want that kind of attention. The group laughed at the phrase "okay to want." Someone commented that she might well not get as much as she wanted, but then we can work with that like anything else. I added that one value in sharing a dream in the group and getting people's responses was that it might help us to deepen group members' understanding of each other.

Maria, whose window-opening dream we studied earlier in this chapter, asked with some annoyance, "Why now? Why did you choose to bring this up at this point? I bet I know." I laughed because I sensed that she was right on target and annoyed at the intrusion of my need into the group's flow. (This group session, by the way, took place a month or two prior to the couple session of the window dream, and turned out to be a factor in her willingness to risk sharing a similar dream with her husband.)

Tony interjected a question about whether or not it would be useful to talk about dreams. Then he added that it was nice to picture me thinking about the group between sessions and coming up with ideas to make things productive. Maria persisted angrily. "There is no way that I'll bring dreams to group. That's way too private and why did you bring it up anyway?" I decided to acknowledge my interest in writing about dreams and to attend to the subjective meaning that this intrusion might have for her. She laughed. "I knew it!" Her anger seemed to calm down as it became clear that I wasn't insisting on her sharing anything she felt was too personal. She did not at this point seem to be too disturbed; she seemed to be focused on the issue of insistence, and whether it was all right for her to say no. Tony was more upset—he was disappointed. He felt he had been given something and then it had been spoiled.

The group's work with these reactions to my intrusion into the process was cut short when Roz jumped in excitedly with a dream. "There was a roach in the bathtub. It was getting bigger and bigger and then it escaped from the tub. Then there was a cat attacking it, but it still kept getting bigger and bigger. It was trying to get away. The cat got the shell and then the body of the bug began to stretch out away from the shell. It was getting away. I thought it would die, but then I became afraid that the cat wouldn't be able to kill it. It was gross. The raw skin was gross and then it snapped free. It got away and got into my washing machine . . . into my clean clothes . . . into my whites. It was in my sweater sleeve. I tried to slam it dead . . . tried to smash it dead against the wall. Then the bug's head started to look like a kitten's head. There was spit flying, but it's not dying. I wanted to wake up to get out of there because the bug wouldn't die. The gross thing was the raw skin."

There was a pause while the group digested the dream and left some room to see if Roz would go further with it. I asked her if she had any thoughts about the dream. She responded that the ugliness under the shell was like a vulnerable and raw part. It was getting into her clean stuff and she was really trying to kill it. When she paused again, I asked the group if they had any reactions to the dream. I clarified that what would be useful is their emotional responses and reactions. I was not looking to figure out and interpret the dream at this point.

Tony said he was uncomfortable listening to the dream, perhaps because Roz seemed removed in telling it. Roz responded that she was so disgusted with it, she wanted to keep it at arm's length. Marilyn, with a little bit of embarrassment, said it made her think of a penis. The way it stretched out and got bigger and the way it was spitting. Tony, still uncomfortable, repeated that Roz was really detached from the dream. "It's like she's telling a story." I added that she treats the dream like a bug that she wants to keep at a distance. Then Roz responded. "It's like I'm not responsible for the dream. No one will understand the horror. I think I stay away from the horror because no one will understand if I really show it."

Very supportively, Marilyn told her, "I would certainly be horrified." Roz continued, "It had to die and it wouldn't. It's like a part of my self. Some vulnerable piece of me." Tony gently commented, "That's what I thought." Roz turned to him and slowed down. "It's like you cut something. It's like being a chicken without a head." "What part of you do you think it's like?" Tony asked with interest. "The needy part of me," Roz replied. "But it had a kitten head," she added. Tony seemed to understand and reflected, "Not a bug's head." Maria interjected, "It was becoming a kitten, a cute kitten." Then Tony said thoughtfully, "It's transitioning. It's transforming to something." Roz mulled these responses over and concluded, "Well, it isn't cute yet!"

After a poignant silence, I asked the group, "If this was your dream, what part of you would be the cut-off part?" For Maria, it was clearly her fear; then she added, "Also the hate part of me." For Marilyn, it was the sense of helplessness. She also felt strongly that she would feel compassion for the helpless creature that was being hurt. Roz was struck by this and her own awareness that she didn't feel any identification with the bug at all. "I feel no compassion for it. It had no expression . . . no appealing expression." Marilyn, again identifying somewhat with the creature and appreciating its value, retorted, "No expression, just a stubborn survival."

Tony concluded that this was a positive dream. "We are all transforming. My life is transforming. It feels awkward. I can feel others' core issues as they respond to the dream and I wonder what mine are. I've been feeling the absence of my father. It was Father's Day last Sunday and I didn't feel like honoring my father. I felt that I'm the father now and I didn't want to acknowledge him." Marilyn was upset with this idea and talked about how her son neglected both Father's Day and his father's sixtieth birthday. She and Tony each explored what this neglect meant to them. For her it was failing to acknowledge a "good" father, while for him it brought out his longing for more engagement with his father and his father's inability to respond to this need. He also talked about how he needs to experience me as actively engaged in the group and is upset if I'm relatively passive at times. I noted this and connected it to his disappointment with my not having brought in the idea of working with dreams after actively considering the group's needs. Tony responded, "I've been getting what I need with other men now . . . and here in the group. That's why I'm angry when Marty is not strong and active. This is the first time I'm really feeling the absence." Roz smiled and remarked, "I guess you have a core issue."

The group continued in a lively manner. Content centered around Marilyn's struggle with food and exercise and her stubborn refusal to give up trying, even though it's very difficult for her. Maria was increasingly quiet and seemed to be withdrawing. When someone commented on this, she acknowledged that she had been having trouble from the beginning of the session. "I want to be connected to you guys. I feel like I'm with you in what you've been talking about, but somehow I'm not really here. It has to do with a memory that I had on a job this afternoon. [Perhaps it also had to do with her reaction to the intrusion of my asking for dreams.] I was at a job site and I went to the bathroom in the basement of the building. It was dirty and smelly. It reminded me of playing in an abandoned bathroom as a kid. It smelled like kids going and peeing and doing dirty things. I remembered feeling scared, but interested."

"Did something happen?" I asked gently. Maria expressed anger at being asked, as she had when I had first asked about dreams. "I had a horrible dream," she said, "and I don't want to bring it into group. It was very sexual and it could have been you in the dream." I asked if the dream and her wish not to talk about it were connected to the fear and hate part of her that she had associated to Roz's bug. "Yeah! Without going into detail, I thought it was you . . . and that Sam [her husband] was in the room watching. It was my boss Arty in the dream, but I remember thinking it could be Marty. Sam came in and I was on my stomach. I was trying to pull the wool over Sam's eyes and he was going along with it."

I reflected, "You were upset that Sam didn't see." "I was really sexual and alive," she responded. "And I was very angry that Sam wasn't saying 'What are you doing?' It was very confusing. I was afraid to tell the dream. It feels shameful that I have such thoughts." I thought some of the shame and incestuous feelings that she reports might have been stimulated by her conflict around whether or not to respond to my need in asking for dreams. I decided not to reflect this in the group session, as the timing did not feel right. We did explore it further in an individual session, and eventually also in the group.

Trying to be helpful, Roz pointed out; "I don't feel responsible for my dreams." "I do," Maria responded, "that I could have that emotion." Tentatively I added, "And you felt hurt that Sam didn't set some limit for you?" Maria continued painfully, "It's like Sam is my mother and she is *not seeing!* It was my fault for hiding something."

Marilyn spoke firmly, yet with tenderness, at this point. "You weren't hiding anything. It wasn't your fault. She just didn't see."

Maria calmed down a little and explained, "I felt powerful. I could make her not see. I wanted Sam to go along and then I was angry that he did. Just like I'm sometimes angry that he seems not to notice me enough as a woman and at the same time I'm often angry when he initiates sex . . . when he wants something from me." Marilyn reflected with a great deal of attunement, "You were glad that he didn't interrupt you. You didn't want to stop, but you needed your mother to limit you. I'm feeling very protective about the part of you that thinks you stopped your mother from protecting you. You weren't that powerful!" Appreciatively, Maria agrees. "That's right, because I could easily feel guilty about that." Roz is also very supportive of Maria as a little girl needing protection. "If it was my daughter, no one could keep me from seeing." Maria took a deep breath at this point and sighed. "I feel more here now . . . more present." Marilyn continued as the group was ending, "I feel bad when a little girl takes too much responsibility." Maria concluded, "She should have stopped us." Marilyn added one further thought. "Also, we don't expect to be protected." As Maria got up to leave she commented, "I felt very confused. I'm okay now."

Discussion

In this session, there was no attempt on my part at completeness or interpretation in the classical sense. Many aspects of both dreams were neither pursued nor investigated. In individual sessions both dreamers would have had more opportunity to stay with their own associative flow and to uncover more material. For example, Maria's anger at her husband for not showing her more sexual attention came out significantly in her individual session the next day. Her ambivalent feelings about my responsiveness, and the intrusion of my needs as a re-creation of her relationship with her father, were explored more deeply in later sessions (both individual and group). The value of working with dreams in group is not the opportunity for completeness and orderly working through, but rather in the aliveness and deepening of group process.

I asked clearly for emotional and subjective reactions, not for experience-distant guesses about what the dream might mean subconsciously to the dreamer, and conveyed this by example, the way I work with most material. Also, I specifically clarified that I was not looking to figure out and interpret the dream. I told the group quite directly that what I thought would be valuable was their emotional responses and reactions.

While the group did not stay overtly focused on the dreamers, the dream material added an aliveness and stimulation that led several members to become open and vulnerable. And in spite of her anger, Maria did in fact offer an experience and a dream that she might well have withheld totally—the play space that had been created in working with Roz's dream may have allowed her to tolerate a greater-than-usual amount of vulnerability. She eventually did allude to issues of shame and secrecy that had kept her hidden early in the group when the idea of working with dreams was suggested. She then also responded to Roz's dream as touching on parts of her self that were connected to fear and hate. Typically of my style of working with dreams, I did not focus on this information at first. I went back to it later at the moment when Maria seemed more open to going further.

As Shapiro (1995) has emphasized, paying particular attention to the degree and quality of affect can improve the timing of analytic interventions. This is equally important, as Harwood

(1998) points out, in a group setting. Maria's fear was quite evident at the beginning of the session, but the quality of her affect was more self-protective than open. Later there was a shift in the quality of her involvement and the availability of her affect. The correct timing of interventions like this one is often based on a sensitivity to shifts in affect and vulnerability.

When I sensed Maria's readiness to explore further, I simply inquired if her previously expressed fear were connected to her hesitation about sharing her dream. On the surface, this was a simple intervention. However, it subtly connected several experiences. The first of these was Maria's deep, yet unexpressed, reaction to Roz's dream. At the same time it related to her hesitation in the here and now and to her conflict about responding to my need. Finally, it touched on her childhood fears and shame about her relationship with her father. These fears centered around her mother's seeming to ignore the oedipal triangle, yet perhaps being dangerously angry or damaged. Interventions like this one are often not completely thought out. They arise spontaneously in the play space if the leader is free and involved.

I look for ways to include the group in the dream—ways to make the dream a group property. That is why I asked the group, "If this was your dream, what part of you would be the cut-off part?" This particular intervention was especially self-psychological in that it led to an exploration of self-states, including Maria's frightened self-state.

Throughout this work in the play space, there is a balancing of reactiveness and responsiveness. In this session the group finds that balance nicely by itself. However, it is not always that easy and it is the responsibility of the leader to return to a balance in this regard when necessary. Tony's reaction to Roz's dream is a constructive expression of reactiveness. He is gentle and aware that Roz might feel attacked or criticized, but the thrust of his expression is his own reaction and not an attempt to be attuned. This turns out to be quite valuable both to him and to Roz, who realizes a few things about her style of presentation that apply to far more than the presentation of the dream. It leads her to take the risk of bringing in a feeling that she fears no one will understand: her feeling of horror. This then becomes part of deepening the group's process.

In contrast to Tony's reaction, the women's response to Maria's dream becomes a significant provision. Their responsiveness contrasts sharply with her transferential expectation that she will be either ignored or punished. The group is protective and warmly responsive. The power of such group responsiveness to ameliorate shame and guilt and to further a healing process is part of what makes group psychotherapy such a valuable addition to individual work.

CONCLUSION

If a dream is offered to the therapeutic process and met with an attitude of serious play by the listening analyst, partner, or group, then exploration, curiosity, and risk taking are encouraged. In the spirit of openness and shared vulnerability, affect is amplified and personal meanings and organizing principles are illuminated and explored. Cooperative exploration, and the deepening of the metaphorical communication among the participants, can enhance the growth of dreamer and listeners both, and can lead to increased intimacy and greater strength in their relationships.

9

An Afterword

Novice therapists and group leaders often want to know what determines a seasoned colleague's choices about how and when to intervene in the analytic process. My own belief is that specific interventions at dramatic moments are not as central to day-in and day-out therapeutic work as the therapist's fundamental attitudes and beliefs, and for this reason I have never liked to formulate technical recommendations. Instead, I try to elucidate the attitudes and understandings upon which an experienced practitioner's interventions rest. These attitudes convey to the patient the therapist's "bread and butter" stance and also underlie the responsiveness that—reliably and consistently, moment to moment, and session after session—the therapist makes available to his patients, and that patients come to count on.

I have described my approach to the psychoanalytic treatment of individuals, couples, and groups. It is essentially grounded in relational self psychology and intersubjectivity, but, perhaps more uniquely, it includes as well a clinical focus on the facilitation of what I have called here "vulnerable moments."

I am convinced that a clinical focus on narcissistic vulnerability and the facilitation of vulnerable moments is central to deepening the therapeutic process, and that the therapist's vulnerable involvement in a relationship is central in both of these. I have therefore tried to highlight throughout this study the concepts of vulnerability and emotional availability as they affect both patient and therapist. The therapist's attitude toward vulnerability is expressed in his empathic immersion in the patient's subjective experience, and in his sensitivity to the vicissitudes of the patient's self-states. These shifts in self experience, particularly those on the vulnerability/protectiveness spectrum, are windows onto selfobject longings, fears, and remembered traumas, and allow the exploration and amplification of this often subtle, and often missed, material. That is why a careful and consistent attention to emerging vulnerability facilitates so effectively the deepening of the empathic bond, and thus of the analytic process.

Every time a therapist overlooks one of these moments, allows it to dissipate, or fails to protect it from distraction or attack, a window of therapeutic opportunity is lost. This book is an attempt to call attention to the role that vulnerable moments can play in therapeutic process, so that their potential for enhancing intensity and intimacy, and through that the facilitating of curative process, can be harnessed.

Despite the risks that by its nature it incurs, vulnerability is central, and intrinsic, to the analytic process. It is an inevitable part of the openness to new experience that is the prerequisite of therapeutic change and merits the therapist's focused attention. In moments of intense vulnerability (and less dramatically in the day-in and day-out tolerance of lower levels of vulnerability in response to the therapist's sustained empathic inquiry and emotional availability), arrested development can be resumed, and new relational experiences taken in.

Structural change in any psychoanalytic process takes place within a relationship. Insight, interpretation, and understanding all play a role, but to have a mutative impact, the context of relationship is imperative. The question is no longer whether insight or affective experience is the more essential. They are both necessary aspects of curative process.

I have used the metaphor of a play space to capture the atmosphere of the kind of interpersonal field and attitudes that encourage the emergence of vulnerability. In the play space, judgments about logic and reality are suspended and playfulness and exploration are enhanced. Intense affective involvement is possible at relatively low risk, but the engagement is real, and it includes the therapist as well as the patient.

For this reason I have paid a great deal of attention to the need for the therapist to be aware of, and even welcome, his own vulnerability if he wishes to facilitate and make optimal use of vulnerable moments. The willingness to experience and reflect upon a wide range of affect and personal associations is a necessary part of what Kohut (1959) meant when he defined empathy as "vicarious introspection, " and is also a component of serious play.

Therapists who are emotionally present and involved without the comfort and protection of a customary role and prescribed behavior are vulnerable. Increasingly, the analytic world recognizes the need for treatment to be responsive to the needs of each unique patient and therapist dyad. Thus, without clear and unchanging roles and techniques, the therapist must repeatedly contain and reflect on not only the patient's anxieties and conflicts but also on his own. The willingness to enter into an entangled and unique relationship with each patient, to facilitate vulnerable moments and to be what Bacal (1985) calls "optimally responsive," is often, on a deep level, a vulnerable experience. But in psychotherapy, as in life, vulnerability is a necessary precursor of growth—and not only for the patient.

References

Bacal, H. (1985). Optimal responsiveness and the therapeutic process. In *Progress in Self Psychology*, vol. 1, ed. A. Goldberg, pp. 202–227. New York: Guilford.

——— (1994). The selfobject relationship in psychoanalytic treatment. In *Progress in Self Psychology*, vol. 10, ed. A. Goldberg, pp. 21–30. Hillsdale, NJ: Analytic Press.

——— (1995). *Beyond empathy*. Presented to the Association for Psychoanalytic Self Psychology, New York, February.

——— (1998a). Introduction: relational self psychology. In *Progress in Self Psychology*, vol. 14, ed. A. Goldberg, pp. xiii–xviii. Hillsdale, NJ: Analytic Press.

——— (1998b). Notes on optimal responsiveness in the group process. In *Self Experiences in Group: Intersubjective and Self-Psychological Pathways to Human Understanding*, ed. I. Harwood and M. Pines, pp. 175–180. London and Philadelphia: Jessica Kingsley and Taylor & Francis.

——— (1999). *Optimal responsiveness: the applications of specificity theory in relational self psychology*. Presented to the Annual International Conference on the Psychology of the Self, Toronto, October.

Bacal, H., and Newman, K. (1990). *Theories of Object Relations: Bridges to Self Psychology.* New York: Columbia University Press.

Bowers, M., Guze, H., and Murphy, R. (1966). Tenderness in psychotherapy: a dialogue. *Voices* 2(1):5–19.

Brandchaft, B. (1994). *Structures of pathological accommodation.* Presented to the Association for Psychoanalytic Self Psychology. New York, March.

Brandchaft, B., and Stolorow, R. (1988). The difficult patient: an intersubjective perspective. In *Borderline and Narcissistic Patients in Therapy*, ed. N. Slavinska-Holy, pp. 243–266. New York: International Universities Press.

Calogeras, R. (1977). Husband and wife exchange of dreams. *International Review of Psycho-Analysis* 4:71–82.

Dicks, H. (1967). *Marital Tensions.* New York: Basic Books.

Ehrenberg, D. (1996). On the analyst's emotional availability and vulnerability. *Contemporary Psychoanalysis* 32(2):275–286.

Fenichel, O. (1941). *Problems of Psychoanalytic Technique.* New York: Psychoanalytic Quarterly.

Ferenczi, S. (1931). Child analysis in the analysis of adults. In *Final Contributions to the Theory and Technique of Psycho-Analysis*, pp. 126–142. London: Hogarth, 1955.

——— (1933). Confusion of tongues between adults and the child. In *Final Contributions to the Theory and Technique of Psycho-Analysis*, pp. 156–167. London: Hogarth, 1955.

Fielding, B. (1966). The utilization of dreams in the treatment of couples. *Psychotherapy and Psychosomatics* 14(2):81–89.

Fosshage, J. (1983). The psychological function of dreams: a revised psychoanalytic perspective. *Psychoanalysis and Contemporary Thought* 6(4):641–669.

——— (1987). New vistas in dream interpretation. In *Dreams in New Perspective: The Royal Road Revisited,* ed. M. Glucksman and S. Warner, pp. 23–44. New York: Human Sciences.

——— (1993). *Countertransference: the analyst's experience of the analysand.* Presented at the 16th Annual Conference on the Psychology of the Self, Toronto, October.

Freud, S. (1900). The interpretation of dreams. *Standard Edition* 4/5.

——— (1914). Remembering, repeating, and working through. *Standard Edition* 12:145–156.

——— (1915). Further recommendations on the technique of psycho-analysis: observations on transference love. In *Collected Papers,* pp. 377–391. New York: Basic Books, 1959.

Friedman, L. (1986). Kohut's testament. *Psychoanalytic Inquiry* 6(3):321–348.

Goldberg, M. (1974). The uses of dreams in conjoint marital therapy. *Journal of Sex and Marital Therapy* 1(1):75–81.

Goldstein, E. (1992). *Self-disclosure and the therapeutic process: what therapists do and don't talk about.* Presented to the Association for Psychoanalytic Self Psychology, New York, January.

Greenberg, R. (1987). Self psychology and dreams: the merging of differences. *Psychiatric Journal of Ottawa* 12(2):98–102.

Hagman, G. (1997). Mature selfobject experience. In *Progress in Self Psychology,* vol. 13, ed. A. Goldberg, pp. 85–108. Hillsdale, NJ: Analytic Press.

Harwood, I. (1998). Can group analysis/psychotherapy provide a wide angle lens for self psychology? In *Self Experiences in Group: Intersubjective and Self Psychological Pathways to Human Understanding,* ed. I. Harwood and M. Pines, pp. 155–174.

London and Philadelphia: Jessica Kingsley and Taylor and Francis.

Harwood, I., and Pines, M., eds. (1998). *Self Experiences in Group: Intersubjective and Self Psychological Pathways to Human Understanding.* London and Philadelphia: Jessica Kingsley and Taylor & Francis.

Kieffer, C. (1996). Using dream interpretation to resolve group developmental impasses. *Group* 20(4):273–285.

Kilian, H. (1993). *On psychohistory, cultural evolution and the historical significance of self psychology—an introduction.* Presented at the 16th Annual Conference on the Psychology of the Self, Toronto, October.

Kohut, H. (1959). Introspection, empathy and psychoanalysis: an examination of the relation between mode of observation and theory. In *The Search for the Self,* vol. 1, ed. P. H. Ornstein, pp. 205–232. New York: International Universities Press, 1978.

——— (1971). *The Analysis of the Self.* New York: International Universities Press.

——— (1972). Letter. In *The Search for the Self,* vol. 2, ed. P. Ornstein, pp. 867–870. Madison, CT: International Universities Press, 1978.

——— (1974) Letter. In *The Search for the Self,* vol. 2, ed. P. Ornstein, pp. 888–891. Madison, CT: International Universities Press, 1978.

——— (1977). *The Restoration of the Self.* Madison, CT: International Universities Press.

——— (1978). Reflections on advances in self psychology. In *The Search for the Self,* vol. 3, ed. P. Ornstein, pp. 261–357. Madison, CT: International Universities Press, 1990.

——— (1981). On empathy. In *The Search for the Self*, vol. 4, ed. P. Ornstein, pp. 525–535. Madison, CT: International Universities Press, 1991.

——— (1984). *How Does Analysis Cure?* Chicago: University of Chicago Press.

Lachmann, F., and Beebe, B. (1993). Interpretation in a developmental perspective. In *Progress in Self Psychology*, vol. 9, ed. A. Goldberg, pp. 45–52. Hillsdale, NJ: Analytic Press.

Lathrop, D. (1966). Experience of tenderness. *Voices*, 2(1):116–118.

Levitsky, A., and Perls, F. (1970). The rules and games of gestalt therapy. In *Gestalt Therapy Now*, ed. J. Fagan and I. Shepherd, pp. 140–149. Palo Alto, CA: Science and Behavior.

Lichtenberg, J., Lachmann, F., and Fosshage, J. (1992). *Self and Motivational Systems: Toward a Theory of Psychoanalytic Technique.* Hillsdale, NJ: Analytic Press.

Lindon, J. (1994). Gratification and provision in psychoanalysis: Should we get rid of "the rule of abstinence?" *Psychoanalytic Dialogues* 4:549–582.

Livingston, L. (2001). Transferences toward the co-therapist couple: triadic relationships and selfobject needs. *Group* 25:1.

Livingston, M. (1975). On barriers, contempt, and the "vulnerable moment" in group psychotherapy. In *Group Therapy 1975*, ed. L. Wolberg and M. Aronson, pp. 242–254. New York: Stratton.

——— (1995). A self psychologist in couplesland: multi-subjective approach to transference and countertransference-like phenomena in marital relationships. *Family Process* 34:427–440.

——— (1996). Countertransference and curative process with

"non-difficult" patients. In *Progress in Self Psychology*, vol. 12, ed. A. Goldberg, pp. 123–140. Hillsdale, NJ: Analytic Press.

——— (1998a). Conflict and aggression in couples therapy. *Family Process* 37(3):311–321.

——— (1998b). Harvest of fire: archaic twinship and fundamental conflict. In *Self Experiences in Group: Intersubjective and Self Psychological Pathways to Human Understanding*, ed. I. Harwood and M. Pines, pp. 58–69. London and Philadelphia: Jessica Kingsley and Taylor & Francis.

——— (1999). Vulnerability, tenderness, and the experience of selfobject relationship: a self-psychological view of deepening curative process in group psychotherapy. *International Journal of Group Psychotherapy* 49(1):1–21.

——— (2001). Self psychology, dreams, and group therapy: working in the playspace. *Group* 25:1.

Livingston, M., and Livingston, L. (1998). Conflict and aggression in group psychotherapy. *International Journal of Group Psychotherapy* 48:381–391.

Meares, R. (1990). The fragile spielraum: an approach to transmuting internalization. In *Progress in Self Psychology*, vol. 6, ed. A. Goldberg, pp. 69–89. Hillsdale, NJ: Analytic Press.

Nell, R. (1975). The use of dreams in couples' group therapy. *Journal of Family Counseling* 3(2):7–11.

Orange, D. (1995). *Emotional Understanding*. New York: Guilford.

Orange, D., Atwood, G., and Stolorow, R. (1997). *Working Intersubjectively: Contextualism in Psychoanalytic Practice*. Hillsdale, NJ: Analytic Press.

Ornstein, A. (1974). The dread to repeat and the new beginning: a contribution to the psychoanalysis of the narcissistic personality disorders. *Annual of Psychoanalysis* 2:231–248.

——— (1991). When the patient is demanding. In *Using Self Psychology in Psychotherapy,* ed. H. Jackson, pp. 153–166. Northvale, NJ: Jason Aronson.

Ornstein, P. (1987). On self-state dreams in the psychoanalytic treatment process. In *The Interpretation of Dreams in Clinical Work,* ed. A. Rothstein, pp. 87–104. Madison, CT: International Universities Press.

Ornstein, P., and Ornstein, A. (1993). Assertiveness, anger, and destructive aggression: a perspective from the treatment process. In *Rage, Power, and Aggression,* ed. R. A. Slick and S. P. Roose, pp. 102–117. New Haven, CT: Yale University Press.

Perlmutter, R., and Babineau, R. (1983). The use of dreams in couple therapy. *Psychiatry* 46(1):66–72.

Racker, H. (1968). *Transference and Countertransference.* New York: International Universities Press.

Richards, A., and Richards, A. (1995). An overview of psychoanalytic theory and technique. *Journal of Clinical Psychoanalysis* 4(4):429–456.

Ringstrom, P. (1994). An intersubjective approach to conjoint therapy. In *Progress in Self Psychology,* vol. 10, ed. A. Goldberg, pp. 159–182. Hillsdale, NJ: Analytic Press.

Sander, F. (1978). Marriage and the family in Freud's writings. *Journal of the American Academy of Psychoanalysis* 6(2):157–174.

——— (1985). Family or individual therapy: the determinants of modality choice. *Hillside Journal of Clinical Psychiatry* 7(1):63–70.

——— (1989). *Marital Conflict and Psychoanalytic Therapy in the Middle Years.* New Haven, CT: Yale University Press.

Scharff, D. E., and Scharff, J. S. (1991). *Object Relations Couple Therapy.* Northvale, NJ: Jason Aronson.

Shaddock, D. (1998). *From Impasse to Intimacy.* Northvale, NJ: Jason Aronson.

Shane, E., and Shane, M. (1994). *In pursuit of the optimal in optimal frustration, optimal responsiveness and optimal provision.* Presented at the 17th Annual Conference on the Psychology of the Self, Chicago, October.

Shapiro, E. (1991). Empathy and safety in group: a self psychology perspective. *Group* 15(4):219–224.

Shapiro, S. (1995). *Talking with Patients: A Self-Psychological View.* Northvale, NJ: Jason Aronson.

Sharpe, S. (1990). *The Oppositional Couple: A Developmental Object Relations Approach to Diagnosis and Treatment.* New York: Basic Books.

Siegel, J. (1991). Analysis of projective identification: an object relations approach to marital treatment. *Clinical Social Work Journal* 19(1):71–81.

——— (1992). *Repairing Intimacy: An Object Relations Approach to Couples Therapy.* Northvale, NJ: Jason Aronson.

Slavin, M., and Kriegman, D. (1998). Why the analyst needs to change: toward a theory of conflict, negotiation, and mutual influence in the therapeutic process. *Psychoanalytic Dialogues* 8(2):247–284.

Solomon, M. (1985). Treatment of narcissistic and borderline disorders in marital therapy: suggestions toward an enhanced therapeutic approach. *Clinical Social Work Journal* July:141–156.

——— (1988). Self psychology and marital relationships. *International Journal of Family Psychiatry* 9(3):211–226.

——— (1989). *Narcissism and Intimacy.* New York: Norton.

——— (1991). Adults. In *Using Self Psychology in Psychotherapy,* ed. H. Jackson, pp. 117–134. Northvale, NJ: Jason Aronson.

Stern, D. (1983). The early development of schemas of self, other, and "self with other." In *Reflections on Self Psychology,* ed. J. Lichtenberg and S. Kaplan, pp. 49–84. Hillsdale, NJ: Analytic Press.

Stolorow, R. (1978). Themes in dreams: a brief contribution to therapeutic technique. *International Journal of Psycho-Analysis* 53:473–475.

——— (1993). Thoughts on the nature and therapeutic action of psychoanalytic interpretation. In *Progress in Self Psychology,* vol. 9, ed. A. Goldberg, pp. 31–44. Hillsdale, NJ: Analytic Press.

——— (2000). Panel on self experiences in groups. American Group Psychotherapy Association annual conference, Los Angeles, February.

Stolorow, R., and Atwood, G. (1992). *Contexts of Being.* Hillsdale, NJ: Analytic Press.

Stolorow, R., Brandchaft, B., and Atwood, G. (1987). *Psychoanalytic Treatment: An Intersubjective Approach.* Hillsdale, NJ: Analytic Press.

Stone, W. (2001). The role of the therapist's affect in the detection of empathic failures, misunderstandings and injury. *Group* 25(1).

Terman, D. (1988). "Optimum frustration": structuralization and the therapeutic process. In *Progress in Self Psychology,* vol. 4, ed. A. Goldberg, pp. 113–126. Hillsdale, NJ: Analytic Press.

Tolpin, P. (1983). Self psychology and the interpretation of dreams. In *The Future of Psychoanalysis*, ed. A. Goldberg, pp. 255–271. New York: International Universities Press.

——— (1989). On dreaming our inclinations. In *Progress in Self Psychology*, vol. 5, ed. A. Goldberg, pp. 39–45. Hillsdale, NJ: Analytic Press.

Ullman, M. (1987). Foreword. In *Dream Interpretation: A Comparative Study—Revised Edition*, ed. J. Fosshage and C. Loew, pp. ix–xiv. New York: PMA Publishing.

Ullman, M., and Zimmerman, N. (1979). *Working with Dreams*. New York: Delacorte.

Warkentin, J., and Leland, T. (1966). Tenderness in psychotherapy: a dialogue. *Voices* 2(1):5–19.

Winnicott, D. (1953). Transitional objects and transitional phenomena: a study of the first not-me possession. *International Journal of Psycho-Analysis* 43:89–97.

——— (1954). Withdrawal and regression. In *Through Paediatrics to Psychoanalysis*, pp. 251–261. London: Hogarth, 1958.

Wolf, E. (1980). On the developmental line of selfobject relations. In *Advances in Self Psychology*, ed. A. Goldberg, pp. 117–130. New York: International Universities Press.

Index

About the Author

Martin S. Livingston, Ph.D., is a training analyst, faculty member, and supervisor at several psychoanalytic institutes in New York City. In these institutes (Postgraduate Center for Mental Health, the Training and Research Institute for Self Psychology, the New York Institute for Psychoanalytic Self Psychology, and the Training Institute for Mental Health), at national conferences, and in the present book, he presents a unique approach to psychoanalysis and psychotherapy. This approach, based on forty years of clinical and teaching experience, stresses a focus on vulnerability within a relational self-psychological understanding of therapeutic process.

Dr. Livingston is co-chair of the Association for Psychoanalytic Self Psychology, editor, or on the editorial staff, of three major group therapy journals, and the author of many articles dealing with countertransference, dreams, couple therapy, and group therapy. He is also author of *Near and Far: Closeness and Distance in Psychotherapy,* and began writing about vulnerable moments in the early 1970s.